Teaching For Christian Wisdom

Teaching For Christian Wisdom

Towards A Holistic Approach to Education and Formation of the Presbyterian Church in Egypt

Samy Estafanos

WIPF & STOCK · Eugene, Oregon

TEACHING FOR CHRISTIAN WISDOM
Towards A Holistic Approach to Education and Formation of the Presbyterian Church in Egypt

Copyright © 2018 Samy Estafanos. All rights reserved. Except for brief quotations in critical publications or reviews, no part of this book may be reproduced in any manner without prior written permission from the publisher. Write: Permissions, Wipf and Stock Publishers, 199 W. 8th Ave., Suite 3, Eugene, OR 97401.

Wipf & Stock
An Imprint of Wipf and Stock Publishers
199 W. 8th Ave., Suite 3
Eugene, OR 97401

www.wipfandstock.com

PAPERBACK ISBN: 978-1-4982-9436-2
HARDCOVER ISBN: 978-1-4982-9438-6
EBOOK ISBN: 978-1-4982-9437-9

Manufactured in the U.S.A.

Contents

Acknowledgments | vii

Introduction: Critical Thinking from Socrates to Egyptian Context | 1

1 Presbyterian Church in Egypt and Critical Thinking | 25
2 John Dewey and the Problem of Thinking of the Presbyterian Education in Egypt—A Scientific Interpretation | 67
3 Critical Thinking in the Christian Traditions —A Theological Norm | 131
4 Teaching for Christian Wisdom—Towards a Holistic Approach to Christian Education in the Presbyterian Church in Egypt | 189

Conclusion | 228

Appendices | 231
Bibliography | 247

Acknowledgments

This research would not have been possible without the help of many professors, friends, and colleagues. This is particularly true of Gordon Mikoski who has been, not only my professor and advisor whose intelligent thinking and deep theological thoughts on the history and philosophy of Christian education were of real help, but also a dear friend and a pastoral counselor. Dr. Mikoski was always there for me when I needed his advice and help. I offer special thanks to great practical theologian Dr. Richard Osmer, not only for his significant theory of Christian education as practical theology, which beautifully organized in his several books, but also for the deep influence that directly left in developing my thoughts and forming my life. I also offer deep thanks to my professor Kenda Crespy Dean. It is true that Kenda was called by all of the PTS students with "life," as she, indeed, is filed with positive energy, love, and hope. Dr. Dean has an influence on shaping my understanding of the teaching theories, youth formation, and discipleship. Practicing the presence of God, forgiveness and reconciliation, the face of the other, and other many issues that I have learned from Dr. Bo Karen Lee; yet, training on prayer and practicing spiritual life was of real spiritual formation of my life.

The idea of teaching in the field of Christian education was primarily inspired to me through Dr. Perry Shaw. For three days in the spring of 2010 in the Arab Baptist Theological School in Lebanon (ABTS), Dr. Shaw and I have spent hours in a thoughtful dialogue, reflecting on the teaching ministry in the Presbyterian Church in Egypt. Special thanks and appreciation should be offered to Dr. Shaw. Especial thanks should be offered to all my colleagues of the PhD seminars in Christian area in the PTS who, since the fall of the 2010 to the spring of 2015, have significantly contributed forming my understanding of both Christian education and practical theology. I offer my thanks to my colleague in the New Testament, Melanie Ann Howard and my colleague in the pastoral care area, Melissa Haupt for their brilliant work in editing this dissertation.

While I thank my beloved family, my wife Yvonne and my children Nada and Nayer who are the most beautiful flowers in my life. As much as I talked with them about John Dewey, my researcher partner, he has become their partner as well. My children, indeed, deserve special thanks, not only for their understanding, but also for their loving support. I also thank all my friends and colleagues for their constant encouragement and support. I want finally to offer my special gratitude to one of the significant Christian intuitions in Egypt and in the Middle East, the Evangelical Theological Seminary in Cairo (ETSC), where I teach in the Christian education area for its constantly support. Along the journey of this study, Dr. Atef Gendy has been more than a President of a seminary, as his readiness to listen, his willingness to support, and his prompt response all are beyond description. I thank all my colleagues in teaching ministry at the ETSC for thoughtfully keep praying for me. I also offer my thanks to many of the ministering team at the ETSC, Eman Salah, Mariam Hanna, and Brice Roger. Special thanks to Manal Elmoteay for her great and professional effort in editing and reediting this work.

Introduction

Critical Thinking from Socrates to the Egyptian Context

Critical Thinking—Selected Definitions

ETYMOLOGY AND DICTIONARY: THE word "critical" derives etymologically from two Greek roots: "kriticos," meaning discerning judgment and "criterion," meaning standards. Etymologically, then, the word implies the development of "discerning judgment based on standards." In a similar way, the *Webster's Online Dictionary* defines critical thinking, as "the mental process of actively and skillfully conceptualizing, applying, synthesizing, and evaluating information to reach an answer or conclusion."[1]

Psychologist Diane F. Halpern:[2] Critical thinking is the use of those cognitive skills or strategies that increase the probability of a positive outcome. It is used to describe thinking that is purposeful, reasoned, and goal directed—the kind of thinking involved in problem solving, formulating inferences, calculating likelihoods, and making decisions when the thinker is using skills that are thoughtful and effective for the particular context and type of thinking task. Critical thinking also involves evaluating the thinking process-the reasoning that went into the conclusion we have arrived at the kinds of factors considered in making a decision. It is sometimes called "directed" thinking because it focuses on a desired outcome.[3]

---

1. *Webster's Online Dictionary*, s.v. "critical thinking."

2. Diane F. Halpern is an American psychologist and past-president of the American Psychological Association. She is Dean of Social Science at the Minerva Schools at KGI and also the McElwee Family Professor of Psychology at Claremont McKenna College.

3. Halpern, *Thought and Knowledge*, 5.

John Dewey (1859-1952): despite roots of "critical thinking" referring to Socrates about 2500 years ago, John Dewey, the American philosopher, psychologist and educator, is widely regarded as the 'father' of the modern critical thinking tradition, which he calls "reflective thinking." In the *How We Think*, Dewey defines this kind of thinking as, "Active, persistent, and careful consideration of a belief or supposed form of knowledge in the light of the grounds which support it and the further conclusions to which it tends."[4] By defining critical thinking as an 'active' process, says Alice Fisher, Dewey is contrasting it with the kind of thinking in which one just passively receives ideas and information from others. For Dewey, critical thinking is essentially an active process in which people think through for themselves, raise questions, and make their relevant information. In defining critical thinking as 'persistent' and 'careful' Dewey is contrasting it with the kind of unreflective thinking we all engage in sometimes, for example when we jump to a conclusion or make a 'snap' decision without thinking about it.[5]

Based on an ancient Greek ideal of "living an examined life" Dewey is deeply convinced that critical thinking is practical in nature and is born in everyday experience. It is based on the skills, the insights, and the values essential to that end. It is a way of going about living and learning that empowers us in quite practical ways. However, Fisher argues that what Dewey says about the 'grounds which support' a belief and the 'further conclusions to which it tends' is the most important thing about his definition of critical thinking. Fisher concludes, Dewey gives huge importance to reasoning, to giving reasons, and to evaluating reasoning as well as possible.[6]

Edward Glaser (1968-Present): building on Dewey's ideas, Edward Glaser, co-author of the "Watson—Glaser Critical Thinking Appraisal," which has become the world's most widely used test of critical thinking, defined critical thinking as:

> (1) An attitude of being disposed to consider in a thoughtful way the problems and subjects that come within the range of one's experience; (2) knowledge of the methods of logical inquiry and reasoning; and (3) some skill in applying those methods. Critical thinking calls for a persistent effort to examine any belief or supposed form of knowledge in the light of the evidence that supports it and the further conclusions to which it tends.[7]

---

4. Dewey, *How We Think*, 9.
5. Fisher, *Critical Thinking*, 7–9.
6. Ibid., 9.
7. Glaeser, *Triumph of the City*, 5.

The significant influence of Dewey of shaping this definition, however, is quite clear. Despite how Glaeser refers to 'evidence' in place of 'grounds,' his second sentence is much the same as Dewey's definition. He was also influenced deeply by Dewey in the centrality of experience and inquiry 'the methods of logical enquiry and reasoning' in constructing the own knowledge.[8]

Robert Ennis (1954–2010): One of the most significant contributions to the development of the critical thinking tradition that has gained wide currency in the field is Robert Ennis' definition, "Critical thinking is reasonable, reflective thinking that is focused on deciding what to believe or do."[9] Three important emphases on critical thinking should be noticed in this definition, 'reasonable,' 'reflective,' and 'deciding what to . . . do,' suggesting that decision—making is part of critical thinking.

Philosopher Richard Paul (1968–Present):[10] "That mode of thinking about—any subject, content, or problem—in which the thinker improves the quality of his or her thinking by skillfully taking charge of the structures inherent in thinking and imposing intellectual standards upon them." They emphasize, "Asking vital questions," "gathering relevant information," "testing well-reasoned conclusions and solutions," "thinking open mindedly," "recognizing and assessing their assumptions, implications, and practical consequences," and "communicating effectively."[11]

Critical Thinking: A Brief History in the Secular World

Socrates (469–399 BCE): The intellectual roots of critical thinking are as ancient as its etymology to the teaching paradigm of Socrates 2500 years ago, who, through using the method of probing questioning has come to the fact that people cannot rationally justify their confident claims to

---

8. Ibid.

9. Norris and Ennis, *Evaluating Critical Thinking*, 12.

10. Richard W. Paul is a leading scholar in critical thinking. In 1980s Paul has worked to advance the concept of critical thinking through his work at the Center and Foundation for Critical Thinking, both of which he founded. He received four degrees and has given lectures on critical thinking at many universities in the USA and abroad: Harvard, the University of Chicago, the University of Illinois, and the universities of Puerto Rico, Costa Rica, British Columbia, Toronto, and Amsterdam. He taught beginning and advanced courses in critical thinking at the university level for over twenty years. He has been the recipient of numerous honors and awards, including Distinguished Philosopher (by the Council for Philosophical Studies, 1987).

11. Norris and Ennis, *Evaluating Critical Thinking*, 17.

knowledge. Socrates believes that "confused meanings, inadequate evidence, or self-contradictory beliefs often lurked beneath smooth but largely empty rhetoric."[12] Socrates has come to the fact that man cannot depend upon those in "authority" to have true knowledge and insight, for individuals may have power and high position and yet be deeply confused and irrational. He pointed to the importance of asking real question that inquire deeply into individual thinking in order to embrace an idea as worthy belief. He also established the necessity of seeking evidence, examining reasoning and claims and assumptions, analyzing basic concepts through practicing. Yet, Socrates' questioning method known as "Socratic Questioning" is the best-known critical thinking teaching method, which reflects the necessity of clarity and logical understanding in the process of thinking.[13]

Plato (427–347 BCE): Unlike his mentor Socrates, Plato was both a writer and a teacher; whose writings are in the form of dialogues, with Socrates as the principal speaker. In the "Allegory of the Cave," which is stated in Book VII of *The Republic,* Plato offers a meaningful allegorical description of the dark situation that people find themselves in with the light of knowing as designs the way for their salvation. Briefly, the Allegory presents most of Plato's major philosophical assumptions. Plato believes that the world that we realize by our senses is not the real world, but only a poor copy of it, the real world can only be apprehended intellectually, knowledge cannot be transferred from teacher to student, rather education should include a way of directing student's minds toward what is real and important, allowing them to apprehend it for themselves. Plato believes that the universe is ultimately good and the enlightened individuals have an obligation to go inside the cave of darkness and save other fellow humans. For him, society must be one whole while the wise Philosopher be the ruler.[14]

Aristotle (84–322 BC): Aristotle, indeed, is a critical inflection point in Western philosophic thought. In his book, *Critical Thinking for College Students,* Jon Stratton states that in the first few lines of his two-volume *Metaphysics,* Aristotle writes that all humans need to know and understand the world. This is not only because it is useful to know, but also because we love to know simply for the sake of knowing. It was after Aristotle pointed this out that the philosophers distinguished two type of thinking. Thinking that involves exploring timeless questions, dedicated to the eternal truth, and meeting the innermost need for thinking is referred to as "theoretical," "abstract," "or "philosophical." Thinking that seeks to affect

12. Paul, Elder, and Bartell, "California Teacher Preparation."

13. Dutton et al., "Critical Thinking."

14. Paul, Elder, and Bartell, "California Teacher Preparation."

practical results in the world is referred to as "practical," "concrete," or "critical" thinking.[15] It is doubtless that Aristotle's theory of logic, which he calls "theory of syllogism," has a deep influence on the history of Western thoughts. For him, syllogisms as the basic tools of reasoning process are pairs of propositions that, taken together, provide a new conclusion. Aristotle concludes that science results from constructing more complex systems of reasoning. Distinguishing between dialectic and analytic, Aristotle says that thinking "is the mark of an educated mind to be able to entertain a thought without accepting it."[16] Calling for cooperative dialogue for constructing the truth, Aristotle also says,

> The investigation of the truth is in one way hard, in another easy. An indication of this is found in the fact that no one is able to attain the truth adequately, while, on the other hand, no one fails entirely, but everyone says something true about the nature of all things, and while individually they contribute little or nothing to the truth, by the union of all a considerable amount is amassed.[17]

For Plato, Aristotle, and skeptics believe that things are not the way they appear to be while only the trained critical mind is able to see deeper through the way things appear to us than the way they really are underneath. Out of the Greek traditions, emerged the need for the people who seek understanding to think both critically and systematically for only this kind of thinking leads to truth.[18]

Thomas Aquinas (c. 1225–74): in the Middle Ages and after, the tradition of systematic critical thinking is strongly evident in the writings and teachings of Thomas Aquinas (*Summa Theologica*). Indeed, listing Aquinas among secular critical thinkers while he is a significant Christian theologian is intentional for the significant effect Aquinas contributed to the critical thinking theory in the entire world. He, indeed, increased man's awareness, not only of the potential power of reasoning, but also of the need for reasoning to be systematic. Do not always reject established beliefs, only those that lack reasonable foundations. Aquinas says,

> The believer and the philosopher consider creatures differently. The philosopher considers what belongs to their proper natures, while the believer considers only what is true of creatures insofar

---

15. Stratton, *Critical Thinking*, 2.
16. Aristotle, *Aristotle's Metaphysics*, Book II, Part 1.
17. Dutton et al., "Critical Thinking."
18. Ibid.

as they are related to God, for example, that they are created by God and are subject to him, and the like.[19]

Renaissance (fifteenth and sixteenth centuries): in this period, a flood of scholars in Europe began to think critically about religion, art, society, human nature, law, and freedom. Having the assumption that most of the human life domains are in need of searching, analysis, and critique, they followed up on the insights of the ancient philosophers and thinkers. Most prominent of these scholars were John Colet, Erasmus, Thomas Moore, and Francis Bacon in England. Bacon, in particular, was explicitly concerned with the way that people misuse their minds in seeking knowledge, recognizing explicitly that the mind cannot safely be left to its natural tendencies. In his book *The Advancement of Learning*, Bacon argues for the necessity of using an empirical study to fully understand the world, which established the foundation for modern science that is based on the information—gathering processes. He was also convinced that most people, if left to their own implements without the guide of education, would develop bad habits of thought "idols," which would lead them to build false and misleading beliefs. Creatively, he classified these idols into: the "Idols of the tribe," which are the ways our mind naturally tends to trick itself; the "Idols of the marketplace," which are the ways we misuse words; the "Idols of the theater," our tendency to become trapped in conventional systems of thought; and the "Idols of the schools," which the problem of thinking when based on blind rules and poor instruction. Bacon's book is considered one of the earliest texts that profound critical thinking.[20]

Rene Descartes (1596–1650): in his book *Rules For the Direction of the Mind*, which considered the second text in critical thinking, Descartes recognizes the need for a systematic discipline of the human mind to guide in thinking critically and for clarity of thinking and precision. Based on the *principle of systematic doubt,* he developed a method of critical thought pointing to the need of locating thinking on well thought through foundational assumptions, believing that every part should be questioned, doubted, and tested. He concluded his theory with "cogito, ergo sum;" "I think; therefore, I am," which he used as the foundation of his entire philosophy. Indeed, the Renaissance's critical thinking model opened the door for the emergence of science, development of democracy, human rights, and freedom of thought.[21]

---

19. Stratton, *Critical Thinking for College*, 1.
20. Ibid., 3.
21. Paul, Elder, and Bartell, "California Teacher Preparation."

Hobbes and Locke (sixteenth and seventeenth century): Rejecting the traditional picture of dominant things in the thinking of their day, they insisted on the necessity of a rational way of thinking of what is considered "normal," believing in the critical mind to open up new horizons of understandable learning. Hobbes adopted a naturalistic view of the world in which everything was to be explained by evidence and reasoning. Locke defended a common-sense analysis of everyday life and thought. He laid the theoretical foundation for critical thinking about basic human rights and the responsibilities of all governments to submit to the reasoned criticism of thoughtful citizens. It was in this spirit of intellectual freedom and critical thought that people such as Robert Boyle and Isaac Newton did their work. Accordingly, it has become a quite fact that egocentric views of the world must be abandoned in favor of views based entirely on carefully gathered evidence and sound reasoning.[22]

Adam Smith (eighteenth century): This time extended the conception of critical thinking, calling people's awareness to the power of critical thought and its tools when it is applied to different aspects of life. Then, he argues that applying it to the problem of economy, it produced Smith's *Wealth of Nations*;[23] applying it to the traditional concept of loyalty to the king, it produced the *Declaration of Independence*;[24] applying it to reason, it produced Kant's *Critique of Pure Reason*.[25]

Auguste Comte and Herbert Spencer (nineteenth century): the understanding and use of critical thought was extended even further into the domain of human social life, as it was applied to the problems of capitalism and produced the social and economic critique of Karl Marx. It was also applied to the history of human culture and the basis of biological life and resulted in Darwin's *Descent of Man* as well as being applied to the unconscious mind, leading to Sigmund Freud's psychological analysis. Its application to the nature of human being led to anthropological studies.[26]

William Graham Sumner (twentieth century): individuals' understanding of the nature and power of critical thinking has increasingly taken more explicit formulations. In his book *Folkways,* Sumner offered a deep study of the foundations of sociology and anthropology in which he pointed out

22. Ibid.
23. Smith, *Wealth of Nations*, book 4, chapter 7.
24. The Declaration of Independence is the usual name of a statement adopted by the Congress on July 4, 1776, which announced that the colonies, then at war with Great Britain, regarded themselves as thirteen newly independent sovereign states, and no longer a part of the British Empire.
25. Kant, *Critique of Pure Reason.*
26. Paul, Elder, and Bartell, "California Teacher Preparation."

to the tendency of the human mind to think sociocentrically while schools' methods uncritically serve for indoctrination.[27] Recognizing the deep need for critical thinking in life and in education, Summer states,

> Criticism is the examination and test of propositions of any kind, which are offered for acceptance, in order to find out whether they correspond to reality or not. The critical faculty is a product of education and training. It is a mental habit and power. It is a prime condition of human welfare that men and women should be trained in it. It is our only guarantee against delusion, deception, superstition, and misapprehension of ourselves and our earthly circumstances. Education is good just so far as it produces well-developed critical faculty. A teacher of any subject who insists on accuracy and a rational control of all processes and methods, and who holds everything open to unlimited verification and revision, is cultivating that method as a habit in the pupils . . . Education in the critical faculty is the only education of which it can be truly said that it makes good citizens.[28]

John Dewey (1859–1952): under the title of "reflective thinking," in a vast number of works, Dewey, has made a significant contribution to the people's understanding of critical thinking both in the nineteenth and twentieth centuries. Dewey points out the importance, usefulness and necessity of this kind of thinking as the best one among others. Calling his approach "naturalistic instrumentalism" he established to the constructive way of forming knowledge through reflecting on one's experience of everyday life. Trusting the natural capacities of the human being to grow continuously, Dewey insisted on locating experience at the center of the learning process. As a fundamental element of learning, Dewey's approach required a learner-centered model of learning so that each learner could construct his or her own knowledge in an environment of democracy and freedom, which he insisted is a "freedom of intelligence." Dewey wrote hundreds of articles and dozens of significant books, such as *Democracy of Education* and *Experience and Education*; however, his popular books *How We Think* and *Logic: The theory of Inquiry*, are the most significant on the topic of critical thinking.[29]

Attesting to this history, however, reflects two fundamental facts. First, it reflects, not only the increased necessity and usefulness of such a kind of thinking, but also the fact that the ability of thinking critically, which

27. Sumner, *Folkways*, 631.
28. Ibid., 632–33.
29. Paul, Elder, and Bartell, "California Teacher Preparation."

is naturally implanted in each human being, can be taught both through other disciplines or as a separate discipline. Second, this brief history of critical thinking also reflects the fact that dominant thoughts and beliefs in all dimensions of life, including spiritual, must not be accepted as they are, but analyzed and assessed for clarity, accuracy, relevance, and logicalness. Knowledge must be subject to the process of interpretation, which involves concepts, assumptions, and implications while students need to be able to articulate thinking about thinking that reflects basic command of the intellectual dimensions of thought.

Critical Thinking—A Brief History in the Bible and Christian Traditions

Old Testament: In his book *Faith-Based Education That Construct: A Creative Dialogue between Constructivism and Faith-Based Education*, HeeKap Lee explains how the critical pedagogy of teaching in the Bible, both in the Old and New Testaments, is the primary foundation of the contemporary school of learning called constructivism. Lee emphasizes that the Bible clearly advocates that there is ultimate truth that leaners need to learn. However, "teacher-as-lecturer" is not the only way; rather, there are many other ways that the Bible offers for learning this truth. In the Garden of Eden, God used *choice* to teach Adam and Eve about good, evil, and redemption. God *challenged* Cain's mind and thinking by presenting contradictions to Cain's ideas. In contrast, God allowed Noah enough time to practice *self-reflection* as he spent about a hundred and twenty years building the ark. Like Noah, Abraham was offered long years to reflect and examine his thought and practice until God's promise came true. Joseph, on the other hand had to go through a *conceptual cluster of problems* to be trained through a problem-solving way.[30]

Further, many of the prophets and apostles used critical thinking to encourage their learners to think and construct their truth themselves. For instance, most of the law that Moses received from God was learned by Israelites through rehearsing and practicing it under the guidance of Moses. Moses instructs parents to educate their children through the concept of 'learning through doing,' "These commandments that I give you today are to be on your hearts. Impress them on your children. Talk about them when you sit at home and when you walk along the road, when you lie down and when you get up" (Deut 6:6–8). Lee continues demonstrating that the critical mode of thinking was used through a vast number of prophets and leaders

30. Lee, *Faith-Based Education*, 41.

in the Bible through many different methods in order to help their audiences construct true knowledge through their own experience. He says,

> Essentially, learning was to happen continuously, inside and outside of the formal classroom setting. Gideon's task was one of teaching through collaboration. Samson spoke in riddles and promoted inquiry through questioning. Samuel used questioning to confront Saul. Likewise, Nathan used questioning to confront David. Sometimes the messages presented by major and Minor Prophets were simple and sometimes they were quite complex—each prophet aligning curriculum according to students' levels of development.[31]

Jesus and New Testament: In his article "The Greatest Constructivist Educator Ever: The Pedagogy of Jesus Christ in the Gospel of Matthew in the Context of the 5Es", William Robertson emphasizes that the teaching methods utilized by Jesus Christ as recorded in the New Testament Gospel of Matthew demonstrated the use of a constructivist methodology as a pedagogical approach. Jesus continually challenged his disciples and followers through the use of experiences, parables, and questions in order to relate the context of his eternal message to their practical and daily lives. In this way, he centered his instruction on developing conceptually correct understandings that had to be discovered and personalized by the learner. For example, in the parable of the Sower (Matt 13:3–9), Jesus described four types of environments where seed could be planted in order to grow into healthy crops. In only one of the four scenarios presented did the seed fall into fertile ground and provide a crop worthy of harvest. In the agrarian society of Israel, many would have had extensive previous knowledge and experience with growing crops from seeds and would also have understood the inherent need for rich soil that was well tended in which to plant and grow crops. For the learners, this parable metaphorically ties their previous learning and experiences to the truths of God, ultimately connecting to the need for personal salvation. As such, this process demonstrates a constructivist educator leading learners through a critical thinking exercise within a problem-solving context. The educational practices utilized by Jesus Christ embodied the foundations of constructivism.

In the Sermon on the Mount, Jesus employed a number of engagement strategies that integrated the familiar settings and experiences of his audience into his teaching. For example, Jesus presented the truths of heaven in a way that allowed the listeners to see themselves in the fabric of his message. This became a key point for having them become engaged in the process of

---

31. Ibid.

personal salvation. He stated, "You are the light of the world, a city set on a hill cannot be hidden nor do they light a lamp and put in under a basket, but on a lamp stand, so that it may give light to all who see it. Let your light so shine before men that they see your good works and glorify your Father in heaven" (Matt 5:18–22). The central idea that each person can experience spiritual salvation was built around topics that were familiar and real in the lives of audiences.

This engagement process helped the learners to see themselves in the teaching of Jesus and to become connected to his message and to the process to follow. This is evident in the parables that Jesus uses in the Gospel of Matthew, in which he uses situations and materials that were familiar and readily available to his followers, such as mustard seeds and salt. Further, by framing his teaching in terms of parables and questions, Jesus facilitated discussion between his followers as they searched for meaning themselves. This sharing within cooperative groups is a basic strategy in constructivism as it allows the teacher to facilitate the learning process, and also helps to develop a common base of experiences on which to help make connections to content.[32]

Christian Traditions: It is not only biblical traditions that strongly promote critical thinking but also Christian traditions. It is clearly known that Saint Augustine was a significant philosopher and critical thinker who kept arguing with the pagans when they attempted to attack the Christian faith. While Augustine offers a great theological account on issues that are hard to be gained intellectually, such as *Trinity*, his book *The City of God* clearly manifests his significant critical thinking skills. In this book, while he intelligently organized comparison between the city of God and the city of man, he refutes pagans' understanding of the history as repeats itself in a circular way and which represents vine understanding of history as a linear way that intentionally directed from creation to judgment in order to fulfill God's will in the world. However, Augustine's ability to argue and refute pagan's claim against Christianity prove, not only his deep philosophical and theological understanding, but also his ability to reflect, analyze, and construct his own thoughts, which were strong enough to give high credibility to his account.

For his philosophical and critical mind, Augustine was able to argue against attacks,

> When they [secularists] are able, from reliable evidence, to prove some fact of physical science, we shall show that it is not contrary to our Scripture. But when they produce from any of

32. Robertson, "Greatest Constructivist."

their books a theory contrary to Scripture . . . either we shall have some ability to demonstrate that it is absolutely false, or at least we ourselves will hold it so without any shadow of doubt. And we will so cling to our Mediator, "in whom are hidden all the treasures of wisdom and knowledge," that we will not be able led astray by the glib talk of false philosophy or frightened by the superstition of false religion.[33]

Thomas Aquinas—the most significant Christian thinker in the Middle Ages, *Luther, Zwingli, Calvin* and other all are models of critical Christian thinkers. Then in the modern era, *Fredric Schleiermacher*, who was known as the father of the liberal theology, his theology was a paradigm shift to the critical use of mind and reason for understandable faith. Then *Karl Barth*, whose theological method reveals a high rational way of thinking, in particular his understanding of the Word of God. Then, Niebuhr and many of the contemporary Christian thinkers who successfully reconciled faith with reason, and theology with philosophy.

Critical Thinking in the Arabic World

In my understanding, the real problem of the East, including Egypt, has always been the incapability to follow the huge scientific, cultural, and philosophical progress of the West. Consequentially, the West is always a step further in all aspects of life, scientific research in particular. While the West has already moved from the post-modernism, stepping quickly into what some call the post-post-modernism, most of the thinkers of the Middle East believe that the East is still swinging between the Middle Age and modern eras.

In his article, "Why the Arabic World Turned Away from Science," Hillel Ofek offers a useful statistic comparison between the West and the Arabic World in scientific progress. Ofek is convicted that the Arabic world is not known for its engagement in the modern scientific project. President Obama, for instance, in his June 4, 2009 speech in Cairo, praised Muslims for their historical scientific and intellectual contributions to civilization of the whole world:

> It was Islam that carried the light of learning through so many centuries, paving the way for Europe's Renaissance and Enlightenment. It was innovation in Muslim communities that developed the order of algebra; our magnetic compass and tools of

---

33. Augustine, *Literal Commentary on Genesis*, 1:121.

navigation; our mastery of pens and printing; our understanding of how disease spreads and how it can be healed.[34]

It is historically true, says Ofek, that the Arabic world through a vast number of significant thinkers in sciences and philosophy did open the door of the Renaissance and Enlightenment for the West by rediscovering and translating the ancient Greek philosophy, Aristotle in particular, into Latin. Averroes, for example, has a great contribution with full commentaries of Aristotle and Plato. The Arabic-Latin translation movements in the Middle Ages, which paralleled that from Greek into Latin, led to the transformation of almost all philosophical disciplines in the Medieval Latin world. The impact of Arabic philosophers such as A-Farabi, Avicenna and Averroes on Western philosophy was particularly strong in natural philosophy, psychology, and metaphysics, but also extended to logic and ethics.[35]

However, Ofek argues the discrepancy between the intellectual achievements of the Middle East then and now, when compared with the rest of the world, is stumbling indeed. In his 2002 book *What Went Wrong?* Historian Bernard Lewis notes that "for many centuries the world of Islam was in the forefront of human civilization and achievement."[36] The reason for this real contribution of the Arabic in the scientific progress and civilization of the world demonstrates that there was no categorical or natural barrier to tolerance, cosmopolitanism, and advancement in the Middle East. Today, the spirit of science in the Muslim world is as dry as the desert.[37]

To understand this anti-rationalist movement, it essentially requires us to return to the history of the relationship of the fundamental religion, Islam in particular, with scientists and philosophers. One of the stories that embodies the tragedy of hatred and antagonism of religion toward philosophers, scientists, and thinkers took place with Averroes himself, one of the great philosophers that opened the door of enlightenment to Europe at the beginning of twelfth century, when the Muslim king had burnt all Averroes' books in philosophy and science, as he believed that all were filled with atheism and anti-religion thoughts. In trying to explain the Islamic world's intellectual laggardness, it is tempting to point to the obvious factors: authoritarianism, bad education, and underfunding. But these reasons are all broad and somewhat crude, and raise more questions than answers. At a deeper level, Islam lags because it failed to offer a way to institutionalize free inquiry. That, in turn,

34. President Obama cited by Ofek, "Why the Arabic World Turned Away from Science."
35. Ibid.
36. Ibid.
37. Ibid.

is attributable to its failure to reconcile faith and reason. With a couple of exceptions, every country in the Middle Eastern parts of the Muslim world has been ruled by an autocrat, a radical Islamic sect, or a tribal chieftain. Islam has no tradition of separating politics and religion.[38]

Critical Thinking: A Brief History in Egypt

Since education is one of the major problems in Egypt today, a significant lack of critical thinking within Egyptian society derives from an educational system that focuses on "memorizing"[39] established knowledge as the primary method in the teaching-learning process; written examinations as the only form of student-assessment; teacher-centered pedagogy; and practice divorced from theory. What Paulo Freire calls "banking education,"[40] and John Dewey calls "rote education,"[41] is the basic educational approach in Egypt today.[42] As a result, mythical thinking, particularly in religious matters, dominates thinking in Egyptian society, including the Christian communities.[43] This pervasive educational approach in Egypt is the medium through which most of the social, economic, and religious problems have fostered and developed.

Christian education in the Presbyterian Church in Egypt is deeply influenced by the problematic situation of Egyptian public education described above. The thoughts and life of the majority of the church leaders have been

---

38. Ibid.

39. I prefer using the word "memorizing" to describe the nature of the pedagogical practice in the educational system in Egypt rather than using the word "parroting." I understand that "parroting" means knowledge transmitting from teacher to student and from student back to teacher without understanding or internalization. While memorizing, in my point of view, is a useful and needed activity in which a kind of understanding is included.

40. Freire and Macedo, *Pedagogy*, 9.

41. Dewey, *Experience and Education*, 18.

42. In their work, "Egypt," in *Issues and Problems in Teacher Education: An International Handbook*, Taher Razik and Diaa El-Din A. Zaher clearly view the picture, "Egypt [is] facing serious problems in education—problems compounded by low literacy rates and an exploding population. Educational quality, particularly in basic education and in technical and vocational education, had seriously declined. Increasing numbers of graduates were unemployable and virtually untrainable. The curriculum was generally irrelevant to the students. School quality was uneven, with better quality schools in urban areas where the wealthy could pay for tutoring. Teachers lacked training in pedagogy. Learning, conducted with martial drills and physical punishment, encouraged rote memorization rather than critical thinking. For many Egyptian children, the result was fragmented information, never to be ground into knowledge."

43. Razik and Zaher, "Egypt," 21.

largely shaped by a lack of using critical thinking and active engagement on the part of the learner. Consequences of this are many; yet, the belief that the Bible must be taken as the literal Word of God; Christian fundamentalism; lack of contextual theological theories that are Egyptian in nature; and lack of using reflective thinking for a deeper understanding of individuals' experiences of everyday life are the main fruits of the problematic educational situation of the Presbyterian church in Egypt.

Nevertheless, the Evangelical Theological Seminary in Cairo (ETSC) stands as one of the most strategic institutions for Christian formation in Egypt. No doubt, the ETSC is more advanced regarding the content, curriculum, and method of education than public and church education; however, since the professional study of most of the teachers at the seminary is theology, the pedagogical practices vary according to the personal creativity of each teacher. Despite this, Fayez Fares[44] has noted that the main method of teaching at the ETSC in the fifties was recitation or a combination of recitation and discussion.[45] Over the years, recitation, discussion, and a combination of lecturing and discussion have continued to be the main methods of education at the seminary today, during which time the teacher always has the final word.

Yet, at the center of this picture, the Christian education area at the ETSC clearly represents the problematic situation of public and church education. Throughout the past ten years for me, both as a student and full-time teacher of Christian education at the seminary, it has been evident through a consensus that was constructed by many graduates that the methods and curriculum of the Christian education area at the ETSC have continued without changes during the past two decades. Through my observations as an educator for years both in the church and teaching ministry of the ETSC, I can easily record the multiple factors that formed the problem of the lack of critical thinking in the process of education and formation of the Presbyterian Church in Egypt. However, in my perspective, "dualistic thinking" of the Egyptian Presbyterians in Egypt is the main factor among all of these. The majority of the Egyptian Presbyterians have a strong position against using philosophy and human reason for a deeper understanding of the Bible and for better education. It was, indeed, not before my study in the area of education and formation at PTS that I realized that the lack of knowledge about the contemporary understanding of practical theology as

---

44. Fayez Fares, a well-known Presbyterian pastor, theological professor, and a publisher of many Christian books, says that the ETSC is considered the first theological institution founded in Egypt after the closing of the old Alexandria Catechetical School in the fifth century.

45. Fares, "Study of Theological Education," 14-15.

an academic discipline was a main reason for this problem. Since practical theology is not taught or known as a scientific discipline, locating Christian education in the broader realm of practical theology was not one of the purposes of the teaching process at this area.[46]

Thesis—Reconciling Dialogue and Critical Thinking

Because of the pivotal role it plays in forming pastoral leaders for the Protestant churches of Egypt, I suggest that any proposal for real changes in Christian formation in the Presbyterian Church in Egypt must begin with a careful and accurate investigation of the teaching-learning process of the Christian education area at the ETSC in the light of the contemporary understanding of Christian education as practical theology.[47] Through their significant works, practical theologians Richard Osmer, Don Browning, James Loder, and others teach us Christian education as practical theology. For them, practical theology involves "praxis," which is a dynamic process of critical theological interpretation that begins with practice, engages in reflection, develops theory, and returns to practice. The final goal of the process is a view to improving practices through concrete proposals for intervention. And, because faith practices are embedded in a network of factors studied by other disciplines,[48] this process requires cross-disciplinary

---

46. Ibid.

47. Although Christians have been in Egypt for nearly 2,000 years, modern Egyptian Christianity is a minority religion in a largely Islamic society. The Evangelical Theological Seminary of Cairo is one of the only theological training centers for evangelical, or Protestant, Christians in Egypt. The seminary was founded by Presbyterian missionaries who began work in Egypt around 1855 and gradually met with a strong response as they eventually reached the areas of El Minya and Assiut, where they had the most success. These areas continue to be strongholds of Orthodox, Protestant, and Catholic Christianity and are the point of origin for most of our seminary students. (A part of the ETSC history on its webpage: http://etsc.org/history.htm).

48. Over the past few years, practical theologians have constructed a new consensus about the subject matter and methodology of the practical theology. Their main focus is to emphasize that practical theology is not a mere application of a theoretical works, but rather "praxis," which is a dynamic process of critical theological interpretation that begins with the practice, reflection, theory, practice. The final goal of the process is a view to improving these practices through concrete proposals. This process is informed by cross—disciplinary reflection because faith practices are embedded in a network of factors studied by other disciplines. Building a sense of spiritual wisdom, that enables faith communities to respond to different life situations with faithful, theologically informed practice.

reflection. Christian education, then, is practical theology, means: praxis, interdisciplinary; and hermeneutical in nature.

The purpose of this dissertation, therefore, is not only to illuminate and address the problematic lack of critical thinking of the Christian education in the Presbyterian Church in Egypt, but also to help shaping a practical theological framework to the whole process. Locating Christian education in the larger realm of practical theology, indeed, would help drawing the Presbyterian educators' attention to the usefulness of practicing Christian education as hermetical, interdisciplinary, and praxis as practical theology, which in turn would help the Presbyterian learners to develop and use critical thinking as an approach of constructing more understanding and deeper Christian faith.

To do so, I argue that by using Osmer's comprehensive approach to "Christian education as practical theology" as a framework, I hope to bring the philosopher, psychologist, and educator John Dewey together in a dialogue with the reformation theologian John Calvin in order to help the Egyptian Presbyterians develop and use critical thinking in the Christian education process. Instead of dualism, divisions, and the constantly tensional conflict that has being created by the process of Christian education, between faith and reason, theology and philosophy, and the divine power and human agency, my intention is to bring john Dewey, for a scientific understanding, and john Calvin, for constructing theological norm, in a dialogue under the umbrella of Osmer's contemporary understanding of Christian education as practical theology in order to reconcile faith with reason, theology with philosophy, Christian with secular, the divine authority with the human agency, and theory with practice, which would help transforming Christian education in the Presbyterian church in Egypt into a critical process.

Method: Osmer's Hermeneutical Circle

The main concern of this research is to transform the pedagogical practice of the Presbyterian education in Egypt to become both theologically and philosophically oriented. Therefore, I intend to use a practical theological approach following Richard Osmer's four tasks of interpretation as the method of this research. Osmer reformulated the contemporary consensus of practical theology as "praxis" in terms of four tasks of interpretation: descriptive-empirical, interpretive, normative, and pragmatic. The *descriptive-empirical* task, with the help of other disciplines, offers an accurate assessment of what is going on in the faith community. The *interpretive* task is at the heart of practical theology, it requires a multilayered awareness of how experiences are snuggled in the reality of life. With the *normative* task, Osmer means to submit possible theological interpretations to the judgment of theological and ethical norms in the Christian tradition as well as to the practices of the church in the present. The *pragmatic* task is essentially a new practice that may lead toward change and a more authentic embodiment of Christ's life in a community of faith.

As he believes that these tasks mutually inform each other in a spiral way, Osmer insists to call his four tasks a "hermeneutical circle." For me, this not only introduces my students to practical theology as interdisciplinary task, which is not known in the Egyptian context, but also promotes a continuous use of philosophical and reflective thinking in different pedagogical practices of the educational process. In the epilogue of *Practical Theology: An Introduction*, Osmer teaches seminarians about how to teach practical theology in a way that encourages competent theological reflection and interpretation among parishioners. He also suggests models of teaching that encourage cross-disciplinary dialogue and thinking (both interdisciplinary dialogue between theological sub-disciplines and interdisciplinary dialogue between theology and other fields of study). Osmer thinks that educators' passion with covering content is the biggest barrier to learning. Practically, Osmer advises educators to make greater use of "case studies and critical incident reports to practice practical theological interpretation in relation to particular situations, practices, and contexts."[49]

Why Osmer?

Despite there being a significant creative discussion on methodology included, some mistakenly call Osmer's work on Practical theology a method, which is an unfair reduction of an extensive study of practical theology and pastoral leadership. Interlacing personal case stories of ministry and leadership with academic reflection on methodological approaches and theories, Osmer creates a fourfold vision of the tasks of practical theology. For me, indeed, Osmer's work first is not a method, nor is it even a theory, but rather a system of thoughts and a comprehensive approach to practical theology. While it includes four tasks of interpreting practical theology, which are all intertwined and feed each other in a hermeneutical circle as a creative method of doing practical theology, his approach also includes theological rationale, interdisciplinary work, and praxis, which in itself is also a hermeneutical circle that begins with practice of the faith

---

49. Osmer, *Practical Theology: An Introduction*, 227.

community, reflection, creating contextual theory, and then goes to practice again. In the meantime, Osmer designs each of the above elements as a complete theory in itself. The first task, *descriptive-empirical*, for example includes an extensive account on empirical research, its scientific nature, types, and the practical ways apply it.

I have also chosen Osmer's approach as a framework, second, because it is both strongly relevant and deeply connected to the purpose and the course of this research. If the purpose of this research is using the contemporary understanding of Christian education as practical theology to illuminate and address the problem of lacking critical ways of thinking in the process of Christian education of the Presbyterian church in Egypt, Osmer's practical theology as both a rational and hermeneutical approach to Christian education is quite useful to achieve my goal. From his 1983 doctoral dissertation "Practical Theology and Contemporary Christian Education" to his latest work *Practical Theology: An Introduction*, representing Christian education as practical theology has become a main concern for Osmer. Therefore, because practical theology is almost an unknown as a discipline and educational approach in the Presbyterian Church in Egypt, using Osmer's approach as practical theology has also become a main concern for me.

Third, using Osmer's approach as a framework for my research is a useful approach because Osmer intends to make it a practice of the whole church, not only of the academics. Reviewing Osmer's *Practical Theology: An Introduction*, Kevin G. Smith says,

> Osmer's primary purpose is to equip congregational leaders to engage in practical theological interpretation of episodes, situations, and contexts that confront them in ministry. A secondary purpose is to equip theological educators to train students in the skills of practical theological reflection.[50]

Addressing the problem of the Presbyterian's alienation from using or developing critical thinking skills, in my perspective, will begin with helping them to think, read the Bible, and read their own life experience theologically instead of the literal way in which they approach their Christian life. With Osmer, my real intention is to make Christian education as practical theology a practice of all members of my faith community in Egypt. In other words, I believe Osmer's approach is useful to guide all Presbyterians in Egypt think both philosophically and theologically instead of being guided by some of the biblical words that are read literally.

50. Smith, Review of *Practical Theology*, 99.

I have chosen Osmer's comprehensive approach to practical theology fourth, because, despite its extensive and deep discussion of all dimensions of the process, it is not obscured or complicated, but rather, comprehensible and easily understood and applied. Indeed, each single competent of Osmer's approach is determined, clear, and practical so that it is helpful to achieve the goals of this research. In short, if the purpose of this research is to guide the Egyptian Presbyterians to develop critical thinking skills in the process of Christian education, I believe that Osmer's approach is as rational, hermeneutical, and critical as I hope my people to be.

Why Dewey?

John Dewey was an American philosopher, psychologist, and educational reformer. He was born in 1859 and died in 1952. He was one of the early developers of pragmatism and functional psychology and his ideas have been influential in education and social reform. Along the course of his writing, Dewey has become the chief prophet of progressive education. In his article, "John Dewey (1859–1952)," Robert B. Westbrook says,

> John Dewey was the most significant American philosopher of the first half of the twentieth century. His career spanned three generations, and his voice could be heard in the midst of cultural controversies in the United States (and abroad) from the 1890s until his death, at the age of 93, in 1952. During this long career, Dewey developed a philosophy that called for the unity of theory and practice. He exemplified this unity in his own work as an intellectual and political activist. His thinking was grounded in the moral conviction that 'democracy is freedom', and he devoted his life to the construction of a persuasive philosophical argument for this conviction and to the pursuit of an activism that would secure its practical realization. Dewey's commitment to democracy and to the integration of theory and practice was most evident in his career as an educational reformer.[51]

I chose Dewey as a scientific partner of my research for many reasons. First, he embraced three careers that are essentially connected and intertwining at the same time, philosophy, education, and psychology. It has become strongly evident that these three are very useful when they are integrated together. Intelligently, Dewey embraced the three of them, integrated them, and uses them to feed each other for the benefit of creating a full, flourished and wellbeing. The second reason for choosing Dewey

---

51. Westbrook, "John Dewey."

as the main dialogue partner of this research is his vast number of significant works. In his lifetime, Dewey wrote hundreds of article and dozens of books and almost all of the subjects that he introduces are of great value to Presbyterian education in Egypt. This rich production, indeed, gives options, alternatives, and great resources and references that are relevant to the idea of the research.

Third, as I believe that Dewey's major themes are extraordinarily relevant to address the problematic reality of the Presbyterian education in Egypt, I was convinced that using Dewey as a main dialogue partner in this research might be helpful to illuminate both the problematic situation and the main factor that formed it in the process. It, indeed, has become evident for most of the world that the Egyptians misunderstood Democracy as just liberation from a dictator regime. This is what actually explains why the great protestors of the youth left El Tahrir Sq. right after Mubarak did step down. Dewey is clearly helpful in aiding the Egyptian education in constructing different view of democracy, experience, anthropology, and creative pedagogy.

Nevertheless, Dewey's Critical theory is what the main purpose of my research is about, a problem that he points to in most of his works and redefines in his significant work *How We Think* and *Logic: The Theory of Inquiry*. Along with Jean Piaget, John Dewey was one of the first major contemporaries to develop a clear idea of what constructivism consists of. He was concerned with the learner as an important agent in the process.

Why Calvin?

One of the main factors of lacking critical thinking in the Presbyterian process of education in Egypt is the significant lack of theological account. For the majority of the Egyptian Presbyterians, the term "theology" itself is unknown. Only pastors and lay leaders that study at seminaries and a few other leaders among the elites of the Church are interested in reading theology. It is even required in many situations to explain what a theological seminary is. However, for the pastors and lay leaders who study theology, the lack of theological knowledge is still problematic since only Calvin and Barth theologies are partially offered by the ETSC.

However, the majority of the Presbyterian leaders appreciate Calvin as the founder of the Presbyterian Church and theology. For a theologically conservative and scripture-centered church such as the Egyptian Presbyterian Church, to convince the church with any kind of teaching is quite difficult without rooting your teaching in the Bible. This indeed, is the first reason for choosing Calvin as a main dialogue partner for this research. In addition to being known, appreciated, and trusted by most of the church leaders, Calvin also deeply liked, appreciated, and rooted the entire of his theology in the Bible. The second reason for choosing John Calvin as a theological partner of this research is the serious account that Calvin offers on the human reason and rationality. Unlike the common impression that many mistakenly have about Calvin maybe because his doctrine of election and predestination, Calvin, not only deeply uses his reason and critical analysis, but also he offers a comprehensive teaching of the usefulness and importance of using reason and critical thinking for deeper understanding of Christian faith and Christian theology. Third, Calvin's understanding of the two kingdoms is a central theme of his theology. His understanding of the relationship of the two kingdoms is a call for a reconciliation of all divisions. Calvin's intention is to view Christians as whole contextual beings that limited with body and physical world while their relationship with God is a spiritual relation, in which God transform human soul, mind, and heart so that becoming able to live and interact in the world in piety and sanctification. The fourth reason that I am taking Calvin, as my theological partner of this research is my conviction that Calvin is the father of the modern democracy. In many ways, the equality of all humans is proven in Calvin's theology. If total depravity means the corruption of the whole human being, it is also means the corruption of all people, which means that all people in a deep need for the glory of God. On the other hand, the priesthood of all believers, which means that in Christ, all have become the children of God, means all are equally brothers and sisters. Rejecting both the chaotic permissive and authoritarian submissive way, Calvin suggests a third order to keep authority from deviation. The new order for Calvin is the participation of all people in discussion and making decisions, which was the first seed for the democracy. Fifth, Calvin's doctrine of God's providence calls Christian to be hermeneutics in everyday life. Believing that God is the sovereign ruler of the world God works "beyond scenes" to guide and direct the world even if the actors do not know. Egyptian Presbyterians, then, are called to see hermeneutical keys to history of God's revelation in the scripture and Jesus.[52]

Chapter Outline

Following Osmer's four tasks of interpretation practical theology, I intend to organize my dissertation in four chapters. In order to define the problem,

---

52. Osmer's notes on Samy Estafanos' comprehensive exam on "Theology and Human Science in Dialogue" (unpublished) Princeton Theological Seminary, September 2012.

in the first chapter, I organize the *descriptive-empirical* in two parts. In the first part, I use a wide range of the secular Egyptian writing on education in order to describe the problem of the lack of critical thinking in general in Egypt. In the second part, following Osmer's data, I apply empirical research in three forms, simple qualitative survey, focus group discussion, and interview on some of Presbyterian leaders and educators in Egypt.

The second chapter focuses on the *Interpretive task*. In order to understand the problem in its deepest pedagogical dimensions and identify the underlying factors that constructed it, I will focus on the educational theory of John Dewey as a scientific interpretation of the problem. In light of Dewey's traditions, I focus on two factors I believe that construct the problem of the lack of critical thinking in the educational process in Egypt. First is the teacher-centered paradigm as a manifestation of the larger problem of the lack of democratic education. Dewey's *Democracy of Education*[53] will offer a useful way to interpret this problem. Second is the lack of attentiveness to learners' life experiences as a necessary component of Christian education. Analyzing this dimension of the problem, I will use Dewey's *Education and Experience*[54] and *How We Think*.[55]

In the third chapter, I will focus on the *Normative task*. In this task, I follow Osmer's primary purpose, which is not only to equip congregational leaders to engage in practical theological interpretations, but also to introduce both educators and learners to the theological heritage as the foundation of Christian education. In the first part of this chapter, I will pay attention to Niebuhr-Dewey debate on the human nature and the power of sin. In this, Niebuhr's theological critique of Dewey's optimistic confidence in the human being will be questioned both by Dewey's philosophical and Valerie Saiving's psychological understandings. In the second part of this chapter, I offer an extensive analysis of John Calvin's theology of human reason in three different statuses, before sin, after in, and after redemption. The purpose of this is not only to find in Calvin's theology what would support Dewey's philosophy of education as continuous growth of the human being, but also to construct a theological norm of the usefulness and necessity of using reason in order to develop critical thinking skills in the Presbyterian education in Egypt.

In the fourth chapter—*pragmatic*, I aim to help the church to construct practice-guiding theories. More concretely, I use the scientific framework of these theories to help build critical thinking skills of the ETSC students.

---

53. Dewey, *Democracy and Education*.
54. Ibid.
55. Dewey, *How We Think*.

These critical and hermeneutical skills will help them to construct a new approach to the Bible and to daily life practice, digging deeper in attaining the Truth through a comprehensive understanding of the whole biblical message, rather than naïve, superficial interpretation of the literal words of the Bible. Yet, I'm aware that not all Western thinkers and educators, particularly secular, are relevant to the contemporary Egyptian context. Therefore, I will both critique and adapt these thinkers in order to contextualize their works to the Egyptian culture and traditions.

CHAPTER I

Presbyterian Church in Egypt and Critical Thinking—Current Status

One has to ask what happened to education and scientific research in the modern Arab world? Today, the contribution of the Arab world to international scientific research is negligible ... In 2009 Turkey produced twenty-two thousand publications as compared to five thousand in 2000 ... During the same period Egypt and Saudi Arabia had a flat trajectory at nearly two thousand, according to a very recent global research report by Thomson Reuters.[1]

It is a real challenge when the Christian minority in Egypt is absorbed in the Islamic majority and, consciously or unconsciously, adopts some or all of its beliefs ignoring weather these beliefs cope or not with the Christian faith ... It is the fact that the Egyptian Church always exists in diverse context and will never be able to choose its society, which urges the church leaders to use every critical means in order to analyze the beliefs and traditions of this context and shape its own Christian identity for the future.[2]

While Western people use a "scientific method" to study the reality and try to solve its problems, knowledge comes out of this scientific method is constantly subject to evaluation. In this way, the validity of knowledge is always examined in light of its usefulness in the real practices. In contrary, the reference of "real practice," of the Egyptian society as a real source of knowledge is substituted with the reference of the literal understanding of the "holy text," as the only source of truth with rejecting any critical or hermeneutical understanding of these texts.[3]

1. Zewail, "Reflections on Arab Renaissance," 39.
2. Zaki, "Towards A Contemporary Arabic Theology," 42.
3. Al Said, *Egyptian Affaires*, 11–12. Al Said was born in Egypt. He has earned his doctoral degree in nuclear physics from Alexandrian University, Egypt. He also served as a professor of computer and knowledge science at Alexandria University, a professor

Egypt Has Always Had Critical Thinkers

Since I learned to read, about four decades ago, I have been hearing that Egyptian education is in a problematic situation. Thousands of articles and books have been published by chat is called "intellectual elites," warning of the risk of a traditional education system, which is unable to form critical learners. Yet, in different fields of theory and practice of the Egyptian society, there were always a "few" critical thinkers, who were singing out of tune.

The Late Egyptian president, Anwar El Sadat (1918–81) was one of the models of critical figures in Egypt. Although he was born in a poor family in a small village, grew up among average Egyptian villagers, and received his education through the public education system, he was the president of Egypt from 1970 until his assassination in 1981. Many scholars of political affairs describe Sadat as possessing an advanced ability to observe, reflect, and critically analyze life circumstances and make successful decisions, which enabled him to make two of the most difficult decisions in modern Egyptian history. He launched a surprise attack on Israel in 1973, and then became the first Arab leader to sign a peace treaty with Israel, for which he earned the Nobel Prize for peace in 1979.[4]

The second significant critical thinker in modern Egyptian history is in literature. Naguib Mahfouz (1911–2006) was born in Cairo to a poor Egyptian family. The life of the public place in Cairo called "Alley" played a significant role in shaping Mahfouz's distinguished works in literature. Despite his advanced skills in math and the sciences, he was elected to study philosophy at Cairo University in 1930, while his interest in philosophy had a great impact in shaping his critical thinking skills, which enabled him to portray the deepest characteristics of the Egyptian personality.[5] Mahfouz published more than forty articles in various magazines and newspapers, most of which dealt with philosophical and psychological issues. He also published about fifty novels, wrote twenty-five film screenplays, and over thirty Egyptian films based on his novels. All his works were translated into English and 40 other languages.[6]

---

and chairman of knowledge management at the Arabic Academy for sciences and technology, a professor of knowledge management at Concordia University, Canada, and a visiting researcher at the University of Michigan. He is also a member of multiple associations of computer science in the USA and Canada. He is one of the founders of the Tahawty group for Egyptian studies and has multiple publications in the same field.

4. Mansur, *Securities Sadat*, 79.
5. "Naguib Mahfouz," www.aucpress.com/t-aboutnm.aspx.
6. Ibid., 2.

Yet, the most controversial work of Naguib Mahfouz is the *Children of the Alley*. Using the narrative framework of a Cairo alley, this 1960— novel describes the spiritual and social history of mankind from Genesis to the present day. The main characters represent God and Satan, Adam and Eve, Cain and Abel, Moses, Jesus, and Muhammad. In thin disguise, the prophets are portrayed as social reformers striving to save their people from tyranny and oppression. Mahfouz then boldly allegorizes the "death of God" in the modern world at the hands of a new prophet, the magician who personifies science. The allegorical style that Mahfouz intelligently uses to portray the way that Egyptians understand religion as hindering the human ability to make progress and to achieve a better life reveals the advanced critical thinking skills he possessed. When he won the 1988 Nobel Prize for this novel, the Swedish Academy placed a strong emphasis on this unique novel, describing it as "an allegory of humanity's historic destiny under the great monotheistic founders of religion."[7] In its citation for the prize, it wrote, "The Nobel Prize in Literature 1988 was awarded to Naguib Mahfouz 'who, through works rich in nuance—now clear-sightedly realistic, now evocatively ambiguous—has formed an Arabian narrative art that applies to all mankind.'"[8]

The third significant critical thinker in modern Egyptian history is in science. Ahmed Zewail (1946–present) was born in the North of Egypt. Like the majority of Egyptians, he enrolled in the public education system in Egypt. Yet, unlike the majority, reading was his first interest, he says, "Reading was and still is my real joy."[9] Zewail developed exceptional critical thinking skills that manifested in his insistence to analyze everything he reads. He says, "Uncle Rizk was special in my boyhood years and I learned much from him—an appreciation for critical analyses, an enjoyment of music, and of intermingling with the masses and intellectuals alike."[10]

However, Zewail says, "For reasons unknown to me, my mind kept asking 'how' and 'why.'"[11] In the mathematics of chemistry, Zewail has found a satisfaction for his critical nature and inquiring mind. Earning his Bachelor degree with a grade of "excellent," he was appointed to teach at Alexandria University in Egypt, where his teaching skills gave him both high credibility and accountability. In 1967, he began a new chapter of his education when

7. El-Gabalaway, "Allegorical Significance."
8. Http://www.nobelprize.org/nobel_prizes/literature/laureates/1988.
9. Http://www.nobelprize.org/nobel_prizes/chemistry/laureates/1999/zewail-autobio.html.
10. Ibid.
11. Ibid.

he got a PhD scholarship to study chemistry at Pennsylvania University, and he then worked as a professor at UC-Berkeley. A few years later, he began work at Caltech University, where he continued his theoretical and experimental research in femtochemistry—the study of chemical reactions across femtoseconds. Using a rapid ultrafast laser technique that allows the description of reactions on very short time scales, he has become the third ethnic Egyptian to receive the Nobel Prize in science in 1999, following Sadat and Mahfouz. In addition to his several publications in chemistry, Zewail earned several prizes and awards, honorary degrees, and academic positions both in the USA and the Arabic world.[12]

The fourth Egyptian figure that reveals that Egyptian society has always had critical thinkers is in law. Mohamed ElBaradei (1942–present) is considered by many as a significant critical thinker in law and an internal diplomat. After earning his Bachelor degree in Law from Cairo University in 1962, and a Doctorate in International Law from the School of Law of New York University in 1974, he was chosen to work in the Egyptian Diplomatic Service in 1964, serving on two occasions in the Permanent Missions of Egypt to the United Nations in New York and Geneva. From 1974 to 1978 he was a special assistant to the Foreign Minister of Egypt while in 1980 he became a senior fellow in charge of the International Law Program at the United Nations Institute for Training and Research. He was also an Adjunct Professor of International Law at the School of Law at New York University from 1981-87. From 1997-2009, ElBaradei began to serve as Director General of the International Association Energy Agency (IAEA).[13] In October 2005, ElBaradei was awarded the Nobel Peace Prize for efforts "to prevent nuclear energy from being used for military purposes and to ensure that nuclear energy for peaceful purposes is used in the safest possible way."[14]

In 2010, a Noble laureate and former diplomat, ElBaradei returned to become a leading voice for reform in Egypt before the recent Egyptian revolution. His critical reflection on the current Egyptian reality and the deep insights that he constructed out of reading behind scenes made the main groups of protestors adopt him as a leader, and almost overnight, he became Egypt's great liberal hope. In El-Tahrir Square, he said more than one time to the revolutionists, "No one can deliver you—deliverance will have to come by the people and from the people."[15]

12. Ibid.
13. Ibid.
14. Ibid.
15. El Bardei in a direct speech to the Egyptian protestors El-Tahrir Square in what is called by the Egyptians "Friday of Anger," January 24, 2011, few days before Mubarak's stepping down.

The last Egyptian figure that clearly proves that the Egyptian society has not been without critical thinkers is in medicine. Magdi Yacoub (1935–present) was born in the East of Cairo. Having studied medicine at Cairo University and qualifying as a doctor in 1957, he moved to Britain in 1962, and then taught at the University of Chicago before coming back to the UK and becoming a consultant cardiothoracic surgeon at Harefield Hospital in 1973. In 1980, he began the Harefield Hospital transplant programme, through which, Yacoub and his team performed 1000 of the procedures, which resulted in the hospital becoming the leading UK, transplant center. In 1986, he was appointed a professor of the National Health and Lung Institute. It is worldwide known that Yacoub performed more transplants than any other surgeon in the world.

For many, Yacoub was not just a traditional surgeon, but also an extraordinary critical scientist who reflected on his performance after each surgery in order to develop the heart and lung transplantation procedures. An article entitled "Magdi Yacoub: The Man Behind the Mask" states, "There are few in the world who would dispute the fact that Yacoub is a brilliant surgeon."[16] Gavin Wright, an anesthetist who has worked with Yacoub for many years at Harefield, says: "Yacoub has always pushed the boundaries of cardiac surgery."[17] Yacoub himself says, "People say you can't do anything unless you have the evidence that this is going to work. I think if you stick to that, literally, then there will be no progress we would all be doing what we did 50 years ago and people would still be dying. You have to make your imagination work but be prepared to put it to the test, under scrutiny."[18]

Egyptian Society Has Always Had a Significant Lack of Critical Thinking

Despite the significant figures mentioned above, Egyptian society suffers a significant lack of using critical thinking for a deeper understanding of life experiences. From a practical theological viewpoint, I believe that when it comes to depending on human reason to reflect and think critically on theory and practice, Egyptian society in general does poorly at understanding texts and contexts. For many Egyptian scholars and educators, a huge cultural, historical, and scientific gap has been established between Egypt and the West. While the West makes use of scientific methods based on and rooted in the use of the human mind and the gift of reason to build a new

16. Naingollan, "Magdi Yacoub."
17. Ibid.
18. Ibid.

civilization and develop a better life, Egypt is still captured by the rigidity of a literal reading of some texts as the only way of judging and living the truth. In the *Egyptian Affaires: Nation between the Culture of Homeland and the Culture of Religion*, Sayed Nasr El Din says,

> In contrast, historical distance continues challenging all abilities of technology. A historical gap is very significant today between the highly civilized nations of the West, where the principles of modernism and post modernism are already utilized and shape all aspects of life, and the Egyptian society that still uses thoughts and imaginations of the ages that are gone—the Middle Ages. The crucial question here is that, what is the reason of this gap? The western values understand and view human as an independent being who is able to construct knowledge of self and universe by using the gift of reason. While Western people use a "scientific method" to study the reality and try to solve its problems, knowledge comes out of this scientific method is constantly subject to evaluation. In this way, the validity of knowledge is always examined in light of its usefulness in the real practices. In contrary, the reference of "real practice," of the Egyptian society as a real source of knowledge is substituted with the reference of the literal understanding of the "holy text," as the only source of truth with rejecting any critical or hermeneutical understanding of these texts.[19]

For El Sayed, any kind of social reform for Egypt is entirely impossible without real cultural and rational reform, which should begin with a careful examination of the problematic reality of education. El Sayed insists that the main problem is that the dominant culture in Egyptian society is the culture of the past, or "Salavist culture." For him, Salavist culture means the imagination of the future as a revival of past, which is thought of as the "golden age." Salavist culture places a very high value on devoting all attention to understanding the heritage of the great predecessors of this golden age while ignoring the great gap between the experiences of past and present cultures and the factors contributing to these experiences. In this sense, memorizing the values and practices of the past always garners the most appreciation, while criticism, analysis, discovery, and creativity are completely ignored.[20]

The fact that critical thinking is not the main way of approaching life and learning for the majority of Egyptian society is more evident through numbers and statistics. El Sayed states a number of important facts based

19. Al Said, *Egyptian Affaires*, 11-12.
20. Ibid., 100.

on certain statistics from the General Council of the Universities in Egypt in 2005. First, while the number of people that earned a Nobel Prize in entire of the Egyptian history is four, the number in the USA is 82. Second, while the total number of college students in Egypt is 1,321,967, only 0.03 percent of them were registered in a scientific discipline; 0.08 percent in engineering; and 0.006 percent in computer and information management. In the meantime, while the total number of the post-graduate students in the Egyptian universities in 2005 was 86,720, only 0.25 percent chose a topic in science, engineering, or computer and information management. In contrast, this number jumped to 50 percent in Japan, for example, in the same year.

In my viewpoint, while multiple factors socially, politically, economically, and religiously contribute to forming it, the poor public education stands out as the most fundamental reason for the problem of a lack of critical thinking in the Egyptian society. The deep link between poor education and lack of critical thinking in Egypt is quite clear for Nobel Laureate, Ahmad Zewail. In his article, "Reflections on Arab Renaissance: A Call For Education Reform," Zewail highlights the fact that poor education is the basis for all of the social, economic, political, and religious problems of the Arabic world, including Egypt. He says,

> One has to ask what happened to education and scientific research in the modern Arab world? Today, the contribution of the Arab world to international scientific research is negligible. In both research investment (R&D spend compared to GDP) and capacity (researcher numbers compared to population), as reflected in research publication output between 2000 and 2009, the predominance of Turkey and Iran is evident; in 2009 Turkey produced twenty-two thousand publications as compared to five thousand in 2000, and Iran produced fifteen thousand papers in 2009, in vast contrast to thirteen hundred in 2000. During the same period Egypt and Saudi Arabia had a flat trajectory at nearly two thousand, according to a very recent global research report by Thomson Reuters.[21]

In the *Renewal of the Arabic Thinking*, philosopher Zaki Naguib Mahmud suggests that Egyptian society suffers a deep problem in its cultural awareness and scientific thinking. Mahmud recognizes the roots of this problematic situation in the insistence of Egyptians to live in the past and learn from its old approaches. Just as groups of learners used to gather around Al shehk (Muslim elder) in the Al Azhar mosque centuries ago and repeat after him what he already memorized from the Qur'an, so too does public

---

21. Zewail, "Reflections on Arab Renaissance," 39.

education in Egypt today make use of a similar method. Despite the large gap of time, different circumstances, different cultures, and the complexity of problems, public education keeps using the same pedagogical practices—indoctrination and memorization. No wonder then, says Mahmud, that the Egyptians who use human reason and critical thinking to justify the truth are few. While these few critical thinkers strive to achieve innovation in their thinking, they are always confronted by ignorance, strong rejection, and persecution. And no wonder also that the Egyptian contributions to the scientific heritage of the world are negligible.[22]

According to Mahmud, the majority of the Egyptians, not only does not know the true meaning of "critical thinking," but also stands strongly against critical thinkers, particularly if they attempt to make any ideological, social, or religious transformations. The late Egyptian president El Sadat, who was the first Egyptian to earn the Nobel Prize for peace after his critical judgment and brave decision, faced much rejection and misunderstanding by major Egyptian groups, while the precious price that El Sadat ultimately paid for the use of his mind to think critically was his life as the fundamentalist army officers assassinated him October 1981.

In literature, not only Arabic thinkers, but also much of the world attested to Naguib Mahfouz's status as one of the best Arabic novelists, a man whose critical mind enabled him to see behind the traditional scenes of Egyptian society. Yet, reading this works literally, the uncritical majority of the Egyptian society spent decades persecuting Mahfouz in every way and characterizing him as atheistic.[23] In the end, like El Sadat, Mahfouz nearly paid for his critical thinking with his life as he was stabbed in the neck and left with a permanent inability to write continuously for more than a half-hour. Ahmad Zewail, Mohamed ElBaradei, and Magdi Yacoub, on the other hand, have been persecuted socially and emotionally since they returned to Egypt a few years ago. As they attempt to be active participants in forming a new Egyptian society that is able to deal with the complexity of the contemporary age through scientific research and critical thinking, the Egyptian fundamentalists insist on both excluding them from social participation and corrupting their image and characterizing them as agnostics.

Nevertheless, rejecting and persecuting critical thinkers is not the only manifestation of the lack of critical thinking in the Egyptian society; legendary thinking[24] and superstitions are another manifestation. In his article "A

22. Mahmud, *Renewal of Arabic Thinking*, 204.

23. Mahfouz, *Children of Alley*.

24. Mythical thinking is the kind of thinking that is not based on scientific rules. It is the belief in magic, sorcery, spirits, reading cup, and palmistry. Some Egyptians, for example, believe that any upside down shoe or sandal inside the house causes

Failed Attempt to Use Science and Logic," Moataz Abdel Fattah[25] insists that science, reason, and critical thinking are all either unknown or disrespected by the Egyptian majority. Science and reason, Fattah says, thrive in an environment that respects the mind and human reason, but any attempt to use them in a society that does not respect them is a "failed attempt." While reason, as a source of knowledge, should lead people to confront centuries of myth and superstitions, science and scientific thinking are so undervalued in Egypt today as to allow anyone to make statements without reference to anything but oneself.[26]

Zaki Naguib Mahmud strongly agrees with Abdel Fattah. In his book *Rational and Irrational in our Arabic Traditions*, Mahmud emphasizes that while scientific thinking links causes to effects, legendary thinking neglects the need to find a cause for each effect. One of the impediments, Mahmud argues, to the progress of the Arabic nations, including Egypt, is to have faith in this sort of thinking following a world that justifies knowledge only through the use of science. Mahmud strongly critiques the Egyptian society for still attributing sickness and death to evil spirits, envy, or superstitions rather than to germs that cause such sickness.[27]

Giving all authority to religion rather than reason is a third manifestation of the significant lack of critical thinking in the Egyptian society. It is well known that Egypt is a religiously centered society. Central to this religious society are the holy texts the Qur'an and the Bible. For the majority of Egyptians, not only are public prayers important, but also the use of religious texts to justify and legalize various practices. From this perspective, most of the Egyptians use a literal reading of texts to prove that critical thinking and philosophical interpretation weaken faith and obedience to

---

depression and calamities; some believe that pinning blue beads or pouring salt protect from envy; some believe that seeing a black cat brings bad luck; and others think that opening scissors widely causes divorce. Yet, one of the most irrational beliefs of some Egyptians today is the notion that camel urine can treat some diseases, a belief which leads some to drink it for healing.

25. Moataz Bellah Abdel Fattah was born in Egypt in 1972. In high school, he was at the top of the country in 1989. He earned a bachelor degree in economics and political science in 1993, then a master in economics and a PhD in political science from the University of Michigan in 2004. He later worked as a professor of political sciences in Cairo University. He published eight books in economics and politics and writes a weekly article in *El Shorouk* newspaper. Shortly after the Egyptian revolution in 2012, he was chosen as an advisor to the prime minister of Egypt Yet, he insisted on resigning as a rejection of military dictatorship. He was chosen as one of the 50 non-parliamentarians elected to the Constituent Assembly of Egypt. Yet, again, he insisted on leaving for the same reason.

26. Abdel Fattah, "Failed Attempt."

27. Mahmud, *Rational and Irrational*, 23.

God. In his book *Owners of Absolute Truth*, philosopher Mourad Wahba[28] suggests that giving religion authority over human reason is the main factor of the persecution of thinkers and intellectuals in the Arabic societies, through the centuries from Averroes to Naguib Mahfouz. For Wahba, the main problem is the belief that the holy text is the literal words of God, so that any attempt to use reason and philosophy to interpret the text for deeper hermeneutical understanding is always against God.[29]

For Farag Foda, who was assassinated by a Muslim because of his position against Islamic fundamentalism,[30] giving authority to a literal understanding of religion rather than to science is the main reason for the nation's backwardness. In his book *A Discourse About Secularism*, Foda pays much attention to the consequences of an insistence on rooting everything in life in religion and ignoring the great human capability to think critically about real life experience. For him, this perspective deceptively leads people to discover an excuse for why they are not responsible for the backwardness of Egypt in social, economic, and scientific matters. Without scientific and critical reflection on their dogmatic religious beliefs, argues Foda, the Egyptians will continue suffer a miserable, dehumanized life.[31]

---

28. Murad Wahba (1926–present) was born in the city of Assuit, Egypt. He studied philosophy at Cairo University and Ain Shams University and received his doctoral degree from Alexandrian University. He worked as a professor of philosophy at Ain Shams University. He is a member of several international organizations, including academic and humanitarian organizations such as the International Federation of Philosophical Societies and Supreme Council of the Egyptian culture. Wahba is the founder and President of the International Society for Averroes and Enlightenment, founded in 1994. He believes that Averroes's philosophy has greatly contributed to the establishment of rational Europe, which resulted in religious reform in the sixteenth century and enlightenment in the eighteenth century as they widely employed the views Averroes preached in the recognition of the role of the mind in understanding the text and in the positive dialogue between people. For Wahba, a revival of the philosophy of Averroes (Ibn Rushed) would work as a tool that bridges the gap between the West and Muslim communities through prevailing dialogue as the basis of peace in any region of the world.

29. Wahba, *Owners of Absolute Truth*, 234–37.

30. Farag Foda (1946-92) was an important Egyptian thinker, human rights activist, and columnist. He earned his Master's degree in agricultural sciences and a PhD from Ain Shams University in Cairo. He published several books and articles. He also made such a great effort to convince people to use their intellectual abilities and critical thinking skills to analyze and understand what they hear or see in the Egyptian society that he was known to walk randomly through the streets of Cairo to meet people and dialectically converse with them concerning Egyptian affairs. He is the founder of the Egyptian Society for Enlightenment. In 1992, fundamental Muslim groups made a "fatwa," which is an Islamic decree, allowing Foda's killing, and in 1992, at age 46; he was assassinated in front of his enlightenment society.

31. Foda, *Discourse About Secularism*, 17–19.

I conclude the first and second sections of this chapter with some concrete points. First, although Egypt has always had critical thinkers,[32] thinking critically, particularly in religious affairs, is always identified as the breaking of God's law, which is literally stated in the holy texts.[33] Second, what really has made the figures described above critical thinkers is their rebellion against the traditional education system in Egypt. Some of them, such as Sir Magdi Yacoub in medicine, left Egypt once they graduated because of the significant difficulties they confronted in their intellectual journey, while others, such as Ahmad Zewail in science, have earned scholarships to study in the West. However, in every case, all of them strongly believed that Egyptian education is incapable of satisfying their deep instinct to reach the highest level of creativity and critical learning. Even for those who remained in Egypt, such as Naguib Mahfouz, Farag Fouda, and Naser Hammed Abu Zaid the education system was not the main source of developing their critical thinking skills, but rather, their insistence on being active learners through reading and researching themselves. Third, despite the positive impact of their thoughts and the vast efforts they exerted to yield social transformation in the Egyptian society, critical thinkers are significantly few in number compared with the Egyptian population—a number that cannot make real changes in Egypt. Fourth, through the years, it has become more evident that critical thinkers are unwelcomed, ignored, or persecuted by the Egyptian society, a fact that strongly suggests that the underlying reasons for this must be carefully examined.

32. Accurate statistics are difficult to find in Egypt. Egypt does not possess a database system of documenting true and trusted information. Therefore, most of the numbers are relative estimates from available media, newspapers, and the internet.

33. Among Islamic scholars, Nasr Hammed Abu Zaid was a professor of Islamic studies and Arabic language at Cairo University and a researcher in English philosophy and humanities. He also taught in the Netherlands and Japan, and he dedicated his life to the call of liberating Egyptians from the authority of the literacy of the Qur'an. Abu Zaid believes that the authoritarian power of the Qur'an extends, to shaping not only people's religious identity but their cultural identity as well, and this gives religion the upper hand over everything in their lives, resulting in text-oriented individuals. Because of this position, Abu Zaid was accused as apostate and atheistic, and the family court demanded that he be forcibly divorced from his wife, a professor of French literature, on the basis that "it is not permissible for a Muslim woman to marry a non-Muslim." Therefore, Abu Zaid and his wife left Egypt forever and lived and taught in the Netherlands until his death in 2011. Regarding his repetitive proclamation, hermeneutics has significantly shaped his critical mind. Abu Zaid published several books, all about using reason and the hermeneutical function of the human mind to construct one's own knowledge.

The Presbyterian Church in Egypt Has Always Had Critical Theologians

Since it was established by American missionaries in 1854, the Presbyterian Church in Egypt, following the enlightenment attitude of reformed theology, has always had critical thinkers as it pays a great deal of attention to the importance and necessity of using human reason for understanding the Bible as the best way to develop a strong Christian faith. While the deep respect for the church's use of human reason has been manifested in many ways, the foundation of the Evangelical Theological Seminary in Cairo (ETSC) in 1863 was due to the recognition of the necessity for rational theological learning.[34]

Indeed, the enlightening role that the ETSC has played in creating Protestant leaders who are able to reflect critically on both text and life experience has been significant throughout the years. Fayez Fares describes the goal of the educational process of the ETSC as training ministers for the Presbyterian Church in Egypt and being a source of enlightenment to the whole community. For this reason, the Seminary is sympathetic to modern intellectual trends and attempts to connect the Egyptian Presbyterian Church with theological and biblical studies going on in other parts of the world.[35]

Among the hundreds of ETSC students who have graduated since it was established in 1863, there have always been figures who have carried the spark of Christian enlightenment to the Egyptian society generation after generation. Most prominent among these figures is Samuel Habib (1928–1997), who was ordained as a pastor of Christian publication of the Presbyterian Church; earned a master of public information from the American University in Cairo (AUC); a MA in Journalism from Syracuse University in NY in 1955; and a D.Min. from the San Francisco Theological Seminary, CA in 1984. Habib also has received three honorary doctorate degrees from Muskingham College, Ohio, USA (1982), St. Xavier University, Nova Scotia, Canada (1994), and Westminster College, Pennsylvania, USA (1995). He was the president of the Presbyterian denomination and the evangelical churches union in Egypt from 1980–1997. Throughout his lifetime, he published and translated about 60 significant works.[36]

It is well known, both in Egypt and other countries, that Samuel Habib was a remarkable critical thinker "who changed the face of human

---

34. Online website of the Evangelical Theological Seminary in Cairo (ETSC).
35. Fares, "Study of Theological Education," 12–14.
36. Coptic Evangelical Organization for Social Serves (CEOSS).

and religious service in Egypt."[37] Through the years, Habib's critical thinking abilities were manifested in multiple ways. First, he was the founder of the Coptic Evangelical Organization for Social Serves (CEOSS). Unlike the traditional thinking of many Presbyterian leaders, Habib intelligently recognizes the entirety of the human being, a holistic approach to Christian salvation, and the inability of spiritual activities alone to reflect the real message of the gospel as embodied in Jesus. While social,[38] economic,[39] and political[40] transformations are important concerns for Habib, education and enlightenment[41] are always top priorities for him. Realizing that more than fifty percent of the Egyptians are illiterate, a fact, which hinders people from growing in Christian faith, Habib, believes that educating people is the first step to making disciples for Jesus. Therefore, he devoted much energy to eradicating illiteracy through the active work of hundreds of CEOSS employees in most of the villages of Egypt.[42]

The second manifestation of Habib's critical thinking skills is the strengthening of cross-cultural and inter-faith understanding, peace building, and dialogue in the region. Unlike the fundamentalist dialogue, which is concerned with eternal damnation in Hell apart Jesus, and the compromising political dialogue, which can lead to the abandonment of Christian identity, Habib critically realizes the need for a dialogue that is based on equality, respect, and openness even as it maintains a Christian identity. A third manifestation of Habib's critical skills is his constant call for democracy, equality, and the empowering of marginal people both in the church and society. His deep theological conviction concerning the equality of all people is the main reason for his fight to empower women, children, and the poor to have a good life and dignity. Habib insists that a society in which seventy percent of females are illiterate will never be able to meet the needs and demands of the critical mind of the contemporary world, and denying the basic rights of children means denying the future of Egypt.[43]

The fourth manifestation of Habib's critical way of thinking is the fight against a literal reading of the Bible. Realizing that the Presbyterians in Egypt are a very scripture-oriented community that strives to find a biblical text to explain everything in life and recognizing that an Islamic

37. Ibid., 35.
38. Habib, *Christ Revolted*, 36.
39. Habib, *Liberation Theology*, 37.
40. Habib, *Church and State*, 38.
41. Habib, *Christianity and Human*, 40.
42. Ibid., 41.
43. Ibid., 38.

understanding of inspiration[44] is fundamentally at the root of Christian belief that the Bible is the literal words of God, Habib emphasizes that the Bible is not the literal words of God but a divine-human work with respect to the human intelligence as created in the image of God. Since he believes that understanding the Bible as the literal words of God is the primary ground in which many Christian problems are rooted and grow, Habib draws the church attention to the need of using human reason for reflecting and thinking critically on the Bible in order to achieve a deeper understanding of the true Christian message of the Bible.[45]

A second critical thinker of the Presbyterian Church in Egypt is Ikram Lamay (1949–present). Lamay graduated from the ETSC in 1971; earned his bachelor degree in law from Cairo University; was ordained as a pastor of three Presbyterian churches in Egypt; and earned a Th.M. and D.Min from the San Francisco Theological Seminary. In 1990, he was appointed as the president of the ETSC until 2000 in addition to being a professor of comparative religions at the same seminary. Indeed, Lamay's critical thinking abilities are manifested in many ways both academically and practically in the Christian community in Egypt. The critical approach that he uses in his writing that is clearly embodied in many books and articles is the first manifestation of Lamay's critical thinking. *Church and Vision*;[46] *How We Think Objectively*;[47] *The Other Face of the Christ's Teaching*;[48] and *Divine Inspiration and Man's Imagination*[49] are examples. As Lamay always insists on the inevitable human responsibility as active participant with God in faith and practice, he argues that Christian faith as we understand it from a critical reading of the Bible and from Jesus' life is never irrational. Both reason and faith are gifts from the same God.

His insistence on making literature and arts basic elements of the educational process of the ETSC is the second way in which Lamay's critical thinking is embodied. Lamay's strategy was not only to invite rational Egyptian actors, secular thinkers, and philosophers for debates and seminars at the ETSC, but also to make attending theaters, watching secular movies, reading Egyptian literature, and visiting historical and scientific places in Egypt one of the requirements for earning an ETSC degree. Lamay's work, indeed, is considered a paradigm shift for the theological teaching of the

44. Parshall, *Cross And Crescent*, 56–57.
45. Habib, *Gospel and Culture*, 89–101.
46. Lamay, *Church and Vision*.
47. Lamay, *How Can We Think Objectively*.
48. Lamay, *Other Face of Christ Teaching*.
49. Lamay, *Divine Inspiration*.

ETSC as its curriculum moved from pedagogical practices that focused only on spiritual dimension toward the formation of the whole person, socially, mentally, emotionally, as well as spiritually.

His academic profession as a professor of comparative religions at the ETSC is a third manifestation of Lamay's critical thinking abilities. Like his professor Habib, Lamay's philosophy of Christian-Muslim dialogue is always based on his conviction of equality and deep respect for the other's faith. While he insists that only Muslims that have the right to interpret Islam, not Christians, Lamay strongly refuses any dialogue that attempts to deceive a Muslim with a corrupted interpretation of Islam in order to convert him or her to Christianity. Being fully convinced that the Holy Spirit alone is able to effect transformation; Lamay always teaches that a Christian should be wholly honest and transparent, even to the extent of helping Muslims to understand Islam correctly, proclaiming the truth of the Gospel with full confidence in the full effect of the Holy Spirit.

The curriculum that he has been teaching for years at the ETSC is another clear sign of Lamay's critical thinking skills. His class "scientific thinking" is, indeed, one of the best-known curricula at the ETSC. In this, Lamay strongly criticizes any attempt at Christian thinking that is not based on scientific and rational bases. In an interview, Lamay explains the importance and necessity of scientific thinking, for Egyptian society in general and for the Presbyterian Church in Egypt in particular, for creating disciples for Jesus who are able to meet the complex needs of the contemporary "age of knowledge." He emphasizes that learning that is based on personal observation, analysis, problem solving, and constructing one's own understanding of truth is the only way to present the message of the gospel in a contemporary framework.[50]

His position towards marriage and divorce among Christians in Egypt is the fourth manifestation of Lamay's critical thinking skills. Unlike the West, marriage in Egypt is a church issue, and the Egyptian Church strongly controls people using its authority to outlaw divorce for any reason other than adultery. This very strict position in the church is rooted in the theological understanding that marriage is a divine, permanent, and indissoluble relationship. Attempting to help the Christians in Egypt to have a different perspective, in his book *Divorce in Christianity*, Lamay emphasizes that the reality of marital relationships in Egypt tells something very different. Significant struggles with life circumstances as well as psychological, sociological, spiritual, and personal problems exist in many marriages. All of these predictable problems for marriage are actual and real; they are not

---

50. Interview with Ikram Lamay, Appendix 2.

only destructive factors for the marriage itself, but also for all members of the family. For Lamay, Christians in Egypt can find theological and practical solutions for the conflict between the theological belief that marriage is a divine and indisputable issue, and their actual and practical life in marriage, which is filled with many tragedies.[51]

A third critical figure in the Presbyterian Church in Egypt is Fayz Fares (1929-2012), a professor of Christian ethics at the ETSC and a senior pastor of one of the biggest Presbyterian churches in Egypt. Through several publications, Fares is known as a significant theologian and philosopher in the Egyptian Protestant community. Earning his Th.M. from Princeton Theological Seminary in 1952 and D.Min. in Christian ethics from the San Francisco Theological Seminary in 1982, Fares attempts, through his theory on Christian ethics, to convince the Presbyterians in Egypt that ethics cannot take fixed unchanging forms of practices, as they are relative, changeable, and take a variety of forms according to the realities of people, time, and context.[52] In this sense, he argues, forming rational disciples who are able to use reason and critical thinking to make an appropriate decision in every situation is the greatest need of Christian education in the Presbyterian Church in Egypt today. Fares examines important issues of the Presbyterian faith such as spirituality, inspiration, Church and State, Christian marriage, divorce, and our journey *With Christ*.[53]

A fourth Presbyterian leader and prominent critical thinker in Egypt is Makram Naguib, a professor of preaching at the ETSC and a senior pastor of a large Presbyterian church in Cairo. Naguib earned a Th.M. degree from Union Presbyterian Seminary in VA and a D.Min from the San Francisco Theological Seminary in 1988. His critical thinking abilities are clearly manifested in his method of assessing ETSC students in their practical preaching every week through his deep, sophisticated understanding of the biblical text and its connections to contemporary life. Yet, his theological interpretation of the political conflict between Israel and the Arabic world is one of the most vivid examples of his strong position against a literal understanding of the Bible.[54] Through most of his works, Naguib introduces the Egyptian Presbyterians to a deeper meaning of the new Israel as the church and a deeper meaning of the gospel as love, reconciliation, and peace which is proclaimed

---

51. Lamay, *Divorce in Christianity*, 13–15.
52. Fares, *Christian Ethics*, 81.
53. Fares, *With Christ*.
54. Naguib, *Conservative or Liberal*, 13–14, 19.

in Jesus, assuring that the kingdom of God is for all nations and races and refuting the idea of Israel as a nationality and political country.[55]

The Presbyterian Church in Egypt Has Always Had a Significant Lack of Critical Thinking

The intention of this section is to present a comprehensive picture of the current problem of the significant lack of development and use of critical thinking from the Christian education process in the Presbyterian Church in Egypt today. To do so, I organize this section in three main parts. In the first part, I describe the problem in its socio-cultural context, as the Egyptian Presbyterian thinkers understand it. In part two, I explain some of the forms through which this problem manifests itself, and in the final part, I explain both educational and theological reasons that contribute to the problem.

Lack of Critical Thinking: Defining the Problem

Despite the fact that the Church has always had a few critical theologians, I am convinced that a lack of development and use of critical thinking as a basic method for education exists to a great extent in the Presbyterian Church in Egypt. While a few thinkers recognize the necessity of a critical thinking for a better life and ministry, the majority of the Presbyterians in Egypt believe that human reason and critical thinking weaken faith and obedience to God. Nevertheless, the few critical theologians in the Presbyterian Church in Egypt are not a product of a certain educational system in the church. Like secular critical thinkers in the Egyptian society, Presbyterian critical thinkers benefitted the most from their rebellion against the traditional ways of teaching and learning in the Church and their focus on alternative methods, such as studying in the West or active self-learning through reading and researching. A very crucial point here is that education is the deep root of this problem; therefore, while there are multiple dimensions of the problem traditionally, culturally, and socially, the Christian education process is at the root of the significant lack of critical thinking in the Presbyterian Church in Egypt.

In a simple form of a qualitative survey that was conducted with 52 Presbyterian leaders, the fact that critical thinking is not an element of the pedagogical practices of the Christian education process in the Presbyterian Church in Egypt is clearly evident. While about 75 percent of the participants

---

55. Naguib, *Religious Thoughts*, 38–47.

believe that they know the expression "critical thinking" and understand what it means, all of them believe that only 18 percent of the Christian educators of the Presbyterian Church understand the actual meaning of the term. Most Egyptians in general and Christians in particular, have convection that "critical" carries a negative meaning that refers always to criticizing others and declaring their weaknesses.

In his book *Conservative or Liberal,* Makram Naguib clearly points to this problem when he states that the word "criticism" is largely misunderstood in the Egyptian context in general and the Evangelical context in particular. The majority of Egyptians, asserts Naguib, assume that this word always aims not only to show negatives and weaknesses, but also to attack and refute the main principles of the faith in God. Being a scripture-centered community, the fear that using reason will corrupt the principles of Christian faith is always prominent when it comes to understanding and interpreting the Bible, as Evangelicals stand firmly against Muslims' claim that the Bible is corrupted.[56] The fundamental way in which Protestants understand Christian theology and biblical text, Naguib argues, contributes to their position against the practice of self-criticism or the use of reflective analysis of thought and practice. This hinders the Church message from being contemporary and relevant to the postmodern age with its great complexities, fragmentation, and uncertainty.[57]

Attempting to make it more evident, three focus groups of discussion were organized in three locations of the Presbyterian Church in Egypt. The aim of these discussions was to examine how the educators in the church understand and use "critical thinking" in the Christian education process as a way of teaching and learning in the Presbyterian Church in Egypt. One of the most important themes of these discussions was highlighted by a primary leader of Sunday school in Minya presbytery who explained that through her years-long ministry among children, she realized that children always show a high level of natural ability in thinking, analyzing, and attempting to find solutions for every problem. Yet, for some reason, these abilities gradually decline as the children grow and enroll in the educational systems, both public and Christian. The Sunday school leader strongly criticized a variety of the educational processes in the church, believing that instead of using every creative pedagogical practice to help the children develop their natural abilities to grow in thinking critically.

---

56. Ibid., 56.
57. Ibid., 57.

These processes hinder them from the use of human reason for a deeper understanding of Christian faith and life experiences.[58]

A second remarkable theme of the focus group discussions emerged from the general Council of Christian education of the Synod of the Nile of the Presbyterian Church in Egypt. Indeed, while this Council includes a president and eight members from the eight presbyteries of the Church in Egypt, all of whom are pastors and Christian educators, discussion with this group revealed a significant lack of understanding of the meaning and usefulness of "critical thinking." One of the disheartening notes of this discussion was that two of the members of the Council clearly admitted to not knowing what "critical thinking" means. However, the rest of the members and the president confirmed the significant lack of critical thinking skills in the church in general which is deeply rooted in the lack of creativity in the Christian education process and the lack of well-trained educators.[59]

In a three-hour interview, Ikram Lamay[60] insisted that while less than 10 Percent of the Egyptian society knows and uses critical thinking, this percentage is far less in the Christian community, including the Presbyterian church. For Lamay, the main factor that creates this problem is a dogmatic belief in the principles of the Christian faith by church communities and the belief that all attempts at different understandings and hermeneutical interpretations of the holy text will result in a weakening of faith and obedience to God.[61] Indeed, Lamay's estimation of this percentage of the existence and use of critical thinking among Christian education leaders of the Presbyterian Church in Egypt is quite similar to the conviction of other Presbyterian leaders in Egypt. Onsi Anis[62] argues that thinking critically is lacking severely as to be nearly nonexistent. While Yousri Elias[63] and Shaher

---

58. Appendix 3, "Focus Group," (Minya Presbytery), 3.

59. Appendix 3, "Focus Group," (General Council of Christian Education of the Synod of the Nile of the Presbyterian Church).

60. Ikram Lamay is one of the notable critical theologians in the Presbyterian Church in Egypt that is mentioned in the third section.

61. Appendix 3.

62. For years, Onsi Anis had been a medical doctor before he followed God's call to study theology and to be ordained as a teaching pastor for Christian education as the ETSC for a few years when he was appointed as a leader of youth ministry and leader training in the Middle East Council of Churches.

63. Yousri is a son of Elias Magar, one of the great pastors in the Presbyterian Church in Egypt; Yousri is the founder of the middle school meeting in the Presbyterian Church in Egypt for twenty-five years. Yousri subsequently helped to spread this ministry to all of the Presbyterian churches in Egypt, when he became the main leader of the general committee for middle school juniors in the Synod of the Nile. He has multiple prospectuses of curricula for serving this age.

Luke[64] think that the Church strongly suffers from a lack of rational thinking, Sameh Hanser[65] thinks that the percentage of Christians that appreciate critical thinking in general in Egypt could be as high as 20 percent.

The negative impact of the disuse of rationality and reflective analysis on the relevance and effectiveness of the church message was a great concern for Samuel Habib. In his book *Christianity and Human Being, Selected Papers*, Habib states that theology in the Presbyterian Church in Egypt suffers a real crisis—it has been eclipsed by a vast heritage from different cultures, which infiltrated this theology throughout the centuries from the pharaoh to Islamic, Coptic, and other cultures. To achieve an understanding of genuine Presbyterian theology, a different approach to the teaching-learning process of the Church is strongly needed. It is the lack of a scientific way of learning and thinking that results in Christians who are unable to deal with the contemporary age and its huge demands and complexity.[66] In a world that subjects everything to scientific rules, Habib continues, the insistence of the church on using the same traditional methods of education and formation will lead to their alienation and exclusion from this "age of knowledge." No wonder, then, that the loyalty of people, youth in particular, to the Presbyterian Church is dramatically declining today.[67]

Indeed, significant lack of using critical thinking by most of the Presbyterian leaders in Egypt has increasingly become evident to me through my personal observation and practice as an educator in the Egyptian Presbyterian Church for years. One of the strong evidence was raised clearly to the surface through a serious of conversations that I intentionally have opened on the Facebook with hundreds of the Presbyterian pastors and leaders in Egypt along the past two years about some of the critical topics, such as divorce in Christianity, electing El Sisi as a military leader for the presidency, ordination of woman as a pastor in Egypt, and homosexuality. In a conservative community such as the Egyptian Christian community, liberal thinking, especially about religious and moral issues, such as woman and sex, is strongly rejected.

---

64. Since 1999, Shaher Luke has been the leader of the general committee of youth in the Synod of the Nile and a leader of Christian education in the Middle East Council of Churches.

65. Sameh Hanser is a medical doctor and leaders' trainer at Haggy Institution in Egypt and North Africa.

66. Habib, *Christianity and Human Being*, 43.

67. Ibid., 69–83.

Lack of Critical Thinking: Manifestations

In my understanding, the problem of the significant lack of use of critical thinking as a basic component in the Christian education process in the context of Protestant communities in Egypt today can be recognized through multiple phenomena. The first phenomenon is the strong position of the majority of Presbyterians against critical theologians of the Church. Categorizing them as unspiritual, or less spiritual. In fact, the majority of the Protestants do not appreciate critical theologians, believing that the use of rationality to justify the truth not only weakens our obedience to God, but also does not give enough space for the Holy Spirit to work freely within us. Particularly in the first ten years of his ministry, Samuel Habib was confronted with strong rejection from the Church. In his book, *Jesus and Historical Criticism: The Story of the Conflict Between Salvation and Social Change*, Andria Zaki asserts that Habib achieved the great revolution in the Presbyterian Church when he recognized that literacy and the development of thinking abilities among Egyptians is a crucial element of the Christian mission. Yet, Zaki asserts, the first decade of Habib's ministry was very hard, as he had no appreciation either from the Church or from his friends, despite the great work he was doing.[68] Sadly, this negative position towards one of the best critical theologians of the Presbyterian Church in Egypt continued until the end of his life when he had a heart attack while trying to convince the Synod of the Nile to adopt new thoughts and a new vision for the Church.

However, it is not necessary for aggression against Christian thinkers to reach the extreme of physical violence or assassination, such as that experienced by secular critical thinkers in the Egyptian society; exclusion and rejection of being labeled unspiritual is another form of persecution. This judgment of the church against critical thinkers clearly identifies its position against the use of human reason for reflective and analytical thinking in order to achieve a deeper understanding of Christian faith and the biblical message. Indeed, what happened with Habib, happened for decades with his student Ikram Lamay. His intellectual attempts at achieving a deeper understanding of the Christian faith, especially in justifying the problematic situation of the church in an Islamic society, was a powerful reason that Lamay was rejected by the majority of the church for a long time. His call for the church to be more flexible in its position on divorce among Christians and for a different form of Christian-Muslim dialogue were neither welcomed nor appreciated by many of Protestants in Egypt for years.

---

68. Zaki, *Jesus and Historical Criticism*, 91.

The second phenomenon that demonstrates the lack of critical thinking in the Presbyterian Church in Egypt is the literal method of reading the Bible. In his book, *Divine Inspiration and Human Imagination*, Ikram Lamay illustrates this problem in the Egyptian context. For him, the Bible is not the problem, but the readers, their cultural background, and their understanding of inspiration. For the majority of Protestants, the dominant image of inspiration is that of dictation or mechanical inspiration, as if God prevented the personality of the writers of the Bible from having any influence and dictated to them issues that are too transcendent to be understood even by the writer's mind. This not only detracts from the Bible's purpose, but also represents the Holy texts as involves multiple contradictions. Lamay argues strongly that this way of reading the Bible as the literal words of God without critical analysis stands against the clear willingness of the divine to work with the human.[69]

Makram Naguib clearly states that our understanding of inspiration is the fundamental issue with which we must start if we are to solve not only church problems, but also the problems of the whole of society. In his book *Conservative or Liberal*, Naguib argues that the fundamental way in which we imagine the authors of the Bible as mere instruments or writing tools without any active role in the process of writing represents the Word of God as a dead, literal dogma instead of a dynamic action of the living God in the world. This perspective also imprisons the Bible in the past, making the Word insufficient for illuminating and addressing our contemporary life problems.[70] In his book *Religious Thoughts and Responsibility of Progress*, Naguib continues arguing that the fundamental understanding of the Holy texts in general as the literal words from God is the main reason for social and spiritual backwardness in Egypt. Focusing on a superficial, literal meaning of the words in the text leads people who are seeking to develop a good life to be absorbed by legendary thinking, unreal imagination, superstitions, miracles, and emotional decisions, instead of critical reflection on their problems in reality.[71]

Describing the threat to the Church in Egypt from a literal reading of the Bible and the belief that it is mechanically inspired by God, Fayez Fares discusses another dimension of the problem. In his book, *The Crisis of Religion and Ethics in the Contemporary Society*, Fares states that thinking that the Bible is beyond any question or inquiry, leads some people to trust in and worship the Bible as they worship God. Taking its words for granted,

---

69. Lamay, *Divine Inspiration*, 9–10.
70. Naguib, *Conservative or Liberal*, 13–14, 19.
71. Makram, *Religious Thoughts*, 12.

they ignore the active human role in constructing meaning in the Bible. Although the Bible itself, Fares assures us, frequently asserts that its authors are human beings who used human language, human skills, and human culture, most Egyptian Protestants unreasonably insist that God literally provided every word and letter in the Bible. This lack of using reason and critical thinking for understanding the depth and diversity of meaning in the biblical words portrays the Bible as a dead book instead of a dynamic divine-human endeavor.[72]

Nevertheless, the problem among a large number of Christians in Egypt of taking the Bible as literally inspired is fundamentally Islamic in origin. In his book, *The Cross and the Crescent: Understanding the Muslim Heart and Mind*, Phil Parshall says that Muslims never allow for any human contribution to the content of the Qur'an, as they believe that Allah authored the text in its totality. The prophet Mohamed, continues Parshall, was purely passive in the face of the revelation that he received from God; he did not write a book, as he was illiterate, but he conveyed the sacred book to humankind. This purity of the revelation of the Qur'an is confirmed by the illiteracy of Mohamed.[73] In his article, "Human Beings in the Care of Religion," Mohamed El Fayomi, says that heavenly books are God-made books such that they have the same anchor and incomprehensible characteristics as God. The attempt of any being to corrupt these books through any change is very risky and worthy of God's wrath.[74]

Living and teaching in a very Islamic context in the Middle East, Perry Shaw[75] sheds light on the problem. Educational philosophy in Islam, Shaw argues, is entirely rooted in the understanding of the Qur'an as the directly spoken word of God, which descended directly from God without error, word for word, letter for letter. Therefore, says Shaw, "It is the Qur'an alone, as the very words of God that gives the only complete sound, and clear source for a life pleasing to God."[76] This notion of the absolute authority of the divinely spoken Qur'an results in the deep con-

---

72. Fares, *Crisis of Religion*, 78.

73. Parshall, *Cross and Crescent*, 56–57.

74. El Fayomi, *Egyptian Man*, 67.

75. Dr. Perry Shaw is Professor of Christian Education and Director of the Educational Ministries Resource Centre at the Arab Baptist Theological Seminary in Beirut, Lebanon. Perry and his family have been living in the Middle East since 1990, serving in a variety of church and seminary-based ministries. Perry is a curriculum and faculty development consultant to regional schools and ministries; his research interests lie in sociological reflection on theological education, intercultural learning theory, and theological and anthropological understandings of Christian leadership.

76. Shaw, "Christian Educator," 91–109.

viction among Muslims that all of what is needed to be known is found in the holy text, the Qur'an. Moreover, for Muslims, right knowledge comes through appreciation and obedience to its words, not through our independent reasoning or critical analysis.[77]

My argument here is that Christian attitudes toward the Bible are inherited from this perspective which understands the Qur'an as the literal words of God, and such positions are a clear consequence of rejecting the use of critical thinking as a way of understanding Christian faith. In his book *Christ and Historical Criticism*, Andria Zaki[78] suggests that the Islamic impact on Christian understandings was shaped by many factors, such as socio-cultural influences, media, and traditions. As more than 85 percent of Egyptians are Muslims and all Egyptians speak the Arabic language, the language of the Qur'an, the educational factor is the main foundation for this understanding. It is mandatory, says Zaki, that all schools teach the Islamic heritage and the Egyptian arts.[79] Samuel Habib describes the deep impact of the Islamic convention of reading the holy text literally on the Christian belief that the Bible is the literal words of God:

> It is a real challenge when the minority is absorbed in the majority's thoughts and, consciously or unconsciously, adopts some or all of the majority's beliefs, despite that these beliefs never agree with the Christian faith . . . church always exists in diverse circumstances along centuries and will never be able to choose its society. Therefore, it should use all critical means in order to disclose and analyze the beliefs and traditions of its context both of the past and present in order to be able to shape its own Christian identity for the future.[80]

---

77. Ibid., 74.

78. Zaki was born in Minya in 1960. After receiving his Bachelor of Theology from the Evangelical Theological Seminary in Cairo (ETSC) in 1983, he received a Diploma in Social Development in 1988 from Coady International Institute, St. Francis Xavier University, Canada. In 1994, he received a Master of Arts in Theological Studies (Major Social Change) at Eastern University, Pennsylvania, USA. And in 2003, he received his PhD in Religions and Theology at Manchester University, Manchester, UK. He is the general director of the Coptic Evangelical Organization for Social Services (CEOSS), Vice-President of the Protestant Community of Egypt (2007–15), President of the Fellowship of Middle East Evangelical Churches, and a part time lecturer at (ETSC). He is the author of two books entitled, *Jesus and Historical Criticism: The Story of the Conflict Between Salvation and Social Change*; *Political Islam* and *Citizenship and Minorities: The Future of Arab Christians in the Middle East*, and he is the writer of forty articles in Arabic published in national and Christian newspapers.

79. Shaw, "Christian Educator," 66.

80. Ibid., 42.

The third serious phenomenon in which the lack of critical thinking in the educational process of the Presbyterian Church in Egypt manifests itself is the alienation of the church from Egyptian society. Ironically, the majority of Egyptian Christians are more loyal to heaven or to the Christian West than they are to Egypt. In the "Theological Thoughts and Minority's Mentality," Zaki explains this exclusivity of Christians in Egypt as a result of being a minority among a Muslim majority, and for Presbyterians, being a minority within the minority. While religious intolerance, social injustice, and poverty are all rooted in the lack of critical education and use of human reason to justify what we learn, the deep influence of these problems on Christians resulted in generating a sense of alienation from earthly life in general and from Egypt as their own home in particular.[81]

In his article "Church Between Alienation and Participation," Ikram Lamay sees this phenomenon at a deeper level, arguing that the crisis of the Presbyterians in Egypt is a crisis of identity. Being a minority among a Muslim majority and a minority within a minority compared to an Orthodox majority creates a great struggle between their Protestant identify, which is western in origin, and their Egyptian identity, which is an Islamic and eastern identity. While reading the Bible in a literal sense, Lamay says, is the underlying reason for this, lack of using reason and critical thinking for a deeper understanding of life experience is at the root of the problem. This lack of thinking critically leads the Egyptian presbyteries to believe that commitment to God clearly means the isolation from all political and social practices, which are not explicitly Christian in nature. This isolation includes the exclusion of arts, secular music, media, and theaters. While we agree that evangelism is the clear message of the gospel, for many, it is limited to the belief that everybody will experience eternal damnation in Hell unless they accept Jesus Christ as the savior and that a true Christian is the one who speaks a certain language, achieves a certain form of practice, and is involved in certain forms of relationships.[82]

In the interview with him, Lamay paid much attention to this problem by arguing that opposing the use of scientific thinking and critical reflection is the rich soil in which multiple problems of the Presbyterian Church are rooted and grow. Among these problems is the isolation of the church from its real mission in transforming Egyptian society, focusing instead either on eternal life in heaven or life in the Christian West, which is not only contrary

---

81. Ibid., 42.
82. Lamay, "Church Between Alienation and Participation," 69–82.

to the real theological meaning of the incarnated God, but also severs the connection between redemption and creation theologies.[83]

In "Theological Thoughts and Minority's Mentality," Andrea Zaki explains how the alienation of Egyptian Protestants is clearly seen not only in the prominent passive position towards participation in the social and political life of the state, but also in the worship in churches. A prominent example of this can be seen in Christian songs. When a singer says, "I am not from here, here is a finite world; not money, not position, not richness, I have another home," these words clearly declare a weak bond between Protestants and their context in the Egyptian homeland. In the same way, argues Zaki, these songs describe the only commitment of the Presbyterians as waiting faithfully for the second coming of Jesus, ignoring the inevitable role that a Christian is called by God to play for achieving a better faith and life in this world.[84]

The fourth phenomenon that embodies the lack of critical thinking skills in the Presbyterian Church in Egypt is in the profuse attention given to miracles, supernatural works, legendries, and superstitions. In "Theological Thoughts and Minority's Mentality," Andrea Zaki argues that as a minority, the Protestants in Egypt are absorbed in dreams of the second coming of Jesus to establish his millennial kingdom on earth and attacking his enemies, instead of critically confronting and finding reasonable solutions for their problems. Zaki believes that waiting for divine intervention to solve our problems in a miraculous way without an active human role is a clear example of the lack of critical and theological understandings of the kingdom of God as a present reality.[85] Because of oppression, lack of freedom, and a significant lack of using the gift of reason, the majority of evangelicals in Egypt seek healing miracles and the appearance of late saints. The best example of this picture is the appearance of Virgin Mary. Many of Christians believe that the Blessed Virgin Mary supernaturally appears in certain churches in Egypt. While it is an entirely Orthodox belief, a remarkable number of Protestants also believe that this appearance is one of the many signs of the supernatural works that God promises to do among God's people. Sameh Maurice, a senior pastor of Kasr El Dopara church in Cairo, one of the biggest Presbyterian churches in the Middle East,[86] not only believes that the Virgin Mary truly appears over some Or-

83. Appendix 2, interview with Ikram Lamay.
84. Zaki, *Towards Contemporary Arabic Theology*, 502.
85. Ibid., 78.
86. Sameh Maurice was medical doctor for many years while he was known Christian leader and speaker in the Kasr El Dopara church. Following God's call, he earned his Bachelor of Theology from ETSC and was ordained as assistant pastor of the church

thodox churches, an appearance which is important to confirm the Christian message in the midst of difficult circumstances, but he also prays that the Virgin marry appear in his church as well. Andrea Zaki thinks that this kind of legendary thinking is always a religious response to adverse circumstances, oppression, and injustice.[87]

A fifth phenomenon that reflects the lack of critical thinking in the educational life of the Presbyterian Church in Egypt is the antipathy toward philosophy. From years of personal observation as a Christian leader, it is quite clear to me that human science in general and philosophy in particular have little or no role in the Christian education process of the Presbyterian Church in Egypt. My personal experience with philosophy is a significant example of this problem. Starting at age 6, I grew up in Sunday school in the Presbyterian Church in Egypt, which runs every afternoon. Through the years, the main foundation of my Christian faith was established in this wonderful school. However, all that we would have learned was a story and memorizing a verse from the Bible. Later, in the middle school and youth meeting, we started to approach deeper subject matter and participate in good discussions, yet the Bible continued to be the only source of our knowledge. Like the majority of the church, I developed a strong position against philosophy because of the concept that any kind of knowledge that is not based on the Bible is corrupted. For most of the leaders in my church, philosophy is not only prideful by definition, but it also leads Christians to be rebellious and disobedient toward God. Indeed, the problematic position of philosophy, in general education in Egypt, helped to support this negative perspective in the church. Arabic translation of some philosophies, such Kant's, is too corrupted to make the comprehension of its meaning understandable. Also, the attempt of Muslim professors, writers, and translators either to Islamize or condemn all philosophies, leads Christians to have a strong negative impression and rejection of philosophy.

The sixth phenomenon in which the lack of critical thinking in the Presbyterian education in Egypt manifests itself is the strong position against arts and literature. If the Bible is the only source of truth in the process of education, the entire of non-Christian sources, such as human sciences, drama, arts, literature, theater, poetry, and music are seen as secular fruits of a corrupt human reason that must be avoided if Christians are truly pursuing good Christian faith and life. While ETSC is the only educational institution where human sciences and philosophy are a fundamental part of the

---

of Kasr El Dopara. A few years ago after the retirement of Minas Abdel Nor, Maurice became the senior pastor of the church and one of the most known charismatic pastors in the Arabic world.

87. Zaki, *Towards a Contemporary Arabic Theology*, 507.

curriculum, arts and literature are almost ignored as an essential component of the educational process. It is the lack of critical and theological reading of the Bible that leads church leaders to focus only on the spiritual dimension while ignore human as a whole being. It is the same reason that leads to the separation of church from state, social transformation from evangelism, and arts and literature from the Bible and theology.

Lack of Critical Thinking: Reasons and Factors

Since American missionaries founded it in 1854, the Presbyterian Church has carried the spark of enlightenment to Egyptian society. However, for many reasons, this spark started to diminish gradually to the extent that distinguishing between the church and society, both in thought and in practice, is now quite difficult. While the church believes that it protects its members from the negative influence of society by alienating itself from all social and political movements, the Presbyterian Church in Egypt is strongly influenced by Egyptian society and has been infiltrated by thoughts and values, which are not Christian.

Central to this dilemma in the Presbyterian Church in Egypt is Christian education. My claim is that the educational process of the Presbyterian Church in Egypt suffers fatal weaknesses in terms of theological foundation, curriculum, pedagogy, educational environment, and the teacher-learner relationship. These problematic deficiencies point to the fundamental problem from which most of the weaknesses of the church arise, that is, a significant lack of developing and using a critical way of thinking a deeper understanding of both text and context. The reasons and factors that contribute to forming this problem are multiple, intertwined, and complicated, including, political, social, economic, and cultural factors. However, I focus my research on two groups, educational and theological factors

Educational Factors

Through my observation as a Christian educator for about three decades, I came to the fact that Christian education in Egyptian Presbyterian Church is deeply influenced by the problematic situation of public education in Egypt. A careful look at both the elementary stage of public education and Sunday school in the Church will clearly illustrate this picture. Focusing on the elementary stage, I identify three main weaknesses of the public education that result in a significant lack of critical thinking as a way of learning and living in the Egyptian society and that negatively impact Christian education in the Presbyterian church: lack of creative pedagogical practices, lack of democracy, and lack of using experience as a way learning.

Lack of Creative Pedagogy

First, we must paint a picture of the educational process of elementary schools in Egypt. While the main goal of this level of education in Egypt is to help students develop basic reading, writing, and arithmetic skills, the curriculum also includes simple scientific principles, geography, and history. However, Arabic language is very fundamental. While the genres of poetry and literatures are part of its curriculum, memorizing multiple passages from the Qur'an is required for all students, including Christians. Teachers in basic education are not necessarily professional educators. In his book *Moral Education in the Egyptian School*, Sedek Afifi states that holding any kind of degree is considered a sufficient qualification for teaching basic education in Egypt, whether the teacher has received educational training or not.[88]

While basic education in the elementary school is a teacher-centered paradigm, its main pedagogical practices focus on indoctrination, rote memorization, and written examination as the sole means of student-assessment. In the classroom, the teacher writes the material on the board or dictates it to the learners word by word. In doing so, the teacher explains some of the words that are difficult to understand. During the whole process, the teacher may stop to answer some of the learners' questions, and in the final stage of the lesson, the teacher asks learners to repeat after him or her. The lesson is repeated several times until students can recite the material by heart, but it is rare in this process that students are asked to analyze, reflect, or solve problems. No wonder, then, that the student that is qualified to get the best grade is the one who successfully regurgitates as much knowledge as s/he can from memory in the written exams.

As the basic method of education in Egypt, memorization has a long history. Prior to the nineteenth century, traditional education in Egypt was completely religious in nature. At that time, mosques and churches operated basic schools in which *alImam,* Muslim prayer leaders, and Christian clergy instructed all male student bodies in memorizing Quranic or biblical passages. The deep religious conviction that memorizing the words of the sacred texts is a great blessing reinforced this activity as the primary method

88. Afifi, *Moral Education*, 37.

of education during this period; therefore, the teacher repeats several passages from memory, asks the student to repeat after him several times, and then requires the student to recite on his own.[89]

Although time has brought changes to the educational system in Egypt such as when Mohamed Ali (an Albanian who ruled Egypt between 1805 and 1848) established a secular education system alongside the Islamic *al-Azhar* system, both *al-Azhar* and secular systems have been dominated by teacher-centered, knowledge-transmission pedagogies.[90] Later, during the British colonization of Egypt (1882–1952), radical advances took place in all levels of public education in terms of the number and quality of educational buildings, the number of teachers, and schoolbooks; yet, the standard educational pedagogy—rote memorization—remained unchanged.[91] Following the 1952 revolution, the Egyptian government headed by Gamal Abdel Nasser (1954–1970) quantitatively expanded school systems to meet the increase of the Egyptian population, a process continued by his successor Anwar Al-Sadat (1970–1981). During the Sadat period, the ministry of education published a working paper that gave more attention to the urgent need for developing and updating Egyptian education, asserting that the curricula did not prepare students for practical, productive lives, and that rote memorization did not create citizens who are qualified to deal with life problems.[92]

Eventually, during the Mubarak regime (1981–2011), despite the government's continued focus on quantitative expansion by extending compulsory education for children between the ages of six and nine to include children between the ages of four and fourteen, in the World Conference on Education for All (Jomtien, 1990), Mubarak emphasized that Egypt's educational problem was the focus on quantity over quality:

> Education should, therefore, change from an outdated mode of teaching dependent on memorization and repetition to a new form of instruction, which would include the student as an active participant in the educational experience and an active partner in the learning process . . . Emphasis on rote learning and memorization has produced individuals who are easily programmed and vulnerable . . . contributing to the prevalence

---

89. Http://countrystudies.us/egypt/71.htm.
90. Http://weekly.ahram.org.eg/2005/766/sc2.htm.
91. Ginsburg and Megahed, "Global Discourses," 99.
92. Ibid., 100.

of many social problems, such as drug dependency, extremism, and fanaticism.[93]

Egyptian Nobel laureate Ahmad Zewail draws more attention to the link between pedagogical practices of education and its ability to create critical thinkers:

> The infrastructure of most of the Egyptian schools is far behind a country like Finland or South Korea. The number of students in public-school classes reaches sixty and more, making it impossible for a teacher to interact well with pupils. University lecture halls are packed with hundreds of students. Teaching also relies heavily on indoctrination, failing to take advantage of pedagogical methodologies that have advanced throughout the modern world. Many of the topics in the curriculum are not suitable, especially when we consider that these students have to compete in the information and space age.[94]

Despite its huge contribution to the problem, Zewail argues, basic education is not the only reason of the failure of the Egyptian education to create critical thinkers. The pedagogical practices of higher education with their constant focus on rote memorization as the main pedagogy has a significant role in forming the problem,

> Teaching methodology in higher education is in need of revamping. Understanding of and respect for facts is essential for the scientific method, which is not only important for education itself but also for integrating rational thinking into the fabric of the culture.[95]

In *Issues and Problems in Teacher Education: An International Handbook*, Taher Razik and Diaa Zaher illustrate the lack of creative pedagogy in public education in Egypt today,

> The curriculum was generally irrelevant to the students. School quality was uneven, with better quality schools in urban areas where the wealthy could pay for tutoring. Teachers lacked training in pedagogy. Learning, conducted with martial drills and physical punishment, encouraged rote memorization rather than critical thinking. For many Egyptian children, the result was fragmented information, "never to be ground into

---

93. Ibid.
94. Ibid., 40.
95. Ibid., 43.

knowledge" . . . encouraged rote memorization rather than critical thinking.[96]

In the same way, the main goal of Sunday school, which runs every afternoon in 70 percent of the Presbyterian churches in Egypt, is to help children to know and memorize the Bible. Sunday school teachers, particularly in rural areas, always carry a vocational high school degree. All Sunday school teachers are volunteers; the pastor is the only paid person in the ministry of the Church. Indeed, while the volunteer Sunday school leaders are very committed, love children, and love ministry, they have to spend a great deal of time every day to make an effective lesson for a large number of children despite the shortage of materials and resources.

For thirty to forty-five minutes, all the children and the teachers gather together in one place to worship and praise God. However, the large quantity of students and limited space make it necessary for students to sit in rows one by one, looking to the leader and not at each other. The most physical movement that students are able to do during the praise time is standing, clapping hands, or moving their bodies in place. In the second section of the meeting, the children are divided into groups according to their age. Teachers always prepare the same lesson for all, which include a story from the Bible, practical application, and a verse for memorization. Such as public education, indoctrination and memorization are the main ways of learning.

For me, the insistence on the central and foundational role of the Bible is a real strength of the process. In an Islamic context, where the Qur'an holds such a central place, memorizing the Bible is a good way to keep and protect Christian identity. These biblical verses, indeed, are the best way to ensure that Christian children continue to be Christian. A sense of appreciating the Bible as the word of God is also built as learners are prepared for a future in which they will encounter Muslims in a university context where they can rely on the strong, apologetic position that they have been taught to counter Muslim claims concerning the corruption of the Bible.

Yet looking to the Bible as a bulwark against corruption of Christian identity in an Islamic society can be a weakness in two ways. First, the belief that the Bible contains answers for all human questions makes it the only source of Christian truth for the majority of Christians in the church, which results in, positioning philosophy against theology, reason against faith, rejecting experience as leading to pride, and regarding traditions as "orthodox" in nature, which call people to seek salvation through human means rather than by grace.[97] Second, because of the belief that the Bible must be taken for

---

96. Razik and Zaher, "Egypt," 91–108.

97. Fares, *Crisis of Religion*, 78.

granted as the literal word of God, memorization of the Bible is often more akin to "parroting," in which words are repeated without critical reflection or deep understanding. This also results in a lack of using research methods in the pedagogy of Christian formation in Egypt.[98] Bible "memorization" in Christian contexts is deeply influenced by the Islamic understanding of the Qur'an as the literal words of God, and this belief results in a large number of theological and biblical misunderstandings.[99]

Lack of Democracy in Education

Multiple social, political, cultural, and religious factors have contributed to the formation of a general dictatorship in Egypt. The nature of the tribal relationships in Arabic culture in general, where there is always the head of the tribe that thinks and makes decisions while all members just obey *him*[100] without discussion, is the main social factor. In this sense, there is a traditional value in always deifying the head of the family, the teacher, and all who are in positions of authority. While poor education is the main cultural factor in the formation of dictators in Egypt, Islamic thought that links good faith and God's obedience with those who never argue or inquire is another significant factor.

Yet, one of the most significant factors that contribute to forming dictatorship in Egypt is the geographical nature of Egypt and the conquest. In his long series, *The Character of Egypt: Studies of the Arab World, and The Contemporary Islamic World Geography,* Gamal Hamdan[101] describes the deep link between the smooth character of the Nile river and the peaceful character of the Egyptians, a connection which was the main reason for their conquest by multiple powers inside and outside of Egypt.[102] A careful examination of Egyptian history clearly illustrates this fact. It is stated histori-

---

98. Ibid., 79.

99. Ibid., 9–10.

100. Pointing to the word *him* here is intentional, as the heads of tribal groups or initiations are usually male, a significant practice of dictatorship in the Middle East, including Egypt.

101. Gamal Hamdan (1928–1993) was born in the North of Egypt and earned his Bachelor degree from Cairo University in geography in 1944. He then earned an MA and PhD in geography from Reading University, UK in 1953, while working as a professor of geography at the faculty of Arts, Cairo University. In 1963, he resigned from the university and spent the rest of his life researching the philosophy of nature and geography. Throughout his academic life, Hamdan published about twenty-nine books, including his prominent series Character of Egypt, and about seventy-nine research and articles.

102. Hamdan, *The Character of Egypt.*

cally that Egypt was conquered repetitively by many nations and powerful individuals: Hyksos, Alexander the Great, the Romans, Muslims, Ptolemy, Coptic, Osmani, Mamluk, French, British, and then Israelis.

Lack of democracy of education in Egypt, then, is a part of a general problem. Like the hierarchy of Egyptian society, the teacher, not only believes that s/he is the knower and all learners should gratefully receive the factual knowledge that s/he deposits in them, but also the teacher always has the final word in any discussion and has an answer for every question. This teacher-centered paradigm is the dominant model of teaching in all levels of public education in Egypt. A culture of shame is also dominant in Egypt where it is shameful for most of people, including teachers, to say, "I do not know." Such a culture makes it difficult for a teacher to accept different themes or thoughts from students and to value them as good knowledge.

In this process, the Egyptian teacher is faced with multiple ideologies and policies. On one hand, the teacher has to follow a certain curriculum with certain content in a certain time, and those who are not committed to such a curriculum risk being punished to the extent of losing their jobs. The number of students, reaching as high as 60–80 per class in some schools and some thousands in college lectures, and the poor equipment in classrooms are a great challenge for group discussions and learning activities due to a lack of space for each learner to be an active participant in the process. Cultural and religious ideologies are another force that shapes the authoritarian attitude of the Egyptian teacher in the educational process. For the majority of teachers in public education who are Muslim, the underlying intention of education is to impart religious values and behavior, even if this is not explicitly stated as such. In his article "Religious Education and Pluralism in Egypt and Tunisia," Muhammad Faour says,

> Some scholars in Egypt use the term "hidden curriculum" to describe the impact of many Islamist teachers on students, either positively or negatively. These teachers impose their own thoughts and attitudes on their pupils in a process that is affected by the prevailing culture within schools and made easier through the dominant teacher-directed methods of lecturing and rote learning as well as the lack of open discourse and critical reasoning.[103]

To guarantee the complete obedience of his followers, the prophet Mohamed commanded, "Do not question nor argue the words of God," a command which continues to be repeated today even though when experts discovered some linguistic mistakes in the Quran, the answer is that God

---

103. Faour, "Religious Education and Pluralism," 7.

planned these mistakes for a particular reason and will. In short, Islam as represented in the Quran means that ultimate truth that is beyond questioning. Therefore, the tendency of the student to accept the teacher's knowledge as a fixed norm is religious in origin.[104]

The weakness of this model of education in Egypt was a real concern for international organizations for decades. The United States Agency for International Development (USAID) has paid an increasing amount of attention to improving the quality of education in Egypt and changing teaching and learning processes from teacher-centered, transmission, and memorization—oriented approaches to student-centered and active-learning approaches. The USAID emphasizes that while this authoritarian model of teaching and the predominance of memorization-oriented and rote learning in schools have been widely criticized by many Egyptian educators since the beginning of the twenty-first century, the Egyptian government devoted little to no attention to improving educational quality through reforming pedagogy and equipping teachers for promoting active learning in a democratic educational environment.[105]

The negative consequences that result from this educational method are numerous: the dehumanization of the learner, who is changed from subject to object, a significant lack of creativity, a lack of teamwork because of lack of flexibility and open—mindedness, and the divorce of theory and practice, science and daily life. However, the most significant consequence is that learners become incapable of handling the demands of complex daily life problems because of a significant lack of reflective skill in observation of their real life experiences.

Christian education in the Presbyterian Church has been deeply influenced by the teacher-centered paradigm of the public education system simply because the educators of the church are the products of public education in Egypt. In her book, *Church and Values System: Theology, Enlightenment, and Social Movement*, Vines Nicola believe that the lack of democracy within the educational process of the Presbyterian education in Egypt is a fundamental reflection of the authoritarian cultural and educational public system, which is the main reason for fanaticism among both Christians and Muslims in Egypt. The image of the Egyptian public teacher is the same one that is typically applied and practiced in Christian education in the church. Therefore, the right starting point for achieving innovation in religious discourse and a tolerant relationship in Egyptian society is developing critical Christians who are able to convey the gospel

104. Wahba, *Fundamentalism and Secularism*, 32.
105. Ginsburg, "Active-Learning Pedagogies."

in a modern, intellectual way. Nicola issues a fervent call to the church to "avoid indoctrination and filling the learners' minds with what has already been inherited in the teachers' minds, as the ultimate truths. Insisting on the authoritarian educational system with indoctrination as the only way of teaching and learning, suppressing any attempt of questioning, and rejecting discourse and criticism, will never make good life."[106]

In many of his works, Samuel Habib pays special attention to the link between the way in which a child is raised and his or her ability to use the gift of reason to justify the truth. Rational education, argues Habib, is not hereditary, but rather, a collection of skills and attitudes that a child develops as s/he is allowed enough space and freedom to inquire, criticize, and express new ideas through discourse. In his book *The Art of Dialogue*, Habib says,

> Dialogue is a supreme art that is achieved through learning, training, and practice. A democratic dialogue is a way of life that one learns through practice in the family, church, school, and society. It is an art that gives priority to mutual understanding and exchanging ideas. The best thing that supports dialogue is the ability to practice a scientific way of thinking to reflect and analyze different situations in order to recognize the multiple dimensions of each situation and make the best decision . . . Good education always helps learners to develop an intellectual flexibility and open-mindedness and avoid fanaticism and rigidity.[107]

In the interview with him, Ikram Lamay expressed his view that the problem of the lack of democracy in the process of Christian education in the Presbyterian Church is a larger issue than it may first appear. Because of the long history of oppression, says Lamay, Egyptians have become subservient and passive. The main problem is that most of those who are in power believe that they possess the ultimate truth; therefore, while they use every means to convince their people of this truth, they continue controlling and abusing them for personal benefits. In his booklet, *How to Think Objectively*, Lamay attributes this weakness to the way that people have been raised from childhood, when parents insist that a polite child is the one who obeys parents without arguing, based on a wrong belief that to question an older is to disrespect him or her.[108] The process of oppression, Lamay argues, does not stop at this level, as many parents use violence, both physical and emotional,

---

106. Nicola, *Church and Value System*, 207.
107. Habib, *Art of Dialogue*, 45.
108. Interview with Ikram Lamay, Appendix 2.

to control their children. Likewise, teachers in schools and educators in the Church insist on treating learners as objects rather than subjects. No wonder, then, that critical thinking barley exists both in society and church.[109]

Lack of Using Experience

In my observations as an educator in Egypt, the only place that I know of using experience as a basic element of education is the kindergarten (KG) stage of New Ramses College (NRC). NRC is a school that was established by American Presbyterian missionaries in Egypt decades ago and that uses the Montessori system for teaching children in KG. Experience is also used as a way of learning in some private nurseries and childcare houses as scattered trials, not as a part of any educational theory or general system. Yet, for many reasons, the public education system in Egypt never makes use of learning through experience. The inability of the poor economy to offer supplies and equipment of the classroom in public education, which is already, not only tiny, but also overcrowded with 60–80 students with no room for physical movement, playing, or using materials. The uncreative pedagogy and a curriculum that focuses only on transmitting prepared knowledge. A third reason is the authoritarian and untrained teachers who are incapable of participating in dialogue, analysis, or argument through practices.

In his book, *Principles of Education: Future Visions for Developing Education in the Twenty-First Century in Egypt,* Ayman El Kholy relates the inability of the learners to develop critical thinking skills within the education system in Egypt to the lack of using personal experience as a tool of education. The focus on "parroting" as a basic way of teaching and learning, without allowing enough space for learners to reflect on their actual life experiences, is one of the main reasons for the lack of using human reason to construct one's own knowledge. Indeed, says El Kholy, education in Egypt does not equip learners to solve real life problems.[110]

As a part of the Egyptian society, the Presbyterian Church in Egypt has been strongly shaped and influenced by this lack of using experience as a fundamental element for learning. A careful observation of the church clearly illustrates that Christian education has developed a strong rejection of the use of an individual's experience as an element of its process. For me, while this rejection serves to widen the gap between theological thought and actual practice within the church, it also fails to create disciples with Christian wisdom. Like public education, Christian education does not

---

109. Ibid.
110. El Kholy, *Principles of Education,* 90–93.

allow learners to reflect and analyze real life problems, which contributes to the alienation of the church from its socio-cultural context in Egypt. Ignoring human experience hinders the ability of the Church to create and develop new theologies that are contextualized and required for the flourishing of human life and church ministry in Egypt.

In addition to the impact of public education, a theological misunderstanding shapes the Presbyterian position against using experience as a basic element of Christian education. The Presbyterian Church in Egypt strongly rejects the use of personal experience in church education for the sake of protecting the church from theological thoughts that are not Presbyterian in nature, such as all Charismatic movements. To speak about personal experience in the church is to fall in spiritual pride, if experience is positive, or beg others' help, if the experience is negative. In an Egyptian Presbyterian perspective, it also leads to a multiplicity of thoughts and attitudes that eventually result in divisions within the church. Consequently, the church focuses its attention entirely on the conceptual understanding of the Bible, neglecting individual emotions as something not spiritual.[111]

The church's rejection of the use of personal experience in the educational process, I would argue, results in multiple negative consequences. First among these is that of dependency. Because educators in the church do not give enough consideration either to training people to reflect on different life situations or to helping them to develop problem–solving skills, the immediate response of the majority of the Presbyterian learners in Egypt have when they experience a problematic situation is to depend on their leaders to solve their problems.

Yet, the most negative consequence of ignoring individual experience in the process of Presbyterian education in Egypt is the lack of a contextual theological theory. While there are multiple publication houses and many writers in the church, most of the published works that emerge from these venues are either translated from western resources or little more than contemplative literature. A lack of challenging motivations, which have been developed through careful observation and reflection on a problematic reality results in real lack of theological theories that emerge from the Egyptian context. It is the focus of the Presbyterian educators on the past experiences represented in the Bible and ignoring present experience with its richness and complexity that result in this problematic situation. This problem, indeed, challenged some of Presbyterian pastors and thinkers of the Middle

---

111. Naguib, *Charismatic Movement*, 62.

East to write *Towards a Contemporary Arabic Theology*[112] as an initial attempt at constructing a contextual theological theory.

Theological Factors

For the many years I spent in ministry prior to starting the Ph.D. program at Princeton Theological Seminary, I was very concerned with the dualistic manner of thinking within the Presbyterian Church in Egypt which manifested itself in an "either . . . or" paradigm: either divine authority or human agency, either evangelism or social transformation, either depending upon the Holy Spirit completely or planning and putting together strategies for the future, either faith or reason, and theology or philosophy. One of the main reasons of this dualistic way of thinking, I believe, is that lack of theological reflection, which is rooted in the lack of the theological foundation of the Christian education process of the church. This, in turn, formed the position of the majority of Protestants against using human reason for understanding of the Christian experience. The lack of Presbyterian theology from the process of education; however, is rooted in two theological concepts; the lack of theological understanding concerning the human reason as a spiritual gift from God and the theological conflict that many of Egyptian Protestants believe exists between the spiritual validity of using human reason and the role of the Holy Spirit.

For the majority of Protestants in Egypt, God has made humans in God's image; yet, what this image entails is difficult to determine. A certain category of attributes that are considered by most Protestants in Egypt to be spiritual and to be a part of the image of God includes love, humility, mercy, giving, and forgiving, while reason, creativity, free-thinking, and willing are not spiritual. This notion that the gift of reason is not spiritual or is not a fundamental component of the "image of God" is supported by the fact that sin so corrupted the human mind that it was rendered unable to make use of reason in order to know and embrace God.

Fayez Fares is one of the significant Egyptian theologians who pay much attention to the nature of the human as a moral, rational, and transcendental being. In most of his works, Fares explains both scientifically and theologically that the human being is more than just a part of the good creation of God. Unlike the corrupted image that most Egyptian Protestants have of humans as incapable of thinking about or achieving goodness, Fares believes that God created humans as the crown of the whole creation because of God's image. To support his claim, Fares uses the text

---

112. Zaki, *Towards a Contemporary Arabic Theology*, 509.

from (Ps 8:3–6): "What is man that Thou art mindful of him, and the son of man that Thou dost visit him? For Thou hast made him a little lower than the angels, and hast crowned him with glory and honor."[113] Criticizing those who think that they glorify God when they humiliate human agency, mind and reason in particular, Fares argues that many naively understand the image of God physically; this image only can be understood spiritually. Since God is the creator of human beings, all human abilities and skills are spiritual by their very nature. While these abilities cannot be reduced to reason alone, reason is both a fundamental element of these spiritual abilities and is never opposed to faith and spiritual life as the majority of Egyptian Protestants think.[114]

In his book, *Self-Awaking in Experiencing God: Enlightening Messages*, Fares maintains this notion by positing that behind the tremendous developments and astonishing achievements within scientific fields is the miracle of human reason that has been created by God as the spark of all creative human thoughts. While all natural laws have existed since creation, it is only when God creates a spark in some minds that humans can discover and use these laws for the creation of a better life. Indeed, when God has created the human being, "God breathed into his nostrils the breath of life; and man became a living soul" (Gen 2:7). Therefore, what distinguishes human from the rest of creation is the human reason and human will, which are the very image in which God has created the human being.[115]

In my interview with him, Ikram Lamay sadly asserts that one of the main problems is the position of the religion against the human nature. Because of a theological misunderstanding, the majority of Egyptian Protestants believe that a strong faith in God is one which guides them to restrain their human nature and to suppress their natural abilities in reasoning and critical thinking, which would lead to the creation of new ideas and new imagination. For Lamay, this perspective stands against the basic understanding of God the creator as the Almighty thinker and of Jesus as the mind of God or "logos." Being full of grace and love, God chooses to work within, through, and with human beings. Therefore, the Holy Spirit uses the gift of reason and human mental and creative abilities to reveal the kingdom of God to the world. And because the kingdom of God does not have fixed forms, God calls Christians to use every intellectual means to represent this kingdom in a way that speaks to the world in a contemporary language.[116]

---

113. NIV translation.
114. Fares, *Christian Ethics*, 119–37.
115. Fares, *Self-Awaking in Experiencing God*, 18–19.
116. Appendix 2, interview with Ikram Lamay.

The second theological reason for the lack of using reason to improve Christian education in the Presbyterian Church in Egypt is the conflict that Protestants believe exists between human thinking and the Holy Spirit. In order to choose a wife, a job, a career, or a ministry, one need only pray in order to discover which one has been planned by the Holy Spirit. This total dependency that many Christians have on prayer and the Holy Spirit is evident not only in making major decisions, but also in a variety of regular activities in daily life. A Christian may sit beside a stranger in public transportation and sense an inner voice calling them to speak with that person about Jesus. Yet This action, in large part, will depend upon a special call from the Holy Spirit, rather than a reflection on this experience using critical thinking to analyze whether situation is appropriate or not, whether the Christian is ready or not, and whether the stranger is ready to listen or not. For many Christians in Egypt, such reflective questions are opposed to the Holy Spirit who knows more than humans and inspires them to act in a particular way.

In her book *Church and Value System: Theology, Enlightenment, and Social Movement*, Vines Nicola identifies the need of the Egyptian Presbyterian Church for what she calls a contemporary-contextual-enlightenment-theology. This kind of theology, Nicola thinks, is constructed when a dynamic intellectual interaction between the gospel, church, and culture takes place. For her, when these three are brought together in a dialogue, it does not mean that the Holy Spirit is absent, since the Holy Spirit is always at work within the congregation. In this interaction, both theologians and the church need to reflective on their experience and traditions in order to construct a deeper understanding of Christian faith and theological thoughts. Nicola asserts that there is no conflict between the Holy Spirit and human reason as both are necessary interactive for a deeper faith and obedience to God.[117]

Conclusion

The fact that a better life is almost impossible without better education is not questioned by any nation in today's world. Egypt has stood among these nations with a long history of honoring education. Yet, while public education suffers serious problems, Christian education in the Presbyterian Church reflects the same difficulties. One of the most significant troubles is the failure of Christian education to create disciples who are able to think critically in order to achieve a deeper understanding life experience.

117. Ibid.

A descriptive analysis of the significant lack of critical thinking in the process of Christian education in Egypt was the purpose of this chapter. While the first section of this chapter briefly described a few significant critical thinkers in Egypt, the second section states that critical thinking is significantly lacking in Egyptian society in general, which manifests itself in many ways. While the third section gives a brief description of a few significant critical theologians in the Presbyterian Church in Egypt, the fourth section provides a thick description of the significant lack of critical thinking from the Church in general. This section was divided into three main parts. The first part was to define the problem of the lack of critical thinking in the Church. The second part explained six phenomena in which the lack of critical thinking manifests itself in the Presbyterian context in Egypt the strong position of the majority of the church against critical theologians, the belief in the literalism of the Bible, the alienation of the church from its socio-cultural context, the focus on legendary thinking and superstitions, the antipathy towards philosophy and human sciences, and the position against arts and literature.

The final part of the fourth section devoted a great deal of attention to the main factors that contribute to the lack of critical thinking in the Presbyterian education in Egypt, which were organized into two main groups: educational and theological. The section on educational factors attempted to portray the deep influence of the public education on the Christian education of the church. This part suggested three educational factors: the lack of creative pedagogical practices, focusing only on indoctrination and memorization as the only methods of education, lack of democracy in education, and a lack of using experience as a basic component in the educational process. Focusing on reformation theology, the theological factors that were highlighted were the lack of understanding of human reason as a basic element of the image of God in the human being and the false concept of a conflict between the Holy Spirit and human reason.

CHAPTER 2

John Dewey and the Problem of Thinking of the Egyptian Education

A Scientific Interpretation

Why, then, should we reconsider John Dewey? . . . How can a champion of scientific method and democratic culture as achievable goals in all walks of life have a work to speak to our post-modern, nihilistic situation? . . . Richard Rorty, Jürgen Habermas, and Richard Bernstein are only a few of the philosophers who are re-discovering the depth and provocative power of Dewey's ideas . . . Dewey's understanding of the relationship between theory and practice is crucial for historical and constructive purposes. Practical theology . . . is a distinctive genre of theology, which is founded in and oriented towards a form of praxis in the present context. Dewey's understanding of the relationship between human *reflection* and experiential contexts represents a potent dialogue partner for practical theology in this regard . . . Not only was Dewey an important influence on Coe, but also he made a significant impact on the Religious Education Movement as a whole.[1]

—Richard Osmer

There is not adequate theoretical recognition that all, which the school can or need do for pupils, so far as their minds are concerned . . . is to develop their ability to think . . . Thinking which is not connected with increase of efficiency in action, and with learning more about ourselves and the world in which we live, has something the matter with it just as thought. And skill obtained apart from thinking is not connected with any sense of the purposes for which it is to be used. It consequently leaves a man at the mercy of his routine habits and of the authoritative control of others . . . And information severed from thoughtful

---

1. Osmer, *Practical Theology*, 15–16.

action is dead ... Since it simulates knowledge and thereby develops the poison of conceit, it is a most powerful obstacle to further growth in the grace of intelligence ... Thinking is the method of intelligent learning, of learning that employs and rewards mind. We speak, legitimately enough, about the method of thinking, but the important thing to bear in mind about method is that thinking is method, the method of intelligent experience in the course, which it takes.[2]

—John Dewey

Dewey's Theory of Critical Thinking

Reflective Thinking—"it alone is truly educative in value"[3]

"Truth" has been a topic of ongoing discussions for humankind for thousands of years. It has also been one of the central and largest subjects of philosophers and thinkers since Plato, who believed in the existence of what is called "two-worlds," "our immanent changing world and the transcendent world with its "Forms," as the true world.[4] To Hegel who created an idealistic ontology called, "absolute idealism," believing in the World Spirit, which is the Absolute Knowing.[5] As a part of the philosophical stream, "truth" is a fundamental and central issue for pragmatist, philosopher, psychologist, and educator John Dewey[6] who was quite Hegelian at

---

2. Dewey, *Democracy and Education*, 135.
3. Dewey, *How We Think*, 2.
4. Kremer, "Dewey and Rorty on Truth," 13.
5. Ibid.
6. John Dewey was born on October 20, 1859, in Burlington, Vermont. While at the University of Vermont, Dewey was exposed to evolutionary theory through the teaching of G.H. Perkins and *Lessons in Elementary Physiology*, a text by T.H. Huxley, the famous English evolutionist. The theory of natural selection continued to have a life-long impact upon Dewey's thought, particularly, its importance of focusing on the interaction between the human organism and its environment when considering questions of psychology and the theory of knowledge. After graduation in 1879, Dewey taught high school for two years, during which time the idea of pursuing a career in philosophy took hold. With this nascent ambition in mind, he sent a philosophical essay to W.T. Harris, then the editor of the *Journal of Speculative Philosophy*, and the most prominent of the St. Louis Hegelians. Harris's acceptance of the essay gave Dewey the confirmation he needed of his promise as a philosopher. With this encouragement, he traveled to Baltimore to enroll as a graduate student at Johns Hopkins University. At Johns Hopkins, Dewey's thoughts were greatly influenced by two thinkers. George Sylvester Morris, a German-trained Hegelian philosopher, exposed Dewey to the nature characteristic of

the beginning of his philosophical career.[7] However, through the course of his academic journey, Dewey departed gradually from the Hegelian conviction of the absolute knowledge, constructing a new belief that ev-

---

German idealism. G. Stanley Hall, one of the most prominent American experimental psychologists at the time, helped Dewey to recognize the power of scientific method as applied to the human sciences. Upon obtaining his doctorate in 1884, Dewey taught philosophy at the University of Michigan for ten years, interrupted by a year at the University of Minnesota in 1888. While at Michigan, Dewey wrote his first two books: *Psychology* (1887) and *Leibniz's New Essays Concerning the Human Understanding*. Both works clearly showed the deep impact of the Hegelian idealism on Dewey, while *Psychology* helped him to link the idealism and experimental science.

In 1894, Dewey was a professor and chair of philosophy, psychology, and pedagogy department at the recently founded University of Chicago. It was during his years at Chicago that Dewey's early idealism gave way to an empirically based theory of knowledge. This change in view led him to write a series of four essays entitled collectively "Thought and its Subject-Matter," which was published at Chicago under the title *Studies in Logical Theory* (1903). During that time, with his wife, Alice, Dewey also founded and directed a laboratory school at Chicago, where he was afforded an opportunity to apply directly his developing ideas on pedagogical method. This experience provided the material for his first major work on education, *The School and Society* (1899).

In 1904, Dewey joined the Department of Philosophy at Columbia University. Dewey spent the rest of his professional life at Columbia where he taught until retiring in 1930. During his first decade at Columbia, Dewey wrote a great number of articles in the theory of knowledge and metaphysics, many of which were published in two important books: *The Influence of Darwin on Philosophy and Other Essays in Contemporary Thought* (1910) and *Essays in Experimental Logic* (1916). His interest in educational theory led to the publication of *How We Think* (1910; revised ed. 1933) and *Democracy and Education* (1916), perhaps his most important work in the field. During his years at Columbia Dewey's reputation grew not only as a leading philosopher and educational theorist, but also in the public mind through his frequent contributions to popular magazines such as *The New Republic* and *Nation*, as well as his active participation in the political affairs, such as women's suffrage and the union of teachers. During that time he traveled the world as a philosopher. Among his major journeys are his lecture in Japan and China from 1919 to 1920, and his visit to Turkey in 1924 to recommend educational policy. Many of his most significant writings during these years were the result of such lectures, including *Reconstruction in Philosophy* (1920), *Human Nature and Conduct* (1922), *Experience and Nature* (1925), *The Public and its Problems* (1927), and *The Quest for Certainty* (1929).

After his retirement, Dewey continued his activities both as a public figure and productive philosopher. A primary focus of Dewey's philosophical pursuits during the 1930s was the preparation of a final formulation of his logical theory, published as *Logic: The Theory of Inquiry* in 1938. Dewey's other significant works during his retirement years include *Art as Experience* (1934), *A Common Faith* (1934), *Freedom and Culture* (1939), *Theory of Valuation* (1939), and *Knowing and the Known* (1949). Dewey continued to work vigorously throughout his retirement until his death on June 2, 1952, at the age of ninety-two.

7. Shook and Good, *John Dewey's Philosophy*, vii. (In a brief autobiographical essay published in 1930, John R. Shook and James A. Good proclaim that Dewey himself acknowledged that Hegel had "left a permanent deposit" in his thought.)

erything in this world is relative. Thus, he opposed the traditional concept of "truth" as fixed, infallible, and ultimate. While he abandoned the idea of supernatural absolute spirit, his thoughts increasingly became liberal and anti-metaphysic.[8] As Larry Hickman[9] writes:

> Dewey's naturalism leads him to argue that everything that is known or knowable exists in relation to other things. There is therefore no such thing as an absolute existence or absolute value. At the level of human life, it is the business of communication (which Dewey terms the most wonderful of all affairs) to generate the meanings by which natural events are enabled to pass beyond their existence as mere occurrences and become pregnant with implications.[10]

Hickman clearly states, "there is not anything absolute, everything is relative and relational in Dewey's philosophy. Dewey himself sees the word 'truth' a misleading term, one that strikes of finality, certainty, and correspondence with reality."[11] Indeed, Dewey is clearly aware of the limits of the human control of nature; thereby, he is aware of the uncertainty arising from these limits. In the *Experience and Nature*, he says, "Man finds himself living in an aleatory world; his existence involves, to put it badly, a gamble. The world is a scene of risk; it is uncertain, unstable, and uncannily unstable."[12] Given this uncertainty, which proves an unavoidable feature of human practice, Dewey, in *Human Nature and Conduct*, applies the same way of thinking to moral affairs, rejecting the philosophical conceptions that he calls "absolutist."[13] For him, "absolutism" is rooted in the presupposition that there are universally applicable moral principles, which means that there are "[r]eady-made rules available at a moment's notice for settling any kind of moral difficulty and resolving every species of moral doubt."[14]

The reasons, however, that Dewey rejects the traditional account of truth as absolute and universal can be summarized as this: First, because truth is the product of the transactional relationship between the living organism and its environment, i.e., between the subject and the object, which means that it is the product of the reshaping, reorganizing, and reconstructing human experience. In this sense, as long as this transactional experience

---

8. Larry Hickman was a director of the center of Dewey studies.
9. Marsoobian and Ryder, *Blackwell Guide*, 162.
10. Ibid.
11. Dewey, *Later Works of John Dewey*, 1:41.
12. Gee, "From Absolutism to Experimentalism," 241–65.
13. Dewey, *Human Nature and Conduct*, 164.
14. Ibid.

is contextual, limited, and changeable, the truth that comes out of it is also contextual, limited, and changeable,

> In its contrast with the ideas both of unfolding of latent powers from within, and of the information from without, whether by physical nature or by the cultural products of the past, the ideal of growth results in the conception that education is a constant reorganizing and reconstructing of experience. It has all the time an immediate end, and so far as activity is educative, it reaches that end—the direct transformation of the quality of experience. Infancy, youth, adult life,—all stand on the same educative level in the sense that what is really learned at any and every stage of experience constitutes the value of that experience, and in the sense that it is the chief business of life at every point to make living thus contribute to an enrichment of its own perceptible meaning.[15]

The second reason for Dewey's belief in provisional truth is his conviction in the inseparable link between the nature of the "truth" that anyone has and the "epistemology" of this truth, i.e., between ontology and epistemology. For him, the objective world exists only according to the way that a being conceives the truth about this reality. In the transactional relationship between subject and object, however, Dewey says, there is a mutual transformational impact between epistemology and ontology, whereby epistemology is always shaped by the philosopher's ontology, and the ontological existence of the reality and world is shaped by the kind of epistemology the philosopher uses to attain the truth about this reality. Because every philosophical theory is produced by a finite and historical human being, the truth that comes out of this finite being cannot be taken for granted.[16]

In this sense, we can understand Dewey's position towards traditional epistemology.[17] If the position of Dewey towards "truth" in the traditional

---

15. Dewey, *Democracy and Education*, 71.
16. Kremer, "Dewey and Rorty on Truth," 7.
17. According to the *Oxford Dictionary* the English term "epistemology" is a combination of the Greek words, episteme, which means "knowledge," and logia, which means "theory." The word means: "The theory of knowledge, especially with regard to its methods, validity, and scope, and the distinction between justified belief and opinion." The term "epistemology" appears to have been used for the first time in the *Institutes of Metaphysics* by J. F. Ferrier (1954). In this work, Ferrier distinguished two branches of philosophy: epistemology and ontology. http://www.oed.com/view/Entry/63546?redirectedFrom=epistemology#eid.

According to the *Stanford Encyclopedia of Philosophy*, "epistemology is the study of knowledge and justified belief." In other words, it is the branch of philosophy that investigates the origin, structural methods, and validity of knowledge. In terms of the origin

concept is outright rejection, it is logical, then, that his position towards the traditional "epistemology" that produces this truth is also outright rejection. In *Experience and Education*, as well as other works, Dewey rejects the different kinds of this epistemology, despite his awareness of the significant role that traditional "epistemology" played as a fundamental branch of philosophy.[18] As Simon Toulmin argues, in his introduction to *The Quest For Certainty*, Dewey's work contains a "radical dismantling of the epistemological tradition" displaying "farsightedness, perception and originality of a kind that could hardly be recognized [at the time it appeared]."[19] In the same introduction, Toulmin quotes Herbert Schneider, Dewey's student and colleague: "the best statement of Dewey's fundamental position . . . took naturalistic philosophy for granted and was not interested in the problem of 'the external world' any more, the way the old fashioned idealists were."[20]

Dewey strongly rejects all varieties of the traditional epistemology,[21] believing that they were the main reason for dualism and divisions in the

---

of cognition, two opposing schools of thought have arisen, namely, empiricism, which asserts that cognition can be obtained through sensation after experience (a posteriori), and rationalism, which asserts that cognition can be obtained through innate ideas before experience (a priori). With regard to the object of cognition, two views have come into opposition, namely, realism, which asserts that the object of cognition exists objectively, and subjective idealism, which asserts that the object of cognition is merely the ideas or representations of the subject. Concerning the method of cognition, such methods as the transcendental method and dialectical method have been proposed. In short, epistemology is concerned with the question, "How do we know what we know?" http://plato.stanford.edu/entries/epistemology.

18. Dewey, *Experience And Education*, 18.
19. Dewey, *Later Works of John Dewey*, 4:vii.
20. Ibid., viii.
21. Epistemological studies have been carried out since ancient times. It was only in the modern period; however, that epistemology became a central theme of philosophy. The philosopher who explained epistemology systematically for the first time was John Locke, whose "Essay Concerning Human Understanding" became known as an epoch-making work. The most important questions with regard to the cognition of an object have been those of the origin, the object, and the method of cognition. In terms of the origin of cognition, two opposing schools of thought have arisen, namely, empiricism, which asserts that cognition can be obtained through sensation, and rationalism, which asserts that cognition can be obtained through innate ideas. With regard to the object of cognition, two views have come into opposition, namely, realism, which asserts that the object of cognition exists objectively, and subjective idealism, which asserts that the object of cognition is merely the ideas or representations of the subject. Concerning the method of cognition, such methods as the transcendental method and dialectical method have been proposed. In the conflict between empiricism and rationalism, empiricism, finally fell into skepticism, and rationalism lapsed into dogmatism. Kant took the position of synthesizing these two opposing positions through his critical method, or transcendental method.

course of education. Both Greek and Modern thinking, Dewey emphasizes, work as the artificial bifurcation of our thoughts, feelings, and actions from the natural world, dividing method from results, teacher from learner, and learner from experience. He asserts, "Instead of seeing the educative steadily and as a whole, we see conflicting terms. We get the case of the child *vs.* the curriculum; of the individual nature *vs.* social culture. Below all other divisions in pedagogic opinion lies this opposition."[22]

Criticizing both traditional and modern approaches to education, Dewey believes that traditional epistemology, which was initiated primarily by Socrates, is defined as an epistemic enterprise that is concerned with the known object as the source of knowledge, which fails to recognize the capacities of the knowing subject. While he views contemporary epistemology, which was initiated by Descartes, as an epistemic enterprise that is concerned with the knowing subject as a sources of knowledge, which fails to recognize the role of the object itself in the process of knowing. And despite he realized the importance of experience in the process of truth formation, Kant, says Dewey, failed to recognize the nature of the subject-object relationship:[23]

> MANKIND likes to think in terms of extreme opposites. It is given to formulating its beliefs in terms of Either-Or, between which it recognizes no intermediate possibilities. When forced to recognize that the extremes cannot be acted upon, it is still inclined to hold that they are all right in theory but that when it comes to practical matters circumstances compel us to compromise. Educational philosophy is no exception. The history of educational theory is marked by opposition between the idea that education is development from within and that it is formation from without; that it is based upon natural endowments and that education is a process of overcoming natural inclination and substituting in its place habits acquired under external pressure.[24]

Analyzing Dewey's distinct position against traditional epistemology, in his introduction to *The Quest for Certainty*, Simon Toulmin says,

> In the first place they set out Dewey's interpretation of the traditional distinction between theoria and praxis in clearer and sharper terms than any of his books... Dewey's work is, on the one hand, directed against traditional epistemological positions,

22. Dewey, *Child and Curriculum*, 469.
23. *Internet Encyclopedia of Philosophy*, http://www.iep.utm.edu/dewey/.
24. Dewey, *Experience and Education*, 17.

of idealist and realist origins alike. Dewey focuses on a critique of their common foundations, viz the split between object and subject, reality and knowledge, world and consciousness."[25]

Then, Toulmin closes his introduction to *The Quest for Certainty*, concluding,

> In these introductory pages, we may look at two main sets of topics. To begin with, we may consider Dewey's criticism of the ways in which central problems in the theory of knowledge have been posed, at least since Rene Descartes and John Locke. By putting John Dewey's arguments alongside those of his younger contemporaries, Ludwig Wittgenstein and Martin Heidegger, we can see just how deeply his critique of traditional epistemology was capable of cutting.[26]

A careful reading of "The Significance of the Problem of Knowledge," says Gordon Scott,[27] will reveal that the main thrust of this work for Dewey "is against traditional foundationalism epistemology: rationalist, sensationalist and Kantian."[28] Scott asserts that Dewey gives a deep insightful analysis of the historical development of the theory of knowledge "epistemology" from Socrates to his time, giving special attention to the conflict between rationalists and sensationalists, which actually is a conflict between reason and action. Scott also emphasizes that the neo–Kantian did recognize this conflict but could resolve it. Dewey concludes, continues Scott, not only with the outright rejection of both epistemologies, but also with an insistence on the need for a new epistemology that is able to reconcile these dualistic divisions. Believing that they were the main reason for the dualism and divisions in the course of education, with Arthur Bentley, Dewey argues against all kinds of traditional epistemologies:

> What has been completely divided in philosophical discourse into man and world, inner and outer, self and not-self, subject

25. Dewey, *Later Works of John Dewey*, 4:ix.
26. Ibid.
27. Professor Gordon did his graduate work in economics at Columbia University and McGill University. In 1966, he worked as professor of Economics in Indiana University in the Economics Department and the Department of the History and Philosophy of Science. In the 1960s, his scholarly interests moved towards the study of the history of economics and broadened to embrace the history of all of the social sciences, and the epistemological problems of social research. In 1990, his book *The History and Philosophy of Social Science* was published by Routledge and *Controlling the State: Constitutionalism from Ancient Athens to Today* was published by Harvard University Press.
28. Scott, "John Dewey and American Social Science," 4.

and object, individual arid social, private arid public, etc. are in actuality parties in life—transactions in our general [pragmatic] procedure of inquiry no radical separation is made between that which is observed and the observer in the way which is common in the epistemologies.[29]

The dualism and division that traditional epistemology caused; however, lead to ignoring the human experience as a fundamental element of learning, and this is Dewey's second reason for rejecting traditional epistemologies. Experience as the transactional relationship between the mind "knower" and the objects of the environment "known," Dewey argues, is the medium where actual learning takes place, and ignoring this vital relationship makes the whole process of knowing "nothing." Therefore, Dewey rejects any view of experience that does not consider its transactional character and separates mind from body, subject from object, and self from world. Raymond Boisvert summarizes Dewey's position:

> Subject and object, terms inherited from epistemology-centered philosophy, were no longer to be understood in the traditional manner. Instead of a subject as spectator examining the realm of objects, there is now the biological environment, which involved participation of organisms in their surroundings. The environment or situation provided the dynamic unity of interacting entities.[30]

A third reason for rejecting all types of traditional epistemologies for Dewey is the conviction that these epistemologies ignore the natural human capacity to grow. Indeed, growth, for Dewey, is the main purpose of education; therefore, the natural capacity of humans to grow should be the main concern of any educational process. In this, Dewey strongly rejects traditional epistemology since it represents knowledge as universal and absolute, as though it emerges from no particular time, location, circumstance, and perspective, and since this traditional epistemology considers this knowledge true in all situations and from all perspectives. Such an epistemology clearly denies that knowledge is socially and historically constructed, and it denies any role for human intelligence in constructing it. Such a denial dichotomizes subject and object, subjectivity and objectivity, and nature and culture in an absolute manner. Since all epistemologies, both traditional and progressive, Dewey thinks, just ignore life experience as a fundamental element of constructing knowledge and ignore human capacity to think,

29. Dewey and Bentley, *Knowing and Known*, 103–4.
30. Boisvert, *Dewey's Metaphysics*, 23.

analyze, and construct "truth," they also suppress human growth. Education, then, is the cultural location where the human capacity for reconstruction can either be facilitated or suppressed. Dewey says,

> The traditional scheme is, in essence, one of imposition from above and from outside. It imposes adult standards, subject matter, and methods upon those who are only growing slowly toward maturity. The gap is so great that the required subject matter, the methods of learning and of behaving are foreign to the existing capacities of the young. They are beyond the reach of the experience the young learners already possess . . . But the gulf between the mature or adult products and the experience and abilities of the young is so wide that the very situation forbids much active participation by pupils in the development of what is taught. Theirs is to do–and learn, as it was the part of the six hundred to do and die. Learning here means acquisition of what already is incorporated in books and in the heads of the elders. Moreover, that which is taught is thought of as essentially static. It is taught as a finished product, with little regard either to the ways in which it was originally built up or to changes that will surely occur in the future.[31]

Nevertheless, if "truth" according to the epistemological traditions before him is absolute, infallible, and right in every situation, "truth," for Dewey, is complex and differs markedly and in many ways from others, particularly, those who presuppose the existence of a mind–independent reality in which truth claims can be justified. "Truth," for him, "is the result of situated processes that were initiated to respond to specific problems;"[32] It is provisional, fallible, and "warranted assertion." Warranted assertion is a new term introduced by Dewey as a substitute for the term "knowledge" or "truth" in order to indicate that knowledge is gained as a result of an ongoing, self-correcting process of inquiry not as internal mental activity.[33]

> Warranted assertion is preferred to the terms belief and knowledge [because] it is free from the ambiguity of these latter terms, and it involves reference to inquiry as that which warrants assertion. When knowledge is taken as a general abstract term related to inquiry in the abstract, it means "warranted assertibility." The

---

31. Dewey, *Democracy and Education*, 18–19.

32. Hildebrand, *Beyond Realism*, 24.

33. According Oxford dictionary, the word "assertion" means "A confident and forceful statement of fact or belief," while the word "warrant" means "Justification or authority for an action, belief, or feeling." In light of this, "warranted assertion" means "justified facts" or "facts that have authority of action."

use of a term that designates potentiality rather than an actuality involves recognition that all special conclusions of special inquiries are parts of enterprise that is continually renewed, or is a going concern.[34]

Moreover, Dewey believes that following any kind of knowledge as a final truth means that we fall in the fallacy and illusions, "[T]he most pervasive fallacy of philosophic thinking goes back to neglect of context." We commit the analytic fallacy, "whenever the distinctions or elements that are discriminated are treated as if they were final and self-sufficient."[35]

A central concern of using this term for Dewey is to assert that there is no one absolute "truth," but many truths, and each of these truths is contextual, limited, and should work as a hypothesis to another examine process. In his own words,

> The profuseness of attestations to supreme devotion to truth on the part of philosophy is matter to arouse suspicion. For it has usually been a preliminary to the claim of being a peculiar organ of access to highest and ultimate truth. Such it is not . . . Truth is a collection of truths; and these constituent truths are in the keeping of the best available methods of inquiry and testing as to matters-of-fact; methods, which are, when collected under a single name, science. As to truth, then, philosophy has no pre-eminent status.[36]

According to the idea of "warranted assertion," Dewey insists that knowledge must be refined and justified by being subjected to continuous testing through life experience. It means that an assertion is only warranted when it succeeds, at the end of the process, to achieve the goal of solving a certain problematic situation. An assertion, for Dewey, then, is a judgment that is obtained after determining the significance of the gathered data; if this assertion leads to the practice that it is supposed to, it is warranted.[37]

Dewey's theory,[38] which he calls "instrumentalism" and later, "naturalism," represents not only a new understanding of truth, but also a new

34. Dewey, *Logic*, 9.
35. Dewey, *Later Works of John Dewey*, 6:5–7.
36. Ibid.
37. Dewey, *Logic*, 143.
38. Despite being considered by many the most productive philosopher in the United States' history, Dewey developed his mature thoughts slowly over the course of his long career, which lasted for more than seventy years. The body of his work is so vast that it has been divided into three periods: early, middle and late. These periods roughly correspond with what many believe to be the three major stages of his philosophy: the

epistemology—a theory that can be perfectly read in three dimensions. First, everyone can know, but fallibilistically rather than foundationally. In other words, everyone can know without a commitment to universality or a correspondence[39] to linguistic "fact." Second, instead of division and dualism, Dewey argues for unifying thoughts and action, goals and methods, truths and inquiry in one process. Third, in many ways and almost in the entirety of his works, Dewey makes it quite evident that true knowledge can never be obtained apart from life experience. Knowing, then, is not an abstract thought; rather, it is an enterprise that is rooted in problems faced by people in context. Finally, at the heart of this theory for Dewey is the process of inquiry or reflective thinking.[40]

Our lives, Dewey emphasizes, should be guided by inquiry which is[41] "the controlled or directed transformation of an indeterminate situation into one that is so determinate in its constituent distinctions and relations as to convert the elements of the original situation into a unified whole."[42] Knowing, Dewey believes, comes about when inquiry leads to an understanding that goes beyond mere comprehension. One might have understanding (i.e., the comprehension of art, chemical elements, or musical notes), but knowing requires having sense of grounds (the "warrant") for asserting one's existence.[43] The outcome of this process, for Dewey, is three different things: knowing, knowledge, and intelligence. Knowing is the process of inquiry, that is, specific instances of applying oneself to solving problems. Knowledge constitutes the firm outcomes of inquiry. Intelligence is the result of the development of capabilities to inquiry in certain ways. As Tom Burke states:

idealistic, experimental, and naturalistic. Following Peirce, Dewey began in the second stage of his philosophy to insist that the method employed by the natural sciences is the method that needed to be applied in philosophy. Although Dewey's naturalism is too rich to be summarized, it could be argued that this philosophy focuses on two basic dimensions. The first is the interaction of living organisms with their environment, and the second is that, like science, inquiry and reflective thinking is the only way to utilize experience in dealing with the world.

39. The Stanford Encyclopedia of Philosophy offers a narrow definition of the correspondence theory of truth as "the view that truth is correspondence to a fact"—a view that was advocated by Russell and Moore early in the twentieth century.

40. Dewey, *Logic*, 104.

41. According to Webster's *Third International Dictionary* (1986), inquiry is an "act or an instance of seeking for truth, information, or knowledge; investigation; research; or a question or query" (1167), while the root word inquire means "to ask for information about, to make an investigation or search, to seek information or questioning" (1167).

42. Dewey, *Logic*, 104–5.

43. Ibid., 143.

Knowledge is the result of successful inquiry, whereas knowing consists in using one's intelligence in given inquires. Intelligence is stabilized knowledge... which can be utilized other inquiries, given the principle of continuity and given the fact that judgment are not abstract decisions but constitute a kind of conduct (assertion)... knowing is to intelligence roughly what asserting is to be disposed.[44]

Critical (reflective) thinking or inquiry represents a new pedagogical epistemology for Dewey. In *How We Think* (1910), Dewey defines critical thinking[45] as an "Active, persistent and careful consideration of a belief or supposed form of knowledge in light of the grounds that support it, and the further conclusions to which it tends." Despite the fact that the notion of inquiry appears in many places in his works, he begins using the term only in his later works. In *The Quest for Certainty*, Dewey asserts, "Thinking is objectively discoverable as that mode of serial responsive behavior to a problematic situation in which transition to the relatively settled and clear is effected[46] In *How We Think* (1933), Dewey explains the patterns of inquiry, which he terms "the five phases of reflective thoughts."[47] It was in *Logic: The Theory of Inquiry*, however, where Dewey provides his most extensive explanation of this process of thinking in response to several attacks of criticism from his contemporaries, most notably Bernard Russell.

Dewey's inquiry, indeed, has its roots in his predecessor, Charles Sanders Peirce (1839–1914). In his essay "The Fixation of Belief," Peirce explains his use of the term "inquiry" as follows: "The irritation of doubt causes a struggle to attain a state of belief. I shall term this struggle Inquiry'"[48] Inquiry, for Peirce, is the struggle to attain a state of "belief" from a prior state of "doubt."[49] The process of inquiry for him occurs only when an individual is challenged with doubt. "Belief" for Peirce is a state that guides our desires and shapes our actions. It is a satisfactory state that establishes some habit that determines our actions. "Doubt," on the other hand, is a state that results when one is confronted with a situation to which prior

---

44. Burke, *Dewey's New Logic*, 256.

45. For Dewey, thinking is problem solving and his paradigm has come to be called, variously, problem solving, critical thinking, reflective thinking, functional thinking, scientific thinking, the complete act of thought, and the method of intelligence (Tanner, "Some Thoughts.").

46. Dewey, *Later Works of Dewey*, 4:181.

47. Dewey, *How We Think*, 200.

48. Frankfurt, "Peirce's Account of Inquiry," 588–92.

49. Peirce, *Writings of Charles S. Peirce*, 8:372.

beliefs make one unfit to respond. For Peirce, any doubt that is exchanged for belief is a kind of inquiry.[50]

The process of Peirce's inquiry, then, occurs only when one is confronted with doubt, and the goal of inquiry is to eliminate doubt and to achieve belief. Yet, doubt and belief for Peirce are mental states, and the process of exchanging doubt for belief is a completely inner process. He says: "the sole object of inquiry is the settlement of opinion."[51] Therefore, under Peirce's view, the fixation of belief is the goal of inquiry. In his process, Peirce also uses a standard criterion to evaluate and adapt all methods of inquiry: the method that tends to result in a kind of belief that is stable and does not generate further doubt.[52]

For Dewey, reflective thinking and inquiry is a questioning process in action.[53] The essential character of inquiry is the encounter with actual problematic situations, which impels us to reflective thought. He says: "We inquire when we question; and we inquire when we seek for whatever will provide an answer to a question asked."[54] In other words, Dewey assures us that questioning is synonymous with inquiry. "Thinking is inquiry, investigation, turning over, probing or delivering into;" all mean to find something new or different from a given situation. Inquiry means questioning, while questioning is a reflective thinking that Dewey distinguishes from other forms of thought, such as stream of consciousness, daydreams, and beliefs.[55]

Unlike Peirce, Dewey understands doubt as an existential condition rather than a mental operation. Therefore, Dewey's inquiry is an active process that interferes with real life, and knowledge is not just a mental thought or concept; rather, it is the actual resolution of a specific problematic, indeterminate situation in daily life. The actual resolution will happen as a result of inquiry and reflective thinking. This idea is based on the belief that thinking is the natural activity of the human being and that this thinking human is living in an uncertain (indeterminate) world, which threatens human existence. The central theme of Dewey's logic involves behavior as well as mental activity in the same process, and he never regards a resolution as an established one unless it occurs in the process of solving the problem that started the thinking process. Dewey understands reflective thinking to be appropriate to treat all kinds of human experiences. Since experience is the

50. Ibid., 8:71.
51. Ibid., 8:375.
52. Ibid., 8:383.
53. Dewey, *Logic*, 13.
54. Ibid., 109.
55. Ibid., 503.

active function of humans within different situations, and since situations are constructed with both biological and social factors, there is no reason why a given indeterminate situation should be a moral situation. A moral inquiry, for Dewey, is the process by which a social condition is disordered or indeterminate. The process of transforming an indeterminate moral situation into a determinate one is as scientific as any other process, which can be treated with the same pattern of inquiry.[56]

Finally, unlike Peirce, Dewey believes that nothing is called stable belief. If belief is the result of the activity of reason in the context of social experience and if experience is always changeable, therefore, belief is also changeable, and the transformation of doubt into belief is not the end of the process of inquiry, as Peirce thinks. Inquiry for Dewey is a continuing process in every field with which it is engaged. The settled resolution of a particular situation by inquiry does not guarantee that the conclusion will continue as settled forever. He says: "there is no belief is so settled as not to be exposed to further inquiry."[57]

It is clear for Dewey, however, that reflective thinking is not the aim of education, but rather, a meaning—making process that helps learners to move from one experience to the next with a deeper understanding as a part of and in relationship with other experiences and thoughts. Carol Rodgers says:

> The function of reflection for Dewey is to make "relationships and continuities" among the elements of an experience, between that experience and other experiences, and between that experience and the knowledge that one carries, and between that knowledge and the knowledge produced by thinkers other than oneself.[58]

This is what he actually means with his significant definition of education as "reconstruction or reorganization of experience which adds to the meaning of experience."[59]

---

56. Ibid., 72.

57. Ibid., 16.

58. Rodgers, "Defining Reflection," 850. Carol Rodgers is an assistant professor of Educational Theory and Practice in the State University of New York at Albany. Her research interests span the history of progressive teacher education, reflective practice in contemporary programs and schools, and inquiry into how teachers learn to see student learning. Her previous publications include "Communities of Reflection, Communities of Support" published in *Research on Professional Development Schools: The Teacher Education Yearbook VIII*.

59. Dewey, *Democracy of Education*, 71.

Goal—Open-ended Growth

Growth is the central notion that pervades the entirety of Dewey's thoughts. Within Dewey's theory, everything else takes place in relationship to the growth of the human being. Dewey states this clearly when he points out, "[T]here is nothing to which growth is relative save more growth."[60] In short, the primary criterion that Dewey offers to assess whether an experience has educational value or not is the general principle of *growth*.

Yet, the kind of growth that Dewey means is one that represents learning experiences that open up opportunities for further growth. Put it another way, growth represents a form of learning that enables human beings to continue learning throughout their lives. On the basis of this understanding, Dewey makes distinctions among educational, non-educational, and mis-educational experiences. While he believes that these distinctions are central to understanding the broader ends of education, he also believes that experiences can be mis-educative when we learn, but do not grow. In this, he borrows the example of a "gang of thieves." The gang teaches its young members how to be thieves, and they learn from practice and education until becoming proficient. However, in the end, these learning experiences are mis-educative, since, although these thieves are becoming more skilled and knowledgeable, their learning limits the depth and breadth of their future experience because they cannot interact freely with others. This limitation severely diminishes their future possibilities for growth.[61]

However, despite being deeply influenced by Hegel, Dewey rejects any notion of *telos* or an absolute end of human affairs, which means that the ends of education (consequences) are connected to the method of education (experiences), and content (subject matter) in a concrete social condition. Ends, then, are not the completion of the process, but a part of a process, one stage in a "continuum." For Dewey, education is not a movement toward a fixed goal, "growth is regarded as having an end, instead of being an end."[62] He asserts, "[T]he conception that growth and progress are just approximations to a final unchanging goal is the last infirmity of the mind in its transition from a static to a dynamic understanding of life."[63]

Nevertheless, instead of fixed goals of education, Dewey uses the term "ends-in-view" to describe this spiral process. Despite the fact that this term points to an end, it actually points to the end of a particular task at hand

---

60. Ibid., 49.
61. Dewey, *Middle Works of John Dewey*, 9:88.
62. Dewey, *Democracy and Education*, 50.
63. Ibid., 56–57.

while reminding us that ends are always provisional and changing throughout the course of educational experiences. Therefore, the term "ends-in-view" is intentionally open-ended, and it represents a series of standards to guide individual practice. This means that the ends and the means of education are the same thing: the continuous growth and learning of the individuals throughout life—it is an open-ended growth. He says,

> For it assumed that the aim of education is to enable individuals to continue their education—or that the object and reward of learning in continued capacity for growth . . . we are not concerned, therefore, with finding an end outside of the educative process to which education is subordinate. Our whole conception forbids. We are rather concerned with the contrast which exists when aims belong within the process in which they operate and they are set up from without."[64]

In this sense, education, for Dewey is not preparing children for life in the future, but rather, education is life in itself. Criticizing both traditional and progressive education, Dewey asserts,

> The main purpose or objective is to prepare the young for the future responsibilities and for success in life, by means of acquisition of the organized bodies of information and prepared forms of skill, which comprehend the material of instruction.[65]

Yet, to grow is to become both more capable of adapting the environment to an individual's activities as well as adapting the activities to the environment. Like Rousseau, education, for Dewey, should aim for the welfare and general goodness of the whole society, a goal, which requires freeing the natural human capacity to grow progressively. Dewey states, "The very idea of education is a freeing of individual capacity in progressive growth directed at social aims."[66] It is the aim of progressive education, Dewey argues, to achieve a state of individual industrial competency for the individual (that is, a state of social efficiency) and to take part in correcting unfair privilege and deprivation.

---

64. Ibid., 91.
65. Dewey, *Experience And Education*, 18.
66. Ibid., 105.

Human Nature—A Whole Being in the Process of Maturity

It would not help very much, however, to simply think that growth, for Dewey, is a synonym of life. Dewey's belief in growth, instead, is deeply rooted in his conviction about the natural capacities of the human being to grow. He conceives of humans as parts of nature that constantly interact with the social and physical environments and sees higher levels of adaptation through the use of intelligence. It is important here to state that adaptation, for Dewey, is not merely a passive accommodation to the environment, but, an active change and control of it,

> Adaptation . . . is quite as much adaptation of the environment to our own activities as of our activities to the environment a savage tribe manages to live on a desert plain. It adapts itself. But its adaptation involves a maximum of accepting, tolerating, putting up with things as they are, a maximum of passive acquiescence, and minimum of active control, of subjection to use. A civilized people enter upon the scene. It also adapts itself. It introduces irrigation; it searches the world for plants and animals that flourish under such condition; it improves, by careful selection, those, which are growing there.[67]

Viewing humans as parts of nature that are able to adapt the environment is not the only concern for Dewey; possessing natural capacities to grow from a state of immaturity to a state of maturity is also an important issue.[68] For Dewey, the word immaturity has both a negative and a positive meaning as it includes the possibility for growth:

> The prefix "im" of the word immaturity means something positive, not a mere void or lack . . . Now when we say that immaturity means the possibility of growth, we are not referring to absence of powers which may exist at a later time; we express a force positively present–the ability to develop.[69]

Yet, immaturity, for Dewey, is characterized by two things: dependence and plasticity. Unlike many, Dewey believes that dependence has a positive side as it clearly implies developing and growing. He notes that the fact that human beings are the most dependent of the animals when born not only points towards interdependence, but also points toward the natural capacity

---

67. Dewey, *Democracy and Education*, 46.
68. Ibid., 41.
69. Ibid., 42.

and need of human being to grow and develop. In this regard, Dewey's deep faith in the natural abilities of the child to grow is quite clear:

> Observation shows that children are gifted with an equipment of the first order for social intercourse . . . the native mechanism of the child and his implies all tend to facile responsiveness. The statement that children, before adolescence, are egotistically self-centered, even if it were true would not contradict the truth of this statement. It would simply indicate that their social responsiveness is employed on their own behalf, not that it does not exist . . . from a social standpoint, dependence denotes a power rather than a weakness; it involves interdependence."[70]

The second characteristic of immaturity, for Dewey, is plasticity. Plasticity, in his view, "is essentially the ability to learn from experience; the power to retain from experience something which is of avail with coping with the difficulties of a later situation."[71] It is the human "capacity to acquire habits."[72] While "a habit is a form of executive skill, of efficiency in doing. A habit means an ability to use natural conditions as means to ends."[73] By habits, Dewey does not simply mean "a change wrought in the organism, ignoring the fact that this change consists in ability to affect subsequent changes in the environment."[74] While education, Dewey argues, is frequently defined "as consisting in the acquisition of these habits that effect an adjustment of an individual and hid environment,"[75] which "express an essential phase of growth,"[76] adjustment "understood in its active sense of control of means for achieving ends."[77]

Nevertheless, Dewey's belief in the natural capacity of the human being to grow, adapt nature, and change from an immature to a mature individual by using intelligence is deeply rooted in what he identifies as the greatest educational resource: the natural impulses of the child. The young human being, Dewey believes, possesses four natural impulses: to inquire or to find out things (i.e., inquiry), to use language and thereby to enter into the social world (i.e., communication), to build or make things (i.e., construction), and to express one's feelings and ideas (i.e., expression). Rather than traditional

70. Ibid., 43.
71. Ibid.
72. Ibid., 45.
73. Ibid.
74. Ibid.
75. Ibid.
76. Ibid.
77. Ibid.

education, which assumes that children are incapable of constructing their own knowledge, Dewey sees these impulses as the foundation for any curriculum. The educational challenge, for him, is to nurture these impulses for lifelong learning and continuous growth. As he writes,

> Keeping in mind these fourfold areas of interest—the interest in conversation, or *communication*; in inquiry, or finding out things; in making things, or *construction*; and in artistic *expression*–we may say they are the natural resources, the un-invested capital, upon the exercise of which depends the active growth of the child.[78]

Values of Thinking—Freedom of Thoughts and Practice

In his work *How We Think*, Dewey devotes almost the entirety of chapter two to "The Values of Thought."[79] First, through thinking reflectively, people act as active subjects who are able to be in control of their acting, instead of being objects that are moved either by instincts according their present emotions or by others. He says,

> Thought affords the sole method of escape from purely impulsive or purely routine action. A being without capacity for thought is moved only by instincts and appetites, as these are called forth by outward conditions and by the inner state of the organism. A being thus moved is, as it were, pushed from behind. This is what we mean by the blind nature of brute actions. The agent does not see or foresee the end for which he is acting, nor the results produced by his behaving in one way rather than in another. He does not "know what he is about."[80]

Thought, Dewey insists, enables an individual to use his or her past experiences to make a better future, "To a being who thinks, things are records of their past, as fossils tell of the prior history of the earth, and are prophetic of their future, as from the present positions of heavenly bodies remote eclipses are foretold."[81]

---

78. Dewey, *School and Society*, 48.
79. Dewey, *How We Think*, 14.
80. Ibid.
81. Ibid., 15.

Secondly, reflective thinking, for Dewey, helps an individual, "to develop and arrange artificial signs to remind him in advance of consequences and of ways to securing and avoiding them."[82] In this, Dewey makes a comparison between a being that lacks a critical thinking, whom he names "a savage," and a being that uses thought to reflect, analyze, and create. Using this comparison, Dewey stresses that, instead of waiting for problems to take place in order to attempt to find solutions for them, critical thinking enables humans to predict the future's consequences through artificial signs that humans make so that they are able to prevent problems before taking place. He states,

> The savage learns to detect the signs of fire and thereby to invent methods of producing flame; Civilized man invents permanent conditions for producing light and heat whenever they are needed. The very essence of civilized culture is that we deliberately erect monuments and memorials, lest we forget; and deliberately institute, in advance of the happening of various contingencies and emergencies of life, devices for detecting their approach and registering their nature, for warding off what is unfavorable, or at least for protecting ourselves from its full impact and for making more secure and extensive what is favorable.[83]

Indeed, I disagree with the name "savage," as it goes beyond differentiating those who do not use thought as a way approaching life and those whose critical thinking is their way of managing their lives, reality and society. However, I agree with Dewey that the way of thinking helps both to plan for and to control the expected consequences of the future.

Finally, using reflective thinking, in Dewey's perspective, "confers upon physical events and objects a very different status and value from that which they possess to a being that does not reflect."[84] It changes the perspective and image that people have about the physical world and events. For a thinking being, "a stone is different to one who knows something of its past history and its future use from what it is to one who only feels it directly through his senses."[85]

For me, however, none of his works with which I am familiar points to the value and necessity of critical thinking more than the passage that I quote at the opening of this chapter. Six years after writing his book *How*

82. Ibid., 15.
83. Ibid., 16.
84. Ibid.
85. Ibid., 17.

We Think, which intensively explores "The Values of thought,"[86] Dewey summarizes his convictions about the value of thinking reflectively in his book *Democracy and Education*. First, known as anti-dualism, Dewey believes that reflective thinking helps individuals to overcome the problem of dualism and division, particularly of theory and practice. This is important for Dewey because it relates education to life. Second, reflective thinking helps educators to focus on developing learners' ability to construct real and useful knowledge, instead of focusing on acquiring abstract information that is inadequate to meet the challenges and complexities of modern life. Third, reflective thinking liberates humans from any kind of slavery to others. It is the freedom of thoughts that does not leave a person "at the mercy of his routine habits and the authoritative control of others."[87] Finally, critical thinking promotes human growth while the lack of its use, Dewey summarizes, "is a most powerful obstacle to further growth in the grace of intelligence."[88]

Pedagogy—The Method of Intelligence

Despite the conviction that his philosophy is a system of thoughts, which cannot be reduced to one dimension or another, many believe that the main focus of Dewey's works is the pedagogy of education. Joseph Ratner says, "The all-important problem, social as well as philosophic, is the problem of method."[89] This, indeed, is how Dewey understands the essence and function of philosophy: not as abstract thoughts or theoretical beliefs alone, but rather, as a theory that should be shaped in practical ways to address life problems. In his words,

> If philosophy is to develop an effective system of operative ideas, then it has to develop a method that is pragmatic and empirical. Philosophy has to become a primarily a method rather than a system. We should think of philosophy as intelligent methods of inquiry rather than an over-arching system of beliefs.[90]

Believing that humans are a part of nature, however, Dewey insists that true knowledge is the knowledge that only comes out from the transaction between the human being and the environment. In *Democracy and*

86. Ibid., 14.
87. Dewey, *Democracy and Education*, 135.
88. Ibid., 135.
89. Ratner, "Introduction to John Dewey's Philosophy," 341.
90. Ibid., 344.

Education, he asserts, "The theory of the method of knowing which is advanced in these pages may be termed pragmatic. Its essential feature is to maintain the continuity of knowing with an activity which purposely modifies the environment."[91] For Dewey, the modification of nature is not just a transaction with the material things of nature; rather, it is the lived experience of the individual within the cultural, social, and environmental contexts in which the individual exists. If the aim of education, then, is human growth that enables an individual to face the complexity of modern life through solving its various problems and if life experience is the medium of learning, then an "intelligent method" of education is necessarily needed in order to achieve this aim through a scientific interpretation of this experience. Therefore, while the traditional method is concerned with imposing ready-made facts onto the minds of learners, what actually Dewey wants to do is to create intelligent minds that are able to construct their own knowledge in any problematic situation by transforming this perplexity into organized and clear situations. He put it in contrast with the traditional methods,

> On the one hand, learning is the sum total of what is known, as that is handed down by books and learned men. It is something that external, an accumulation of cognitions as one might store material commodities in a warehouse. Truth exists ready-made somewhere. Study is then the process by which an individual draws on what is in storage. On the other hand, learning means something, which the individual does when he studies. It is an active, personally conducted affair. The dualism here is between knowledge as something external, or, as it is often called, objective, and knowledge as something purely internal, subjective, and psychical. There is, on one side, a body of truth, ready-made, and, on the other, a ready-made mind equipped with a faculty of knowing.[92]

In order to construct such a mind that equipped with a faculty of knowing, thinking intelligently is the only way for Dewey. In his book *Philosophy Goes to School*, Mathew Lipman emphasizes that "thinking" is the method of learning for Dewey. Quoting Dewey, "all which the school can or need do for pupils, so far as their *minds* are concerned . . . is to develop their ability to think,"[93] Lipman says, "Thinking *is* the method of intelligent

---

91. Ibid., 345.
92. Dewey, *Democracy and Education*, 288.
93. Ibid., 135.

learning, of learning that employs and rewards mind."[94] And despite the fact that "reflective education" is rooted in Socrates' philosophy, Dewey is the one that shaped it into a pedagogical theory of education:

> For surely it was Dewey who, in modern times, foresaw that education had to be defined as the fostering of thinking rather than as the transmission of knowledge; that there could be no difference in the method by which teachers were taught and the method by which they would be expected to teach; that the logic of a discipline must not be confused with the sequence of discoveries that would constitute its understanding; that student reflection is best stimulated by living experience, rather than by a formally organized, desiccated text; that reasoning is sharpened and perfected by disciplined discussion as by nothing else and that reasoning skills are essential for successful reading and writing; and that the alternative to indoctrinating students with values is to help them reflect effectively on the values that are constantly being urged on them.[95]

Nevertheless, an "intelligent method" of education, for Dewey, is not possible without science. This is why his method of education is called a "scientific method" of solving problems. If science is the foundation of modern innovation and true knowledge it is necessarily needed to be used as the method for doing philosophy if we are to transmit philosophy from mere intellectual abstractions to a practical field that can help to shape a better life for human beings. Science, for Dewey, indeed, signifies human intelligence; "Science represents the office of intelligence . . . pursued systematically, intentionally, and on a scale due to freedom from limitation of habit. It is the sole instrumentality of conscious, as distinct from accident, progress."[96] It also is the core of all kinds of human progress in modern time. He concludes his views in this statement: "Ultimately and philosophically, science is the organ of general social progress."[97] Richard A. Brosio points out that "Dewey's pedagogy is the mastery of the scientific method."[98] An educator, however, does not teach the scientific method by having learners memorize its characteristics; rather, the scientific method means "we know an object when we know how it is made, and we know how it is

---

94. Ibid., 135.
95. Lipman, *Philosophy*, 4.
96. Dewey, *Democracy and Education*, 228.
97. Ibid., 239.
98. Brosio, *Relationship of Dewey's Pedagogy*, 40.

made in the degree in which we ourselves make it."⁹⁹ In the process of being an active partner in the making of an object, one is constantly confronted with new and different problems. A good method of education, then, is a method that both assesses learners in solving these problems and, more important, prepares them to face further problems in the future. Therefore, "the ground or basis for a belief is deliberately sought and its adequacy to support the belief examined."¹⁰⁰

Although a focus on reflective thinking as the method of education can be discerned in most of his works, Dewey only starts to use the term literally in his book *How We Think* (1910). In this work, the central conviction for Dewey is that learning is learning to think. Yet, "The better way of thinking is reflective thinking."¹⁰¹ He defines reflective thinking as the "*Active, persistent and careful consideration of a belief or supposed form of knowledge in light of the grounds that support it, and the further conclusions to which it tends.*"¹⁰² This kind of thinking, involves a process of translation "from a situation in which there is experienced obscurity, doubt, conflict, disturbance of some sort into a situation that is clear, coherent, settled, harmonious."¹⁰³ In *The Quest for Certainty*, Dewey asserts, "Thinking is objectively discoverable as that mode of serial responsive behavior to a problematic situation in which transition to the relatively settled and clear is effected."¹⁰⁴ In *Democracy and Education*, reflective thinking, for him, is the sole method to obtaining true knowledge: "While we may speak, without error, of the method of thought, the important thing is that thinking is the method of an educational experience. The essentials of method are therefore, identical with the essentials of reflection."¹⁰⁵

Yet, in order for him to organize his pedagogy into a specific practical method, Dewey explains the patterns of reflective thinking or inquiry in *How We Think*, and *Logic: The Theory of Inquiry*, identifying "the five phases of reflective thoughts,"¹⁰⁶ which he considers essential functions of this particular intelligent process.

1. *Suggestion—the habit does not work*: It is a doubtful situation that is seen as problematic, and some vague suggestions are considered as

99. Dewey, *Later Works of John Dewey*, 4:428.
100. Dewey, *How We Think*, 1–2.
101. Ibid.
102. Ibid., 9.
103. Ibid., 101.
104. Dewey, *Later Works of John Dewey*, 4:181.
105. Dewey, *Democracy and Education*, 192.
106. Dewey, *How We Think*, 200.

possible solutions. Situation, for Dewey, however, is the environmental context in which an organism exists and acts: "What is designated by the word 'situation' is not a single object or event or set of events. For we never experience nor form judgments about objects and events in isolation, but only in connection with a contextual whole. This latter is what is called a 'situation.'"[107] For him, a problematic situation it is a state of *perplexity*, doubt, and indetermination while he believes that all kind of reflective thinking and inquiry begin with a genuine doubt. He calls it a "forked-road situation, a situation that proposes alternatives."[108] Like Peirce, Dewey thinks that Cartesian doubt was insincere, as we cannot intentionally place ourselves in doubt, but rather, we are driven into doubt when our ways of acting fail us in doubtful situations. Dewey explains that an "unsettled or indeterminate situation might have been called a problematic situation. This name would have been, however, proleptic and anticipatory."[109] Osmer asserts that this phase of practicing reflective thinking begins with what Dewey calls a "felt difficulty," which "leads to special forms of observation, hypothesis–formation, and experiential texting, construed in a variety of ways."[110] While he calls it a "forked-road situation, a situation that proposes alternatives,"[111] at one point, Dewey describes it as a time of "suggestions." Osmer maintains, by "felt," "Dewey does not mean something that is primarily subjective. The difficulty arises in the situation, not merely . . . in internal consciousness in this initial phase the problem remains indefinite."[112]

2. *Intellectualization—defining the problem*: Dewey argues that one never starts in a settled problem but rather, in a problematic situation in which one is often not aware of what the problem is. From this understanding, we can realize two points. First, for Dewey, we are not able to realize exactly what the problem is until we attempt to find some solution to the problematic situation. It is true that most of the reflective process consists precisely in the intellectual process of understanding what the problem is. A teacher, for example, who wants to know why learners cannot achieve learning objectives, will probably realize how to address the problem only when she or he understands the situation.

107. Dewey, *Democracy and Education*, 288.
108. Ibid., 20.
109. Dewey, *Logic*.
110. Osmer, *Practical Theology*, 33.
111. Ibid., 20.
112. Ibid., 45.

Second is that Dewey's understanding reflects the importance and necessity of the role of the learner in the process of illuminating and addressing the problem. The learner is an active participant in the process, not just a receiver.

As Dewey points out, says Osmer, problem definition is a crucial element in discerning what is going on and what should be done, which is not possible without thinking reflectively. The purpose of inquiry, then, is to transform an indeterminate situation into a specific problem, and then to convert this situation into an object of study.[113] Questioning itself, says Dewey, does not constitute the problem; rather, problems arise from experience and are mediated by questioning. It is notable here that while Dewey is quite concerned with questioning, he asserts that knowledge has no role in constructing the problematic situation which already exists: "It is of the very nature of the indeterminate situation which evokes inquiry to be questionable . . . we are doubtful because the situation is already doubtful."[114]

3. *Hypothesis-formation:* for Dewey, this is the phase of analyzing thoughts and creating an idea that will lead to the process of resolving a given problematic situation. Dewey calls this "the guiding idea" or "hypothesis."[115] In describing this phase, Osmer explains two. First is the relationship of facts to hypothesis-formation. It is not a static relationship, says Osmer; it is not as though we have a clear set of facts that present themselves to us, giving rise to a hypothesis, but, "The criteria of what constitutes a fact is functional and is controlled by the purpose and aim of the investigation being undertaken."[116] Dewey believes that knowledge arises from everyday experience is more real and primary than the data that are gathered by highly developed scientific procedures. Second, is Dewey's understanding of the means-ends relationship. To understand what this means for Dewey, Osmer suggests that we first understand what he means by "ends-in-view." For Dewey, says Osmer, an ends-in-view is "the result of the initial deliration and problem-definition of reflective experience. It refers to a specific, intended plan of action or mode of interaction in light of the specific features of the situation."[117] It is an anticipated outcome or course of

---

113. Osmer, *Practical Theology*, 111.
114. Ibid., 109.
115. Dewey, *How We Think*, 109.
116. Osmer, *Practical Theology*, 48.
117. Ibid., 49.

action that serves as a guiding idea that directs action and observation to and moves the situation towards an intended "end."[118]

While Dewey calls this end a "consummatory experience," between the "end-in-view," as the anticipated course of action that leads to certain consequences, and the "end," as the actual consummatory experience, lies the "means."[119] Osmer agrees with many that nothing is more important for Dewey than his conviction that means and ends cannot exist separately. To hypothesize a sharp separation between means and ends is to fail to recognize the contextual and temporal nature of all ends, particularly in the process of reflective experience in which human intelligence is used to form an end-in-view and to follow it through to the resolution of a problematic situation. In short, hypothesis-formation is the phase that is responsible for creating ideas, which will lead to the resolution of the problem that we already defined.[120]

4. *Reasoning—in the narrower sense:* In this phase, attempting to find some coherence within these hypotheses, an individual who is confronted with a problematic situation compares the ideas or hypotheses that she or he framed in the third phase. This phase is comprised of elaborating the meaning of ideas in relation to each other. For Osmer it is "an active process of reflection on the proposed course of action that is to be taken."[121] In this process, a person might recall additional facts from memory, other cultural resources, or other people. Then, the tenability of a working hypnosis can be evaluated and tested in the light of the knowledge and resources available to the individual or community. These thought experiments are important, not because they allow for a return to the beginning again, but also because they can lead to the reformulating of a working hypothesis.[122]

5. *Testing the Hypothesis by Action:* In this phase, the working hypothesis is tested by trying to realize it in practice through reconstructing the problematic situation. For Dewey, it is only in the practical testing of the hypothesis in real life activity that makes it possible to draw conclusions about its validity. This is why Dewey calls the previous phase "reasoning in a narrow sense," as he believes that proper reasoning is only actualized as a part of the testing process of the hypothesis.

118. Ibid.
119. Dewey, *How We Think*, 110.
120. Osmer, *Practical Theology*, 47.
121. Ibid., 51.
122. Miettinen, "Concept of Experiential Learning," 72.

The situation is reconstructed according to the requirements of the hypothesis in order to see whether the consequences that are deducted[123] from the hypothesis become real in practice. Osmer says, "This means that the idea must lead to overt action which gives experimental correlation or verification."[124]

Although the testing of the hypothesis does not always lead to the confirmation of the hypothesis, for Dewey it makes the process of learning possible. The consequences can be compared to the initial suppositions that were included in the hypothesis, which makes this process different from just trial and error. What really matters here is Dewey's conviction that the outcome of the process is both direct and indirect. The direct or immediate result of the process is that the problematic situation is reconstructed and resolved, which helps to control the activity. The indirect and intellectual outcome is the production of a meaning that can be used as a resource for formulating solutions to problems in the future. Dewey says, "and may well be that by-product, this gift of the goods, is incomparably more valuable for living a life is the primary and intended result of control, essential as that control to having a life to live."[125]

Though sometimes understood by readers as a linear process, Dewey makes it clear that these are "phases" not steps. The overall process is more recursive than sequential, and the order in which the phases occur (and reoccur) is thoroughly contingent. In his introduction to *Intelligence in the Modern World: John Dewey's Philosophy*, Joseph Ratner says:

> Inquiry is not like a race and the beginning of inquiry is not the line that is left behind at the top of the gun. With every step taken in the course of inquiry there is a new beginning issuing from a new ending; but beginning and ending do not follow upon each other–they intercept and unite. In walking along the right foot does not follow upon the left–both are working through the whole stride. What is an ending or a beginning depends upon the functional positions determined within the moment of inquiry.[126]

For Dewey, however, the attitudes that learners bring to the process of reflective thinking can open or block the door to effective learning. Dewey

---

123. Induction and deduction, for Dewey, is an important issue in this process; yet, for the sake of space, I offer just brief comparison between the two in the appendix.

124. Osmer, *Practical Theology*, 52.

125. Miettinen, "Concept of Experiential Learning," 72.

126. Dewey, *Intelligence In Modern World*, 212–13.

argues that careful awareness of our attitudes and the ability to discipline them for the sake of the thinking process is one of the thinker's responsibilities. The reason for this is Dewey's recognition of the tendency of all humans to see what we desire to be true or what we fear is true, rather to accept the evidence or the grounds that support what emerges from the process of reflection. This is why he cautions against the risk of the belief "which is in harmony with desire."[127] In *Democracy and Education*, Dewey offers five attitudes that are necessary for a successful thinking. He says, "Some attitudes may be named, however, which are central in effective intellectual ways of dealing with subject matter. Among the most important are, directness, open-mindedness, single-mindedness (or whole-heartedness), responsibility. Readiness."[128]

1. *Directness*: Dewey thinks that this attitude is described best not through positive terms, but through negative ones, i.e., by what it is not. In this way, directness is not self-consciousness, distractedness, or constant preoccupation with how others perceive one's performance. These terms, for Dewey, indicate, "A person is not immediately concerned with subject matter. Something has come between which reflects concern to side issues. A self-conscious person is partly thinking about his problem and partly about what others think of his performances."[129] Rather, Dewey says, "Confidence is a good name for what is intended by the term directness."[130] Yet, it should not be confused with "the confidence, which may be a form of self-consciousness—or of 'cheek.'"[131] It is not the focus of an individual on thinking or feeling about his or her attitude as it is not a reflex. Rather, it is the straightforwardness with which one goes at what he has to do. Although directness does not mean self-absorption, it does not also mean self-detachment. Indeed, a teacher's growth may well pass from self-absorption, to forgetting oneself, to self-awareness, which, primarily, includes observing and reflecting on his or her thoughts, emotions, and actions. This growth enables him or her to ask, "Where was the learning in today's work?" Instead of asking, "What did I teach today?"[132]

   In *How We Think*, Dewey concludes his understanding of teachers' directness as:

127. Ibid., 30.
128. Dewey, *Democracy and Education*, 192.
129. Ibid., 153.
130. Ibid.
131. Ibid.
132. Ibid., 154.

> *The teacher must have his mind free to observe the mental responses and movement of the student . . .* The problem of the pupils is found in the subject matter, the problem of the teachers is *what the mind of the pupils are doing with this subject matter.* Unless the teacher's mind has mastered the subject matter in advance, unless it is thoroughly at home in it, using it unconsciously without need to express thought, he will not be free to give full time and attention to observation and interpretation of the pupils' intellectual reactions. The teacher must be alive to all forms bodily expression of mental condition—to puzzlement, boredom, mastery, the dawn of an idea, feigned attention, tendency to show off, to dominate discussion because of egotism, etc.—as well as sensitive to the meaning of all expression in words. He must be aware not only of *their* meaning, but of their meaning as indicative of the state of mind of the pupil, his degree of observation and comprehension.[133]

2. *Open-Mindedness*: Dewey describes this attitude as "hospitality" to new ways of seeing and understanding. This hospitality is the attitude of a mind that welcomes suggestions and relevant information from all sides, and it works as means of guiding the development of a situation and the growth of a human being. Dewey states,

> But intellectual growth means constant expansion of horizons and consequent formation of new purposes and new responses. These are impossible without an active disposition to welcome points of view hitherto alien; an active desire to entertain considerations, which modify existing purposes. Retention of capacity to grow the reward of such intellectual hospitality. The worst thing about the stubbornness of minds, about prejudices, is that they arrest development; they shut the mind off from new stimuli. Open-mindedness means retention of the childlike attitudes; closed-mindedness means premature intellectual old age.[134]

For him, however, open-mindedness should be differentiated from empty-mindedness. As he puts it, open—mindedness is not a matter of saying, "Come right in; there is nobody at home."[135] To say it another way, open-mindedness is not the blind acceptance of every

---

133. Dewey, *How We Think*, 275.
134. Dewey, *Democracy and Education*, 154.
135. Dewey, *How We Think*, 30.

idea without intelligent critique; rather, it is the willingness to interact with different perspectives, joined with the "possibility of error even in the beliefs that are dearest to us,"[136] and the acknowledgement of the limitations of one's own perspective.

3. *Single-Mindedness or Whole—Heartedness*: In *Democracy and Education*, Dewey offers a detailed explanation of the subject matter, which can be seen as three interrelated tensions: the actual content that a teacher is teaching (e.g., French), the learner's acquisition of the content that the teacher is teaching, and how the teaching affects the leaners' process of learning. This triangular relationship of teaching, learning, and content interact to form a dynamic nexus that is held in tension by the force of the context, including the classroom, school, community, and external environment. This process, Dewey argues, would not constitute good teaching with curiosity about and enthusiasm for that subject matter alone. He says, "Absorption, engrossment, full concern with the subject matter for its own sake, nurture it. Divided interests and envision destroy it. Intellectual integrity, honesty, and sincerity are at the bottom not matters of conscious purpose but quality of active response."[137] Without them, indeed, a teacher will have no energy, no fuel, to perform reflective inquiry. Without the teacher's full engagement and energy to observe and to gather information about learners and their learning processes, reflective thinking becomes crucial.[138]

4. *Responsibility*: By this term, Dewey means the disposition to consider in advance the probable consequences of any projected step, to accept them deliberately, and to acknowledge them in action, not just confess them verbally. Indeed, it asks, "What are the real–life implications of my thinking?"[139] It also means that thoughts and action are inseparable,

> Is to consider the consequences of a projected step; it means to be willing to adopt these consequences when they follow reasonably from any position already taken . . . [learners must ask] for the meaning of what they learn, in the sense of what difference it makes to the rest of their beliefs and to their actions.[140]

---

136. Ibid.
137. Dewey, *Democracy and Education*, 155.
138. Ibid., 154.
139. Dewey, *How We Think*, 32.
140. Ibid., 32.

Being responsible also means the acknowledgement that the meaning we are acting on is our meaning and not a meaning that resides "out there." Failure to create real meaning in the attempt to know a thing, then, is the worst consequence of the excessive complication of a school subject. Dewey says,

> The most permanent bad results of undue complication of school subjects and congestions of school studies and lessons are not the worry, nervous, strain, and superficial acquaintance that follow . . . but the failure to make clear what is involved in really knowing and believing a thing. Intellectual responsibility means severe standards in this regard. These standards can be built up only through practice in following up and acting upon the meaning of what is acquired.[141]

5. *Readiness*: While the first four attitudes consist of the essential elements of what Dewey calls the "readiness" to be engaged in the reflective thinking process, Dewey himself asserts that these attitudes do not necessarily cover the range of attitudes necessary for the process. This, indeed, is the reason that Carl Rodgers added two more attitudes through his reading of Dewey: curiosity and the desire for growth. Without these, Rodgers says,

> The courage required for truly reflective work would be absent . . . Truly to inquire in one's practice in a whole-minded, open-minded, direct, responsible way demands the courage to release not only what one holds dear but the elements of one's very identity.[142]

Dewey's concern, indeed, is not only the intellectual curiosity and perseverance of learners, but also what he calls "the desire to go on learning,"[143] and whether "One is willing to endure suspense and to undergo the trouble of searching."[144]

---

141. Dewey, *Democracy and Education*, 157.
142. Rodgers, "Defining Reflection," 842.
143. Dewey, *Experience and Education*, 49.
144. Rodgers, "Defining Reflection," 866.

Curriculum—Human Experience

It is eminently known that the world of everyday life is the starting point for Dewey's philosophy. Unlike most of the traditional philosophies before him, the main concern for Dewey is not the "a priori" conceptual knowledge, nor general universal principles of human behavior. Rather, it is the construction of knowledge through the process of inquiring during the daily life activities of human beings. Dewey did not search beyond the realm of ordinary experience to find a more fundamental reality since the everyday world of experience is the reality that humans already had in the past and have access to in the present. His impression of the success of physical science, in solving practical problems, understanding, predicting, and controlling the environment, shaped his conviction that the scientific systematizing of human experience is the best way, not only of problem solving, but also of attaining the intellectual ability to deal wisely with future experiences.

A careful look at his works reveals that experience is given notable consideration in every single one of Dewey's works. In his article, "John Dewey (1859-1952)," Robert B. Westbrook[145] emphasizes that Dewey's logic that education always emerges from actual experience began when he developed the Laboratory School at the University of Chicago (1896-1904), not to educate teachers for the purpose of attaining knowledge, but rather, to change the traditional philosophy which considers education as pure thoughts apart from actual life experience.[146] In his work, *How We Think*, Dewey emphasizes that to think critically, you need to go through an action; to reflect is to analyze a real perplexing situation and certain problem for which you seek a solution. It is the experience of this problematic situation that motivates the kind of thinking that is critical for analyzing and solving situations. This means that unless one has meaningful life experiences to draw upon to help clarify perceived problems, "confusion remains mere confusion."[147] In *Democracy and Education*, in addition to pointing to experience in nearly every chapter, Dewey dedicates a whole chapter to explaining the nature of experience and its relation to the process of thinking. He devotes a great deal of attention to the importance

---

145. Robert Westbrook (United States of America) was a Graduate of Yale (BA) and Stanford (PhD) Universities, He taught at Scipps College and Yale before taking up the post of Associate Professor of History at the University of Rochester (New York). He is the author of numerous articles and essays on American cultural and intellectual history, including *John Dewey and American Democracy* (1991) and *Pragmatism and Politics*.

146. Westbrook, "John Dewey."

147. Dewey, *How We Think*, 5.

and benefit of using experience in the course of education by stressing that experience must be continuous in two phases: not only during individual action, but also after action. In *The Need for a Recovery of Philosophy*, he tries to locate the human being as a part of this nature, insisting that experience is "an affair of the intercourse of a living being with its physical and social environment."[148] In *Experience and Nature*, Dewey articulates his view of experience: "Things interacting in certain ways are experience; they are what are experienced. Linked in certain ways with another natural object—the human organism—they are how things are experienced as well."[149] In *Experience and Education*, he summarizes his entire philosophy of experience as inseparable from good education: "A philosophy of education based upon a philosophy of experience,"[150] and, "All genuine education comes about through experience."[151]

The nature of experience for Dewey, however, cannot be fully grasped unless we understand his view of the human being as a part of nature. Osmer thinks that Dewey's philosophy is a philosophy of nature, which aims to create a place for the human being in nature and to confirm the role that intelligent inquiry can play in acquiring human values. Osmer says,

> A philosophy of nature attempts to show how it is that nature, in this inclusive sense, has given rise to the complex reality of human experience. It is not a priori but a posteriori, not offering first principles or foundational elements but an account of an evolutionary, natural process.[152]

In his article, "Two Concepts of Inquiry," Robert Talisse argues that Dewey's strong belief in the philosophical implications of the Darwinian Theory of evolution constantly calls him to reconstruct conception of experience of the traditional philosophy, which understands experience as passive knowledge that constructed in mind when this mind receives some impressions of external objects through human senses.[153] In the same sense, Richard Field corroborates the effect of Darwinism on Dewey's conception of experiences:

> The theory of natural selection continued to have a life-long impact upon Dewey's thought, suggesting the barrenness of

148. Dewey, *Middle Works of John Dewey*, 10:6.
149. Dewey, *Later Works of John Dewey*, 6:12–13.
150. Dewey, *Experience and Education*, 29.
151. Ibid., 15.
152. Osmer, *Practical Theology*, 21.
153. Talisse, "Two Concepts of Inquiry," 69–81.

static models of nature, and the importance of focusing on the interaction between the human organism and its environment when considering questions of psychology and the theory of knowledge.[154]

Indeed, Dewey's insistence on this reconstruction, clearly illustrates that experience is one of the most, if it is not the most, essential principles of his philosophy of education.

What does Dewey mean by the term "experience, then? Reflecting on Dewey's philosophy of experience, Osmer asserts, helps us to understand experience in two ways: "experience is either something that goes on inside a person or is the data functioning as evidence in scientific inquiry."[155] In the former, experience is something that "I" have or undergo, i.e., the subjective response of an individual to a particular occurrence. It refers to the feelings and cognitive structures that determine the experiencer's appropriation of the external world. This view, says Osmer, "is post-Kantian in its emphasis on the mental categories of the experiencer as constitutive of that which it experienced."[156] Second, Osmer continues, experience is a "derivative of certain reductionist tendencies in science. This position represents experience as a carefully refined and measured datum."[157] This understanding is closely associated with the rise of the scientific method of the Enlightenment and Empiricism and views experience as "carefully controlled and measured proof."[158] When a person hears that "we learn from experience," it means either that we learn when we are subjectively affected or that we learn when we form generalizations from our particular encounters.[159]

Despite these two meanings of experience being included in Dewey's philosophy of experience, says Osmer, "neither is adequate to grasp what he means by this concept."[160] Osmer's concept, indeed, clearly critiques these positions. For him, experience is not something subjective that "I have," nor is it refined statements or observations that emerge from a highly controlled process of reflective inquiry. It is not something "within" or "outside of" the experiencer; it is not in the subject "human being," nor in the object "environment." Rather, it is a transactional process, "not merely

---

154. Field, "John Dewey (1859–1952)."
155. Osmer, *Practical Theology*, 24.
156. Ibid.
157. Ibid.
158. Ibid.
159. Ibid., 25.
160. Ibid.

between subject and object but constituting them within an unfolding context."[161] In Dewey's words,

> "experience" is what James called a double-barreled word. Like its congeners, life and history, it includes what men do and suffer, what they strive for, love, believe, and endure, and also how men act and are acted upon, the ways in which they do suffer, desire and enjoy, see, believe, imagine—in short processes of experiencing... it is "double barreled" in that it recognizes in its primary integrity no division between act and material, subject and object but contains them both in an unanalyzed totality.[162]

Dewey rightly believes that experience has active and passive dimensions. It is the individual's experience of active striving that leads to meaning, which is made explicit in the resolved situation. In the passive phase, however, experience is the undergoing of the action's consequences. By this understanding, experience is not only cognitive, but it is also an active-passive affair by which we make some changes in the environment and situations, and in return, situation and environment create change in us. Dewey asserts,

> When we experience something we act upon it, we do something with it; then we suffer or undergo the consequences. We do something to the thing and then it does something to us in return: such is the peculiar combination. The connection of these two phases of experience measures the fruitfulness or value of the experience ... experience as trying involves change, but change is meaningless transition unless it is consciously connected with the return wave of consequences, which flow from it. When an activity is continued into the undergoing of consequences, when the change made by action is reflected back into a change made in us, the mere flux is loaded with significance. We learn something.[163]

In *Experience and Education*, Dewey makes it clear that experience is more than its traditional definition; it is not a mere observation or interaction. Rather, "we have to understand the significance of what we see, hear, and touch. This significance consists of the consequences that will result

---

161. Ibid., 27.
162. Dewey, *Reconstruction in Philosophy*, 139.
163. Dewey, *Democracy and Education*, 92.

when what is seen is acted upon."[164] For him, in short, "Experience is not what happens to you, it's what you *do* with what happens to you."[165]

Not every experience, however, is educative for John Dewey. Though he states, "all genuine education comes about through experience," Dewey quickly adds that this "does not mean that all experiences are genuinely or equally educative . . . for some experiences are mis-educative."[166] In order for Dewey to distinguish an educative from mis-educative experience, he identifies two primary criteria, which can determine the value of experience: the principle of continuity, or "experiential continuum," and interaction. These two, "in their active union with each other provide the measure of the educative significance and value of an experience."[167] All experiences, he argues, have an impact, i.e., an element of *continuity*; therefore, to know the kind of experience one has is to know the impact of this experience. Dewey argues that experiences in traditional education have largely negative influences on future experiences. He says that learners who go through traditional experience are "rendered callous to ideas" and lose "the impetus to learn."[168] Dewey refers to an experience with such continuity as *mis-educative*, as it "has the effect of arresting or distorting the growth of further experience."[169] On this basis, an experience that causes callousness toward learning could be a repetitive experience that places a student in a "groove or rut," an experience that leads to carelessness, or an experience that is individually enjoyable but thoroughly disconnected; all of these are mis-educative, as they lead to an inability to make sense of future experiences.[170] In contrary, any experience that promotes learners' desire towards further experience is classified by Dewey as an educative experience. In short, an educative experience cultivates a "desire to go on learning."[171]

The second criterion, by which we can evaluate educative experience, for Dewey, is *interaction*. If the principle of continuity means "every experience both takes up something from those which have gone before and modifies in some way the quality of those which come after,"[172] the principle of interaction means, "an experience is always what it is because of

---

164. Dewey, *Experience and Education*, 21.
165. Kegan, *Evolving Self*, 11.
166. Dewey, *Experience and Education*, 25.
167. Ibid., 48.
168. Ibid., 26.
169. Ibid., 25.
170. Ibid., 25.
171. Ibid., 48.
172. Ibid., 35.

a transaction taking place between an individual and what constitutes his environment."[173] It is important here to notice that Dewey recognizes that environment includes not only a person's physical surroundings, but also the "persons with whom he is talking . . . or the book he is reading, or the toys with which he is playing."[174] "In a certain sense every experience should do something to prepare a person for later experiences of a deeper and more expansive quality. That is the very meaning of growth, continuity, reconstruction of experience."[175] Indeed, Dewey strongly criticizes traditional education because of its focus on the objective dimension of experience, while his strong criticism of progressive education is because of its focus on the subjective dimension of experience. This is his reason for focusing on the interaction between the living organism and its environment and between the subject and object.

Nevertheless, the central role that experience plays in education for Dewey, is quite clear. Indeed, his deep conviction is that the educational process is one of continual recognition, reconstruction, and transformation.[176] Learning is broader than the perception of senses as it is not only concerned with the representation or existence of an organism in its environment, but also with the organism's daily activities. According to this perspective, knowledge is not simply pure ideas that exist in the mind apart from the organism's life activities. Rather, it is ideas that enable the organism to deal practically with environmental situations. In this case, knowledge is only true when it successfully guides the organism's action toward its purpose.[177] Knowing is not a matter of attaining an accurate picture of how "things really are," but rather, it is the ability to control and direct environmental conditions using human reason and intelligence to reflect upon and construct one's own knowledge in any situation.[178]

Teacher—A Guide and Facilitator

In his critical analysis of both traditional and progressive education, Dewey clearly rejects the image that the two models offer of the teacher as a dictator; instead, he views the teacher as an intellectual leader. He says,

173. Ibid., 43.
174. Ibid., 44.
175. Ibid., 33.
176. Dewey, *Democracy and Education*, 50.
177. Ibid., 288.
178. Ibid.,45.

The older type of instruction tended to treat the teacher as a dictatorial ruler. The newer type sometimes treats the teacher as a negligible fact, almost as an evil, though a necessary one. In reality the teacher is the intellectual leader of a social group. He is a leader, not in virtue of official position, but because of wider and deeper knowledge and matured experience. The supposition that the principle of freedom confers upon liberty upon the pupils, but that the teacher is outside of its range and must abdicate all leadership is merely silly.[179]

In *Experience and Education*, he says that teachers should have confidence when they plan the learner's experience, as learners need assistance from teachers in making sense of their world. In order for the teacher to do so, it is important, Dewey suggests, that the teacher observes learners and determines what kind of experiences they are interested in and invest in planning and organizing for learners' activities. It is the teacher's responsibility, then, to shape the curriculum based on knowing the learners and their abilities. The learners also need the teacher to decide whether the experience is educative or mis-educative.[180] The teacher, Dewey insists, must use a "greater insight to help organize the conditions of the experience of the immature [students]."[181]

However, despite his confidence in the learner–centered paradigm, Dewey, believes that the teacher has a significant role in the process, for s/he should work as a guide and facilitator inside the classroom, creating a social environment that is able to promote the natural abilities of the learners to think and grow. Teachers are thus "the organs through which pupils are brought into effective connection with the material."[182] Believing that a child learns best when s/he interacts with others, Dewey suggests that the teacher should give the child a space both to work alone and cooperatively with peers and adults. In his *Creed*, Dewey asserts, "[E]ducation comes through the stimulation of the child's powers by the demands of the social situations in which he finds himself."[183] He also says, "I believe, finally, that the teacher is engaged, not simply in the training of individuals, but in the formation of a proper social life."[184]

---

179. Dewey, *Later Works of John Dewey*, 8:377.
180. Dewey, *Experience and Education*, 18.
181. Dewey, *Logic*, 346.
182. Ibid., 121.
183. Dewey, *My Pedagogic Creed*, 3
184. Ibid.

Yet, for Dewey, the teacher's role as a guide and facilitator does not mean exercising authoritarian control over learners, but rather, it means providing an aid to learners' freedom. Dewey states, "Since freedom resides in the operations of intelligent observation and judgment by which a purpose is developed, guidance given by the teacher to the exercise of the pupils' intelligence is an aid to freedom, not a restriction upon it."[185] A teacher is an intellectual leader who should be qualified to promote learners' natural capacities to grow in a free environment, and who "Must survey the capacities and needs of the particular set of individuals with whom he is dealing, and must at the same time arrange the conditions, which provide the subject matter or content for experiences that satisfy these needs and develop these capacities."[186]

Indeed, the role of the teacher in Dewey's "new education" classroom is essential and vital, while the way that teachers perform this role is extremely different from those in a traditional classroom. For Dewey, it is crucial that learners are not mere receptacles into which the teacher deposits knowledge; rather, the teacher facilitates an educational environment that allows learners to play an active role in constructing their own knowledge. Since the model of education that Dewey promotes is experience-based, education for him is a social process, whereas "teacher loses the position of external boss or dictator but takes on that of leader of group activities."[187] He states,

> In sum, I believe that the individual who is to be educated is a social individual and that society is an organic union of individuals. If we eliminate the social factor from the child we are left only with an abstraction; if we eliminate the individual factor from society, we are left only with an inert and lifeless mass. Education, therefore, must begin with a psychological insight into the child's capacities, interests, and habits. It must be controlled at every point by reference to these same considerations. These powers, interests, and habits must be continually interpreted— we must know what they mean. They must be translated into terms of their social equivalents—into terms of what they are capable of in the way of social service.[188]

---

185. Dewey, *Experience and Education*, 71.
186. Ibid., 58.
187. Ibid., 69.
188. Dewey, "My Pedagogic Creed," 77–80.

The teacher, therefore, cannot impose his own goals upon learners, which, for Dewey, would be "fatal" to real progress, as it opposes learners' real growth. In Dewey's words,

> To talk about an educational aim when approximately each act of a pupil is dictated by the teacher, when the only order in the sequence of his acts is that which comes from the assignment of lessons and the giving of directions by another, is to talk nonsense.[189]

Rejecting the traditional image of the teacher as the one who knows everything in an authoritarian way while learners do little more than gratefully receive what the teacher deposits, Dewey insists that when teachers impose their aims onto learners' minds, this results in, not only a mechanical educational process, but also in the enslavement of learners. For him, "[E]xternally imposed aims" are "responsible for the emphasis put upon the notion of preparation for remote future and for rendering the work of both teacher and pupil mechanical and slavish."[190]

Nevertheless, some might think that the role of the teacher in Dewey's education is easier than that of the traditional one. In traditional education, it is, indeed, not necessary for teachers to "become intimately acquainted with the conditions of the local community, physical, historical, economic, occupational, etc., in order to utilize them as educational resources."[191] According to Dewey, the role of the leader in a democratic classroom is arguably more difficult, for leading such a classroom requires teachers to be understanding of the needs of the learners, to have a plan for learners' success, and to have the abilities required for a dialectical education. He states, "[P]rogressive education is more difficult to carry on than was ever the traditional system."[192] In short, for Dewey, the concept of leading the classroom indicates that the teacher is a democratic leader, and this kind of leader needs:

> To be intelligently aware of the capacities, needs, and past experiences of those under instruction, and secondly, to allow the suggestions made to develop into a plan and project by means of the further suggestions contributed and organized into a whole by the members of the group.[193]

189. Dewey, *Democracy and Education*, 101–2.
190. Ibid., 110.
191. Ibid., 21.
192. Ibid., 18.
193. Ibid., 80.

Learner—Centered Paradigm

Like Vygotsky, Montessori, and Piaget, Dewey's philosophy is based on the conviction that education should be child-centered, both active and interactive, and involve the social world of the child and his every day experience. This conviction, indeed, is deeply rooted in his trust in the natural capacities of the child to observe, analyze, and grow.[194] In *My Pedagogic Creed*, Dewey offers clear statements of most of his educational and philosophical convictions. He states, "The child's own instinct and powers furnish the material and give the starting point for all education."[195] Therefore, learners should be given enough space and freedom to use their own intelligence to reflect on their experience in order to "recognize in concrete what surroundings are conducive to having experiences that lead to growth."[196]

What is linked to the child's ability to learn and grow is Dewey's conviction that the child's interests should be considered as a basis for constructing any curriculum. In fact, this conviction leads to another deep conviction for Dewey: that education is life in itself, not just preparatory learning for future life. In his *Creed*, he states, "I believe that education, therefore, is a process of living and not preparation for future living."[197] It is the act of education, which should illuminate and address what the child needs to know in that time and context. Dewey portrays this situation in some questions:

> How many students, for example, were rendered callous to ideas, and how many lost the impetus to learn because of the way in which learning was experienced by them? How many acquired special skills by means of automatic drill so that their power of judgment and capacity to act intelligently in new situations was limited? How many came to associate the learning process with ennui and boredom? How many found what they did learn so foreign to the situations of life outside the school as to give them no power of control over the latter? How many came to associate books with dull drudgery, so that they were "conditioned" to all but flashy reading matter?[198]

Freire's critical educational theory suggests that the educator needs to first engage learners in their contextual experiences. Only through

---

194. Dewey's view of anthropology was discussed in detail above.
195. Dewey, *My Pedagogic Creed*, 291.
196. Dewey, *Experience and Education*, 23.
197. Dewey, *My Pedagogic Creed*, 2.
198. Dewey, *Experience and Education*, 26-27.

engaging learners in the terms of their own experiences is an educator able to build in concepts of learning that dialogue with those experiences in order to develop conscious critical thinking skills. Only in such practice does power reside with the learner, not the educator. Freire calls this, an "authentic education."[199] Arizona State University offers a definition of "learner centered education" that is not too far from the Frierian concept of empowerment:

> Learner-centered education places the student at the center of education. It begins with understanding the educational contexts from which a student comes. It continues with the instructor evaluating the student's progress towards learning objectives. By helping the student acquire the basic skills to learn, it ultimately provides a basis for learning throughout life.[200]

Educational Environment: Democracy

Education for Dewey is a very social process in which the individual is both a part of and constructed with nature and society. Yet, although agreeing with the natural approach to education promoted by the French philosopher Jean Jack Rousseau, Dewey criticizes this approach for not giving enough attention to the social dimension of the child's life, for making the "natural" opposed to the "social," and for making "nature" itself the goal of education. This is the reason; indeed, that Dewey's goals of education are intimately tied to his social goals.[201] If learners, Dewey notes, are to strive for a truly democratic life, the educational process itself should be practiced in a thoroughly democratic environment. In his words,

> A society which makes provision for participation in its good of all its members on equal terms and which secures flexible readjustment of its institutions through interaction of the different forms of associated life is in so far democratic. Such a society must have a type of education, which gives individuals a personal interest in social relationships and control, and the

---

199. Freire and Macedo, *Pedagogy of Oppressed*, 109.

200. Arizona Faculties Council, "Definition of Learner-Centered Education." http://www.abor.asu.edu/4_special_programs/lce/guiding_prin.htm.

201. Rousseau's approach to education is best known through his work *Emile: Or on Education*.

habits of mind, which secure social changes without introducing disorder.[202]

Indeed, Dewey's faith in democracy as the ideal of the good life is a central element of his philosophy of education. Osmer writes, "Dewey placed his faith in the ideal of a democratic life at all levels of human community."[203] Yet, democracy, for Dewey, is not a mere fact, rather, is a moral ideal, "an ideal which unifies and transforms a person's desire and thoughts by committing them to an imaginative presentation of human possibilities that provides direction and passion from one situation to the next."[204] In this sense, says Osmer, "democracy serves a religious function in Dewey's philosophy,"[205] as it discloses the ideal possibilities for human existence to which he was deeply committed. Osmer quotes John Randall,

> Such a democratic community, Dewey is convinced, most fully realizes the possibilities inherent in man's fundamentally social nature . . . to be captured morally and imaginatively by such an ideal, to acknowledge its rightful claim over our desires and purposes, to live in its light, is to live religiously.[206]

Dewey's faith in democracy, however, is rooted in two assumptions. The first is his deep belief in the equality of all people. He argues that despite the biological diversity and social differences of human beings, educational, cognitive, emotional, behavioral, religious, and economic background cannot be denied. Assuming an absolute mathematical or numerical equality for human beings is denying the richness of human variety, as people differ in accordance with their natural talents and their social positions. Dewey states,

> Belief in equality is an element in the democratic credo. It is not, however, belief in equality of natural endowments. Those who proclaimed the idea of equality did not suppose they were enunciating a psychological doctrine, but a legal and political one. All individuals are entitled to equality of treatment by law and in its administration. Each one is affected equally in quality if not in quantity by the institutions under which he lives and has an equal right to express his judgment, although the weight of his judgment may not be equal in amount when it enters into

202. Dewey, *Democracy and Education*, 99.
203. Osmer, "Practical Theology and Contemporary Christian Education," 99.
204. Ibid., 103.
205. Ibid., 99.
206. Randall, "Religion of Shared Experience," 110.

the pooled result to that of others. In short, each is equally an individual and entitled to equal opportunity of development of his own capacities, be they large or small in range. Moreover, each has needs of his own, as significant to him, as those of others are to them. The very fact of natural and psychological inequality is all the more reason for establishment by law of equality of opportunity, since otherwise the former becomes a means of oppression of the less gifted.[207]

Dewey's second assumption arising from his trust in democracy is his belief in the capacities of human nature. Dewey has confidence in the ability of people to arrive at cooperative, intelligent behavior while addressing and solving common problems. Two notes, however, are important here. The first is Dewey's assumption that humans are social beings, which means that they are naturally driven to each other. As Dewey puts it, they "cling" together. In this, Dewey stands against the liberal belief in the self-centered and self-assured individual. The second is Dewey's conviction that men and women are intellectually and morally able to come to terms with each other, an attitude of cooperativeness, which gives rise to social frameworks supporting public discourse, deliberation and decision-making. In Dewey's words,

> The foundation of democracy is faith in the capacities of human nature; faith in human intelligence and in the power of pooled and cooperative experience. It is not belief that these things are complete but that, if given a show, they will grow and be able to generate progressively the knowledge and the wisdom needed to guide collective action.[208]

What is the meaning of democracy for Dewey, then? To understand Dewey's philosophy of democracy is to return back to his philosophy of experience as a fundamental element of education. As he makes it evident in many places, experience can "grow in ordered richness,"

> Democracy is belief in the ability of human experience to generate the aims and methods by which further experience will grow in ordered richness... Democracy is the faith that the process of experience is more important than any special results attained, so that special results achieved are of ultimate value only as they are used to enrich and order the ongoing process. Since

207. Dewey, "Democracy and Educational Administration," 60.
208. Ibid., 59.

the process of experience is capable of being educative, faith in democracy is all one with faith in experience and education.[209]

A democratic society is the sort of society that enables growth and transformation to take place. For this reason, Dewey begins his description of democratic life with emphasizing, "shared experience." In Dewey's understanding, this term has two meanings. First, it refers to the important roles that language and communication play in human life. To be a self is to engage in shared activities and language. Second, it refers to a deeper meaning, as he states, "[S]hared experience is the greatest of human goods."[210] Dewey points to the enrichment and broadening of meaning that can take place in a democratic social transaction. Randall states, "[L]ife, he holds, achieves its richest significance when human beings undertake and undergo things together, with the conscious interplay of finding out each other's interests and views that attends a community of purpose."[211]

For Dewey, however, democracy is not only a moral ideal, but also a way of life. Unlike the understanding of many today, democracy for Dewey is not a form of government or elections, but rather, it reaches far beyond the political rules regulating the activities of states, authorities, and public administrations. Democracy, for Dewey, is a form of life, a form of associational behavior among individuals that can be practiced in every sphere of organized social life, and its methods of organizing social behavior can be applied to all social structure,

> In the first place, democracy is much broader than a special political form, a method of conducting government, of making laws and carrying on governmental administration by means of popular suffrage and elected officers. It is that, of course. But it is something broader and deeper. The political and governmental phase of democracy is a means, the best means so far found, for realizing ends that lie in the wide domain of human relationships and development of human personality. It is, as we often say, though perhaps without appreciating all that is involved in the saying, a way of life, social and individual. The keynote of democracy as a way of life may be expressed; it seems to me, as the necessity for the participation of every mature human being in formation of the values that regulate the living of men together: which is necessary from the standpoint of both the

---

209. Dewey, *Experience and Nature*, 202.
210. Ibid.
211. Randall, "Religion of Shared Experience," 109.

general social welfare and the full development of human beings as individuals.[212]

For him, "the keynote of democracy as a way of life . . . [is] the necessity for participation of every mature human being in formation of the values that regulate the living of men together."[213]

> Now this idea cannot be applied to *all* the members of a society except where there is adequate provision for the reconstruction of social habits and institutions by means of wide stimulation arising from equitably distributed interests. And this means a democratic society.[214]

For Dewey, democracy is also a learning process. He believes that the relationship between democracy and education must be reciprocal and mutual if we are to create intelligent citizens who are able to face the challenges and complexity of contemporary life. Indeed, democracy can be sustained both by human behavior that can be learned and by social knowledge that can be acquired through securing enough freedom for an individual to do so. For Dewey, however, democracy is not merely acquiring knowledge of political facts; rather, learning democracy is an active process of social involvement, of broadening learners' minds through intelligent interaction with others and groups, and of reflection on their experience. Democracy, then, is the way of creating intelligent individuals who are capable of constructing an understanding not merely gaining knowledge. Dewey says,

> This is because unfortunately, knowledge to so many people means 'information.' Information is knowledge about things, and there is no guarantee in any amount of 'knowledge about things' that understanding-the spring of intelligent action-will follow from it. Knowledge about things is static. There is no guarantee in any amount of information, even if skillfully conveyed, that an intelligent attitude of mind will be formed.[215]

Dewey's understanding of learning democracy, indeed, has a broad meaning, covering all activities in society that lead to intelligent and cooperative problem solving in all aspects of life, such as state politics, community affairs, work, and family. For him, however, central to learning democracy is the education system in the schools. He writes,

---

212. Dewey, "Democracy and Educational Administration," 57.
213. Dewey, "Crucial Role of Intelligence," 400.
214. Dewey, *Democracy and Education*, 91.
215. Dewey, "Democratic Faith and Education," 48.

> That democracy and education bear a reciprocal relation, for it is not merely that democracy is itself an educational principle, but that democracy cannot endure, much less develop, without education in that narrower sense in which we ordinary think of it, the education that is given in the family, and especially as we think of it in the school.[216]

To conclude, democracy, for Dewey, is not a form of government concerned with elections and protecting minorities, an institution, which he calls "political democracy," but rather, a form of life and a way of living for individuals, an ethical ideal, and a personal commitment, which he calls "a social idea." Such a democracy helps individuals to be self-directing, capable of making their own goals, and aware of both their rights and responsibilities. Creating democratic character in individuals, then, requires a democratic society of equality and mutuality, which provides individuals enough freedom to grow as full beings. Dewey says that there is "no form of social life that can allow for greater human development than democracy."[217] In this way, people will practice democracy as a "shared experience" of common life, which helps to maximize both individual and social common good.[218] Yet, preparing people to be active citizens in a democratic society begins with education. Therefore, Dewey is against all kinds of authoritarian procedures that require learners to be passive recipients of any "dogma of knowledge," but rather, insists that both learners and teachers should work together in equality and mutuality to discern truth. He also rejects the term "epistemology" as static theory of gaining knowledge, preferring the term "theory of inquiry" or "experimental logic" as a dynamic and democratic way of constructing knowledge through experience and critical thinking.[219] For Dewey, all kinds of freedom begin with "freedom of intelligence" and "freedom of thought."[220]

---

216. Dewey, "Democracy and Education," 36–37.
217. Dewey, *Democracy and Education*, 218.
218. Ibid., 219.
219. Ibid.
220. Dewey, *Experience and Education*, 61.

Dewey and the Educational Problem of the Presbyterian Church in Egypt

A New Pedagogical Approach

I believe that applying Dewey's complex philosophy to Egyptian education in recent times is difficult. Political, social, economic, and religious forces highlight the fact that applying Dewey's scientific method requires a radical change of multiple systems of the Egyptian society, a process that is quite difficult at the present time. Yet, with John Dewey, I believe that transforming Egyptian education is the starting point for changing all aspects of life in Egypt. The purpose of this research; however, is to assist Christian education in Egypt to transform its process into an intelligent practice. And despite the huge challenges, I see Dewey's critical thinking theory useful to guide the Presbyterians in Egypt to illuminate and address lack of critical thinking in the process of education. Dewey's thoughts, indeed, would help achieve better education that is relevant and valuable for modern Christian education in the Egyptian Presbyterian Church. I state here six dimensions in which the Presbyterian problem in Egypt might be interpreted in the light of Dewey's theory of reflective thinking.

First, Dewey's theory might help the Presbyterians in Egypt to have a right anthropological position towards the child and a right understanding of the human as a critical being in nature. The conviction that a child is an incomplete adult who will only achieve his or her completeness with age is one of the wrong beliefs that result in, not only a teacher–centered paradigm, but also the oppression of children in the process of education. Dewey writes,

> The fundamental factors in the educative process are an immature, underdeveloped being; and certain social aims, meanings, values incarnate in the matured experience of the adult. Such a conception of each in relation to the other as facilitates completest and freest interaction is the essence of educational theory.[221]

Indeed, Dewey rejects this notion, insisting that the child is a whole human being, but independent and in the process of maturity. He states,

> Our tendency to take immaturity as mere lack, and growth as something, which fills the gap between the immature and mature, is due to regarding childhood comparatively, instead of intrinsically. We treat it simply as a privation because we are measuring it by adulthood as a fixed standard. This fixed

---

221. Dewey, *Child and Curriculum*, 468.

attention upon what the child has not, and will not have till he become a man.²²²

Like Friere,²²³ the main concern for Dewey is to change learners from dehumanized passive objects into active, humanized subjects. In his words, "Growth is not something done to them; it is something they do."²²⁴ Dewey's conviction of the maturity of the child as a whole human being despite his or her immaturity has its deep roots in his conviction of what he calls "the greatest educational resource—the natural impulses of the child,"²²⁵ which are inquiry, communication, construction, and expression. Instead of the traditional view, which assumes that the child is incapable of make his or her own knowledge; through these impulses, Dewey believes that the child is capable of constructing the own knowledge, which establish for a new curriculum for the Presbyterian education in Egypt.

Second, Dewey's theory might help the Presbyterians in Egypt to set different goals for Christian education. As a part of public education, the main goal of Christian education in the Presbyterian Church in Egypt is to prepare children for future life. While encouraging children to have faith in Jesus, to grow as his disciples, and to obey the call to be servants of God are all excellent goals, all of these goals speak from an adult's experience to an adult's understanding of things will happen in the future. This, indeed, alienates learners, not only from their actual life experiences at that age, but also from the educational process itself, which results in a learning process that is neither joyful nor comprehensive. Dewey, instead, insists on a form of education that makes a full life a primary goal in itself. According to *Experience and Education*, education is a process of living not a preparation for future living; only the experience of everyday life is generative of true education and true knowledge. Thus, it is essential to encourage students to live, to enjoy life, and to learn how to use their life experiences as a medium for learning. This is particularly relevant to the Egyptian context because of the richness of church practice and individual experience. In *Creativity*, psychologist Csikszentmihalyi teaches that joy promotes understanding and creativity.²²⁶

Third, Dewey's reflective thinking would strongly help Egyptian Presbyterians to recognize and face dualism as a serious and fundamental problem for Christian education in Egypt. As it was mentioned earlier, the Presbyterians

222. Ibid., 41.
223. Freire and Macedo, *Pedagogy of Oppressed*, 91
224. Dewey, *Democracy and Education*, 42.
225. Ibid., 43.
226. Csikszentmihalyi, *Creativity*, 110.

insist on putting things in conflict, as an either . . . or pattern: either divine or human, evangelism or social transformation, depending upon the Holy Spirit or planning and creating strategies, faith or reason. Without full awareness of what it is doing, the church in Egypt puts itself in conflict with the world, refusing arts and music, condemning the use of philosophy and reason for Christians, and rejecting all sources of education that are not Christian. Indeed, Dewey, who is well known for being anti-dualism, is quite useful for illuminating and addressing this problem.

Comparing his theory of thinking with other theories, in *Democracy of Education*, Dewey emphasizes that while his theory calls for continuity the others "state or imply certain basic divisions, separations, or antitheses, technically called dualisms."[227] In this text, Dewey points to the manifestation of dualism in four dimensions, which I understand as being quite similar to Egyptian dualisms. First is the dualism that exists in social groups and classes within a group like the dualism between rich and poor, men and women, noble and baseborn, ruler and ruled. Second is the dualism of knowledge as something external and objective versus knowing as something purely internal, subjective, and psychical. In other words, this is a dualism of subject matter and method of education, activity and passivity of knowing. Third is the dualism, or the opposition, of intellect and emotions where emotions are conceived as being purely personal and having nothing to do with the work of intelligence in apprehending facts and truths. Fourth is the dualistic separation of knowing and doing, theory and practice.[228]

Indeed, Dewey's theory of reflective thinking perfectly interprets the Egyptian problems of dualism as a serious factor both contributing to and resulting in the lack of critical thinking skills in the process of Christian education among the Presbyterians in Egypt. Dewey says that this dualism, which is not only dividing people, but also dividing the human being into sectors, works as a barrier that leads to "absence of fluent and free intercourse."[229] In his words,

> I became more and more troubled by the current intellectual scandal that seemed to me involved in the current (and traditional) dualism in logical standpoint and method between something called "science" on the one hand and something called "morals" on the other. I have long felt that the construction of logic, that is, a method of effective inquiry, which would apply without abrupt breach of continuity to the fields designated by

227. Dewey, *Democracy and Education*, 287.
228. Ibid., 289.
229. Ibid., 297.

both of these words, is at once our needed theoretical solvent and the supply of our greatest practical want.[230]

Fourth, Dewey's reflective thinking would immensely help Egyptian Presbyterians to illuminate and address the problematic pedagogy of Christian education. It has been made clear in the first chapter that a lack of creative pedagogy is one of the main factors in the dwindling of critical thinking in the process of Christian education in the Presbyterian Church of Egypt. While basic education operates with a teacher-centered paradigm, its main pedagogical practices focus on indoctrination, rote memorization, and written examination as the sole means of student-assessment. Throughout the entirety of his works, Dewey strongly rejects this kind of learning, calling it "rote education."[231] The negative impact of this method on education is huge, says Dewey. Not only does it dehumanize learners, deny them enough space to grow, and refuse to help them to use their intelligent abilities to construct their own truth, but also it imprisons their minds in the past as they simply memorize the ready-made knowledge of adults' past experiences. In *Experience and Education*, Dewey is clear:

> The subject matter of education consists of bodies of information and of skills that have been worked out in the past; therefore, the chief business of the school is to transmit them to the new generation . . . The main purpose or objective is to prepare the young for future responsibilities and for success in life, by means of acquisition of the organized bodies of information and prepared forms of skill, which comprehend the material of instruction.[232]

In his critique of the traditional methodology, Dewey also helps the Presbyterian education in Egypt to realize the negative consequences of a teacher-centered pedagogy of education. Such consequences include turning learners into mere passive recipients and never helping them to build intelligent minds. Furthermore, such pedagogy acknowledges neither the natural capacities of the young nor interaction with their life experiences. Instead, Dewey insists on the necessity and usefulness of a child-centered paradigm for creating intelligent and independent learners, as it makes learners fully engaged with not only the subject matter at hand, but also with intelligent reflection on their life experiences. He states,

---

230. Dewey, "From Absolutism to Experimentalism," 23–24.
231. Dewey, *Experience and Education*, 20.
232. Ibid., 17–18.

> Since the subject matter as well as standards of proper conduct pre-handed down from the part, the attitude of pupils must, upon the whole, be one of docility, receptivity and obedience... The gap is so great that the required subject matter, the methods of learning and of behaving are foreign to the existing capacities of the young. They are beyond the reach of the experience the young learners already possess... The gulf between the mature or adult products and the experience and abilities of the young is so wide that the very situation forbids much active participation by pupils in the development of what is taught... Learning here means acquisition of what already is incorporated in books and in the heads of the elders.[233]

Dewey's theory of reflective thinking might help Egyptian Presbyterians to recognize the static education as a product of an uncreative pedagogy of education, which cannot cope with the challenges of the daily life changes and the complexity of the contemporary age. He says,

> Which is taught is thought of as essentially static. It is taught as a finished product, with little regard either to the ways in which it was originally built up or to changes that will surely occur in the future. It is to a large extent the cultural product of societies that assumed the future would be much like the past, and yet it is used as educational food in a society where change is the rule, not the exception.[234]

Fifth, Dewey's reflective thinking would greatly help Egyptian Presbyterians to illuminate and address the problem of curriculum of Christian education in Egypt. While Presbyterian education over the years has developed a strong sense of rejection of using a learner's experience as a useful element in the educational process, most of Dewey's works illustrate that the main principle of his philosophy is that a process of inquiry occurs in the midst of vital experience. The Presbyterians in Egypt insist on focusing on the intellectual as the best way of forming disciples of Jesus, with little or no regard for the other dimensions of the human being, including emotional, physical, social, sexual, and spiritual dimensions. Dewey, however, insists that life experience is the only thing that engages a learner as a whole being in the process of learning. While the Christian education of the Presbyterian Church in Egypt gives full attention to the body of information that is externally imposed upon the minds of learners as a curriculum, Dewey insists that meaningful questions are inspired by genuine curiosity about

---

233. Ibid., 18–19.
234. Ibid., 19.

real-world experiences and challenges. It is not something that can be delivered from "outside" but active participation in a real life experience that helps to construct true knowledge.[235]

Despite the richness of life experiences in the faith community of the Presbyterian Church in Egypt, its education never considers creating or finding a systematic way for using these experiences as a fundamental element of education. I believe that Dewey is useful for showing that this rejection serves to widen the gap between the church's theological thoughts and practice, or, in other words, between the life of the church and society. Like general education in Egypt, which does not utilize life experiences, the education of the church is alienated from the context in which it exists. This not only results in using external curricula that do not meet with the needs and challenges of the learners' real life thus diminishing their joy and interest in the process, but it also results in a lack of constructing theological norms that are contextual in nature. Dewey, indeed, should convince Egyptian Presbyterians that what is needed is "a philosophy of education based upon a philosophy of experience,"[236] and that "All genuine education comes about through experience."[237]

Sixth, Dewey's reflective thinking would greatly help Egyptian Presbyterians to illuminate and address the problem of a lack of democracy in education in Egypt. Unlike most of the Egyptians, I think that both the January 25, 2011 and June 30, 2013 revolutions have failed to achieve their goals: bread, freedom, human dignity, and social justice. In my understanding, Mubarak's regime before the revolutions established a "police state" that prized security over freedom, dignity, and justice. However, during the years of what was wrongly called the "Arabic Spring," the Egyptians were gradually forced to cry for security over freedom. It seems to me that the main reason for this failure is a lack of understanding of the true meaning of democracy.

Indeed, I see Dewey's theory of thinking, which is grounded in reflecting on one's own experience in a democratic society and free educational process, to be useful in illuminating the failure of the Egyptians, in general, to recognize the inevitable link between true democracy and education reform. Contrary to the understanding of most Egyptians, it is clear for Dewey that democracy is not just freedom from an authoritarian regime but rather, a personal way of life that begins with a democratic educational process. I believe that Dewey can help Egyptian Presbyterians to create in individuals a democratic character that is not only aware of both

---

235. Dewey, *How We Think*, 71.
236. Dewey, *Experience and Education*, 29.
237. Ibid., 15.

rights and responsibilities, but also aware that true freedom is the freedom of intelligence and freedom of thought. This, indeed, is not possible without a democratic environment of education in which learners are given a sufficient safe space not only to share their experiences, but also to reflect and learn from these experiences. He says, "Beings who are born not only unaware of, but quite indifferent to, the aims and habits of the social group have to be rendered cognizant of them and actively interested. Education, and education alone, spans the gap."[238]

Finally, Dewey's reflective thinking would greatly help Egyptian Presbyterians to illuminate the problem of the lack of philosophy of education. While antipathy toward rationalism and philosophy is a notable conviction of a majority of Christian educators in Egypt, Dewey insists on the necessity of the philosophy for an effective education. While Egyptian educators focus the entire education on teaching a body of knowledge and certain procedures for children, youth, and marriage, Dewey believes that a philosophy of education should go beyond knowledge and procedures. While Egyptian educators insist on rejecting the use of philosophical ideals as ways of thinking, Dewey insists on the need to make philosophy a general theory of education if we seek both individual and social transformation. He says,

> If we are willing to conceive education as the process of forming fundamental dispassion, intellectual and emotional, towards nature and fellow-men, philosophy may even be defined as the general theory of education. Unless a philosophy is to remain symbolic—or verbal—or a sentimental indulgence for a few, or else mere arbitrary dogma, its auditing of past experience and its program of values must take effect in conduct.[239]

If Dewey views education "as a deliberately conducted practice"[240] and philosophy as the "general theory of education,"[241] then the relation between philosophy and education for Dewey is not a relation of two theories or two kinds of practices, but rather, it is a relation of theory and practice. It is one of Dewey's central beliefs that this is the case. Dewey is convinced that "philosophy is at once an explicit formulation of the various interests of life as propounding of points of views and methods through which a better balance of interests may be effected."[242] He is equally certain that it's essential aim is the "modification of emotional and

238. Dewey, *Democracy and Education*, 3.
239. Ibid., 338.
240. Ibid., 387.
241. Ibid., 389.
242. Ibid., 387.

intellectual dispositions"²⁴³ in order to bring about "harmonious readjustment of the opposed tendencies."²⁴⁴ Dewey, in short, believes that philosophy is deeply connected to "thinking." He says,

> It is of assistance to connect philosophy with thinking in its distinction from knowledge. Knowledge, grounded knowledge, is science; it represents objects, which have been settled, ordered, disposed of rationally. Thinking, on the other hand, is prospective in reference. It is occasioned by an unsettlement and it aims at overcoming a disturbance. Philosophy is thinking what the known demands of us—what responsive attitude it exerts. It is an idea of what is possible, not a record of accomplished fact. Hence it is hypothetical, like all thinking.²⁴⁵

From an educational viewpoint, I see this perspective of Dewey's theory of education as philosophy as the most useful dimension for Presbyterian education in Egypt. It is the understanding and embracing of education as philosophy that would help the Presbyterians in Egypt to unite and overcome conflicts of thought in Egypt, conquering the problem of dualism, which is the main reason for division and contradiction in the process of both Christian education and social practices. Dewey points to the necessity of this unity:

> The reconstruction of philosophy, of education, and social ideals and methods thus go hand in hand. If there is especial need of education at the present time, if this makes urgent a reconstruction of the basic ideas of traditional philosophic systems, it is because of the thoroughgoing change in social life accompanying the advance of science, the industrial revolution, and the development of democracy.²⁴⁶

Educational Assessment

Despite the significant impact that his works left both on philosophy and education, Dewey has been always critiqued. Henry Miller, for instance, said in 1952, "There is a great need for a review of the educational philosophy of John Dewey and his prodigious influence on teaching-learning process. Such a critique should be a searching, systematic but balanced, and scholarly

243. Ibid.
244. Ibid.
245. Ibid., 380–81.
246. Ibid, 285.

rather than merely journalistic."[247] In his book, *The Ideal and The Community*, Isaac Baer Berkson[248] postulated that Dewey's experimental philosophy of education with its emphasis on naturalism, behaviorism, and individualism, slights moral values since moral values are derived from historical traditions and communal living rather than from individual.[249] It is true, says Berkson that Dewey writes a great deal about society, but his conception of society does not go beyond interaction among individuals. Furthermore, it remains on the psychological level and fails to give adequate weight to the role of the community. Moreover, the experimentalism overemphasizes the factor of experience, leaving little room for mind, ideals, and institutions, which should be the heart of the learning process.

Not only Miller, Berkson, and other conservatives critiqued Dewey's philosophy of education, but also progressive educators, such as Bertrand Russell.[250] Indeed, Russell critiqued the nature of content, the role of democracy in education, and the process of individual development of Dewey's education. While Dewey adopts a "pragmatic truth" that believes that whatever worked is true as long as it functions and when it no longer works, it is replaced by a new truth, Russell rejects this view, arguing that this means that truth is reduced to whatever the majority believed it to be, a conclusion that suggests that knowledge is determined by power and this represents a misapplication of democracy.[251] Russell's rejection of Dewey's thoughts, indeed, is rooted in his distrust of what he called the "herd instinct"—the tendency of the majority of human beings to go unthinkingly in a single direction. Because of this instinct, Russell argues, we cannot know the extent to which education could be democratized.[252] While Russell sees the importance of democracy in education, he also insists on the limits of its process because of differences in the intelligence and cleverness levels of children. He says,

247. Miller, "Scholarly Critique of Dewey," 133–40.

248. Isaac Berkson was born on December 23, 1891 in New York City, and died there on March 10, 1975. His main interests were in Jewish philosophy and education.

249. Berkson, *Ideal and Community*, 45.

250. According to Stanford Encyclopedia of Philosophy, Bertrand Russell (1872–1970) was a British philosopher, logician, mathematician, social critic, and political activist, who was anti-war. He led the British revolt against idealism in the twentieth century. He earned the Nobel Prize for literature. Together with G.E. Moore, Russell is generally recognized as one of the main founders of modern analytic philosophy. Russell was interested in teaching and learning throughout most of his life. He wrote two major books on the subject: *Education and the Good Life* in 1926 and *Education and the Social Order* in 1932. Russell continued to write about education throughout his career.

251. Rockler, "Russell vs. Dewey," 5.

252. Ibid.

> The error of democracy lies in regarding all claims to superiority as just grounds for the resentment of the herd. In the modern world, much work which is necessary to the community requires more ability than most men possess and there must be ways of selecting exceptional men to do this work.[253]

For Russell, it is not only Dewey's view of democracy, but also its practice in the field that makes it problematic. In one of his chapters, entitled "The Herd in Education," Russell emphasizes that election campaigns have more and more become media events, which are designed not to enlighten people, but rather to manipulate the "herd."

Russell also disagrees with Dewey on the aim of education. While the process of education is the most important element for Dewey, Russell thinks that the content of education should receive more attention. While Dewey believes that growth is the only purpose of education, Russell describes four characteristics that education should develop as other goals of education: vitality, which is psychological rather than mental and focuses on the pleasure of feeling alive, courage, which is the absence of fear and the ability to understand one's limits, sensitivity, which is the appropriate response to particular emotional events in life, and intelligence, which is the ability to think for oneself and to know how to learn.[254]

As I examine Dewey's philosophy of education, I might agree with some of the educational critiques that were raised against his progressive thoughts. Dewey, indeed, seems to be very romantic and optimistic towards the political, social, and religious forces that might make the operation of his thoughts harder than he imagines in actual practice. In a society such as Egypt in particular, education is one of the major processes that political power forcibly shapes and directs for the purpose of supporting its dictatorial regimes. Educationally liberating people from rules in Middle Eastern countries, including Egypt, means ceding power along with its immense benefits and luxuries. Another challenge to Dewey's thoughts is the accumulation of social traditions. The tribal attitude that has been inherited in Egyptian society throughout the centuries and supported with Islamic beliefs is one of the real forces. In Egyptian society, the elder, whoever he is, is the leader who always has the final word. The father in the family, the teacher in the school, the manager, and the president are the people who always possess the truth. As a part of Egyptian society, Christian education leaders possess the same identity, thoughts, and practice, which give little or no space for free learning from the learner's side. A third challenge

---

253. Russell, *Education and Social Order*, 55.
254. Rockler, "Russell vs. Dewey," 7.

to applying Dewey's theory in Egypt is the fundamental religious forces. Indeed, it is not only Islamic, but also Christian fundamentalism that poses a real challenge since it might oppose embracing and applying Dewey's progressive education in Egypt. Yet, Dewey's conviction is that liberating any society begins with liberating its individuals, and liberating individuals begins with liberating their intelligence and their thoughts. This is the progressive and pioneer role that the Presbyterian Church in Egypt should play in order to lead Egyptian society towards liberating the Presbyterians' thoughts through education.

Despite the challenges, however, I find much to appreciate in Dewey's thoughts, believing that contextualizing his theory in the Christian education process of the Presbyterian Church in Egypt would help to illuminate and address a number of the problems of its process. The first strength that I appreciate is not only Dewey's understanding of the active nature of the child, but also his awareness of the important differences in individual children. In *Democracy and Education*, Dewey agrees with Rousseau on the idea of individual differences:

> The general aim translates into the aim of regard for individual differences among children. Nobody can take the principle of consideration of native powers into account without being struck by the fact that these powers differ in different individuals. The difference applies not merely to their intensity, but even more to their quality and arrangement.[255]

Indeed, Dewey does not believe that children are born naturally good, nor did he believe that they are born sinful. Rather, his view of children is practical and empirical. For him, children differ in their interests and capacities; they have a natural tendency toward both good and evil; they are active, social creatures whose interests should be identified and guided in freedom,

> Keeping in mind these fourfold interests—the interest in conversation or communication; in inquiry, or finding out things; in making things, or construction; and artistic expression—we may say they are natural recourses, the uninvited capital, upon the exercise of which depends the active growth of the child.[256]

To consider these differences is to meet the different abilities of learners to understand and develop their truth, skills, and critical mind. Given this powerful plea for recognition of the child's imaginative life, I believe

255. Dewey, *Democracy and Education*, 122.
256. Dewey, *School and Society*, 30.

with Dewey that engaging children in these activities helps teachers finding a convenient approach of interaction with each learner, helps curriculum to meet each learner's ability to understand, and enriches their inner experiences and imagination, which help create critical thinkers and creative minds. Dewey asks,

> Why are we so hard of heart and so slow to believe? The imagination is the medium in which the child lives ... Shall we ignore this native setting and tendency, dealing not with the living child at all, but with the dead image we have erected, or shall we give it play and satisfaction?[257]

The second aspect that I greatly appreciate is Dewey's concept of growth. It is, indeed, central for Dewey that a child's immaturity is not to be condemned, but rather, to be valued and appreciated for its potential. However, he states in *Democracy of Education* that it is a mistake to think that growth is a movement towards a fixed goal. Instead of being an end, growth is regarded as having an end. Dewey wants education to proceed in such a way that learners would remain always eager for further education. For Dewey, growth should create future possibilities for further growth. He ask, "does this form of growth create conditions for further growth, or does it set up conditions that shut off the person who has grown in this particular direction from the occasions stimuli, and opportunities for continuing growth in new directions?"[258] In fact, such an understanding helps educators not only to respect the child as a whole human being, but also to opens the educational door to a world of opportunities and endless potential for the continuing transformation of both individuals and societies into a thriving life.

A third strength that I appreciate in Dewey's theory of thinking is his insistency on a child-centered curriculum with daily life experience as the main content. In regard to the child and curriculum, Dewey criticized both the new and the old educational process, insisting, "The child and curriculum are simply two limits which define a single process."[259] Later, in *Experience and Education*, he rejects the either/or approach to the child and curriculum, insisting that child, curriculum, and subject matter should be interactively linked together. In this, he has a special interest in and different view of geography as the foundation for "occupations." He says, "The unity of all sciences is found in geography. The significance of geography is that it

---

257. Ibid., 38.
258. Dewey, *Later Works of John Dewey*, 13:19.
259. Dewey, *Child and Curriculum*, 279.

presents the earth as the enduring home of the occupations of man."[260] For him, the basic content and structure of any curriculum should emerge from the activities of life. From an educational viewpoint, this is, indeed, a fundamental principal, as it helps Egyptian educators not only to overcome the problem of lacking good curricular materials, but also to create contextual curricula that might meet with the actual learners' needs.

A fourth and more important strength that I appreciate in Dewey is the inquiry and scientific method of education. What I really appreciate is that inquiry is not an aim, but rather, a means by which growth—the goal—is achieved and maintained. As he realized that traditional epistemology was a primary problem for education, Dewey believes that inquiry and critical thinking is the best practical pedagogy for aiding in the development of intelligent learners who are independently able to deal with life perplexities. If experience is the medium and content of the curriculum, as Dewey insists is the only way of true learning, then inquiry and critical thinking are the methods of interpreting this experience. What Dewey actually hopes to achieve is not just a community of people saturated with information or fixed knowledge, but rather, people who exhibit habits of mind that facilitate future intellectual and moral growth. While most people mistakenly equate knowledge and truth, Dewey regards knowledge as larger and more encompassing than truth. For him, knowledge is that information or understanding which is useful in guiding inquiry in order to construct one's own truth. While truth, he believes, is warranted assertion, which is not eternal, absolute, or fixed. For me, this reasonably fits with both human limitations and the constant and increasing changes of the world.

Dewey's conviction about the necessity of democracy for good education is the fifth dimension that I appreciate in his philosophy. I value in Dewey not only his belief in democracy as a way of life more than a form of government, but also the deep connection he makes between true democracy and education. We are not to learn democracy through our free communication, which allows for the transmission of habits of acting, thinking, and feeling, but we should practice democracy practically in class in order to create democratic characters. In this, Dewey never mentions the transmission of knowledge, facts, or truths, as he is concerned with the desire to communicate, not with the products of past communication: "There is more than a tie between the words common, community, and communication. Men live in a community in virtue of the things which they have in common; and communication is the way in which they come

---

260. Dewey, *School and Society*, 13.

to possess things in common."[261] For Dewey, teachers in democratic societies should not pass on knowledge, like bricks, to their students. Rather, teachers should engage students in patterns of communication that will help them to develop democratic habits of association as well as the necessary habits of the mind. In short, democracy, in Dewey's view, is always a work in progress and not a fixed entity. For me, this notion lends life and credibility to everything we do.

What I most appreciate in Dewey is that he puts great emphasis on individuals' capacity to engage in critical thinking and believing. I concur with him that critical thinkers, aided by the methods of intelligence, will improve society while democratic society will support and nurture critical thinkers. As a society becomes more democratic, it educates in order to guide the critical thinking that will support its own growth. In this regard, school, argues Dewey, should be organized as a small democratic society where democratic ideals, pluralism, and competing ideas stimulate critical thinking.

Conclusion

A scientific interpretation of the lack of critical thinking in the process of Presbyterian education in Egypt was the intention of this chapter. The Egyptian problem was discussed in detail in light of Dewey's theory of reflective thinking. In the first section of this chapter, I discussed Dewey's theory of reflective thinking in detail: Dewey's rejection of the traditional view of "truth," as an absolute end, followed with his rejection of the traditional "epistemology" that resulted in this truth, Dewey's understanding of "truth," as provisional, followed by his understanding of "epistemology," as warranted assertion and instrumental, Then, in the fourth part, I introduced Dewey's view of reflective thinking, which he believes is the best way of thinking. The second part of the first section of this chapter pointed to Dewey's conception of the value of using critical thinking for liberating individuals, and helping them to achieve personal growth. In the third part, I examined Dewey's understanding of the goal of education to be unlimited growth while the fourth part explained using scientific thinking as a method of making philosophy and practicing education. Then, in the fifth part, I discuss Dewey's portrayal of the role that the teacher should play as a guide and facilitator in the process of education while in the sixth part, I examined his insistence on the learner being an active partner who, with the help of the teacher, has to construct his or her own truth. In the seventh part, I highlight Dewey's assertion that the use of experience is a central element in the process. In the

261. Dewey, *Democracy and Education*, 7.

final part of the first section, much attention was given to democracy as an essential environment of education.

The second section of this chapter was designed to interpret the problem of the lack of critical thinking in the Presbyterian education in Egypt in light of Dewey's philosophy and the main factors that formed it. The belief that a child is an incomplete human being, Presbyterian education believes in the preparation of the young for future life while this education is divorced from life experiences, a situation that results in a lack of interest and joy for learners in this process. Having an authoritarian teacher that resulted in a teacher-centered education, which focuses on indoctrination and memorization as method of education, where learners suffer from a sever lack of democracy resulting in creating dependent learners who just accept ready-made truths and neither pay attention to life experience as an important element for education nor construct critical thinking skills. In this section, I argue that using Dewey's theory of reflective thinking is useful for the transformation of Christian education in the Presbyterian Church in Egypt into a process that is able to form disciples who possess Christian wisdom and meet the challenge of social changes in the contemporary age.

In the third section of this chapter, I highlighted some of the criticisms of Dewey's educational theory. I started this criticism with pointing to some of the significant philosophers, such as Miller, Berkson, and Russell, who engaged in a critical debate with Dewey from the time of the appearance of his instrumental theory until now. These thinkers and others who disagree with Dewey in some of his educational and philosophical thoughts have devoted more attention to the issue of the democracy of education, believing that freedom should be limited in the process. Then, I pointed to some of Dewey's thoughts that might be troublesome in the Egyptian context. However, I explained in more detail some of the Dewey's strengths, which I believe make his theory useful and essential to Presbyterian education in Egypt.

It is obvious, then, that interpreting the Egyptian problem in the light of Dewey's scientific theory is both necessary and useful to help understand its depth, dimensions, and the underline factors that formed it. However, interpreting Dewey's theory in the light of Christian faith and the sinful human nature reveals the fact that there is much that is missing for the human being to achieve the good life. It also reveals the inability of Dewey's theory alone to solve the human problem, which reveals the need for not just an appropriation, but rather, a critical appropriation of this theory both in the light of the Egyptian context and reformed theology. In the next chapter, with focus on Reinhold Niebuhr, I offer a theological assessment of Dewey's philosophy of education, and, with more focus on John Calvin's theology of reason, I will try to construct a theological norm for using critical thinking for a more successful and effective process of Presbyterian education in Egypt.

CHAPTER 3

Critical Thinking in the Christian Traditions

A Theological Norm

Life is a battle between faith and reason, in which each feeds upon the other, drawing sustenance from it and destroying it.[1] . . . God grant me the serenity to accept the things I cannot change, the courage to change the things I can, *and the wisdom to know the difference.*[2]

Men are not irrational creatures" without "the seeds of the knowledge of God.[3] . . . For we see implanted in human nature some sort of desire to search out the truth to which man would not at all aspire if he had not already savored it. Human understanding then possesses some power of perception, *since it is by nature captivated by love of truth.*"[4]

The human soul consists of two faculties . . . Intellect and will. Let the office, moreover, of the intellect be to distinguish between objects, as each seems worthy of approval or disapproval; while that of the will, to choose and follow what the intellect pronounces good: but to reject and flee what it disapproves . . . *Let it be enough for us, that the intellect is as it were the leader and governor of the soul.*[5]

There is within the human mind, and indeed by natural instinct, *an awareness of divinity*. This we take to be beyond controversy. To prevent anyone from taking refuge in the pretense of

---

1. Http://www.brainyquote.com/quotes/quotes/r/reinholdni159158.html.
2. Ibid.
3. Calvin, *Calvin: Institutes*, I.v.15.
4. Ibid., II.ii.12.
5. Ibid., II, fol. 23.

ignorance, *God himself has implanted in all men a certain understanding of his divine majesty.*[6]

Faith is a form of knowledge—not an abstract, bookish sort of knowledge but a personal knowledge . . . faith Calvin is talking about is very different from "blind faith." *True faith is not content merely to accept what others say without question.*[7]

Dewey's Naturalistic Rationalism and the Corrupted Human Nature

Niebuhr's Critique

WHEN NIEBUHR, WHO WAS just thirty-eight, was asked to write a review of Dewey's occasional papers "Characters and Events" for *The World Tomorrow*, Dewey had just celebrated his seventieth birthday and had published his work, *The Quest for Certainty*, based on his lectures in Gifford in 1929. In this review, Niebuhr praises Dewey for being one of the rare philosophers that are willing to "descend from their ant-hill of scholastic hairsplitting to help the world of men regulate its common life and discipline its ambitions and ideals."[8] In his book, *Does Civilization Need Religion?* Niebuhr praised Dewey for being "a statesman for the reason that, though he has not had actual political responsibility, he had helped to form political thought and guide political conduct."[9] He also noted that Dewey's seventieth birthday celebration "gave his friends an opportunity to rejoice in the triumphs of his spirit and purpose in philosophy, in education and in social reform."[10] Despite all his subsequent criticism of Dewey, Niebuhr's willingness was to situate Dewey among the "social minded educators."[11] Then, in the *Characters and Events*, Niebuhr chose to include Dewey along with Bertrand Russell in a select party of two, whose "extraordinary contemporary influence" in the task of "molding the political and social thought of their people."[12]

---

6. Ibid., I.iii.1.
7. Johnson, *John Calvin*, 63.
8. Rice, *Reinhold Niebuhr and John Dewey*, 3.
9. Ibid., 5.
10. Ibid., 3.
11. Ibid.
12. Ibid., 4.

In the early thirties, however, Niebuhr started to attack Dewey's philosophy in a socio-political perspective, showing that what Dewey attempts to apply on the ground is just a romantic ideal that cannot cope with the selfish power struggle between groups and nations even though when individuals have the potential to do good. In his book, *Moral Man and Immoral Society*, Niebuhr distinguishes between the moral potentialities of individuals and of organized groups, or "individual man" and "collective." Corporations and sovereign states, says Niebuhr, are *by their nature* all but incapable of unselfish conduct; instead, they are always competing for power. He says, "As individuals, men believe that they ought to love and serve each other and establish justice between each other. As racial, economic, and national groups they take for themselves, whatever their power can command."[13] In the introduction of this book, Niebuhr also strikes with John Dewey, "social injustice cannot be resolved by moral and national suasion alone, as the educator and social scientist (meaning Dewey) usually believes. Conflict is inevitable, and is this conflict power must challenged by power."[14] Niebuhr states,

> Even a nation composed of individuals who possessed the highest degree of goodwill would be less than loving in its relation to other nation. It would fail, if for no other reason, because the individuals could not possibly think themselves into the position of the individuals of another nation in a degree to insure pure benevolence. Furthermore such Goodwell as they did possess would be sluiced into loyalty to their own nation and tend to increase that nation's selfishness.[15]

In his article, "After Capitalism—What?" Niebuhr offers an emphasis such as of the *Moral Man and Immoral Society*, he states,

> There is nothing in history to support the thesis that a dominant class ever yields its position or privileges in society because its rule has been convinced of ineptness or injustices. Those who still regard this as possible are rationalists and moralists who have only slight understanding of the stubborn inertia and blindness of collective egoism.[16]

Again, Niebuhr insists that even religion and intellectual ideals cannot do anything to resolve this problematic situation.

13. Sumner, *Folkways*, 9.
14. Ibid., xv.
15. Ibid., 74.
16. Dewey, *Later Works of John Dewey*, 9:400.

> The inability of religious and intellectual idealists to gauge properly the course of historical events results from their constant over-estimate of idealistic factors in political life. They think that an entire nation can be educated toward a new social ideal when all the testimony of history proves that new societies are born out of social struggle, in which the positions of the various social groups are determined by their economic interests.[17]

However, what in the early thirties originally seemed to be just a politico-social debate between Niebuhr and Dewey and was meant to attain a new social order, has later turned into a religiously motivated attack from Niebuhr on Dewey's philosophy. In *An Interpretation of Christian Ethics*, Niebuhr argues that the only a "prophetic" Christian analysis of life which underscores the realism of the doctrine of original sin can solve our problems—as opposed to "the naturalistic rationalism of John Dewey."[18] Daniel F. Rice states, "One of the major disagreements Niebuhr had with Dewey regarded Dewey's naturalism and the ease with which he believed scientific method could be applied to human studies. Niebuhr's choice of terms to describe Dewey's position was *naturalistic rationalism*."[19] Declaring the corruption of human nature and that God is "both the ground of existence and the essence which transcends existence," wherein "lies the foundation for ethic which enables men to give themselves to values actually embodied in persons and existence, but also transcending every actuality."[20]

Niebuhr's use of prophetic Christianity, which he himself says might serve as a "proof against the disappointments and disillusions of naturalistic morality, in which there is always a touch of romantic exaggeration of the goodness of man and a corresponding cynical reaction,"[21] to critique Dewey's "naturalistic rationalism" is not enough to convince. Niebuhr continues criticizing Dewey in his Gifford Lectures in 1939 published later in two volumes under the title, *The Nature and Destiny of Man: A Christian Interpretation*. In the preface of the first volume, Niebuhr explicitly states, "the study is based upon the conviction that there are resources in the Christian faith for an understanding of human nature which have been lost in modern culture."[22] Being known by many as a theologian of sin, it is not

---

17. Ibid., 404.
18. Niebuhr and Santurri, *Interpretation of Christian Ethics*, 127.
19. Rice, *Reinhold Niebuhr and His Circle of Influence*, 49.
20. Ibid., 130.
21. Ibid., 131.
22. Niebuhr, *Nature and Destiny of Man*, xvi.

surprising, then, that the Christian doctrine of sin comes in for Niebuhr's confrontation with John Dewey.

Building on Augustine's theology in the *Evil and Augustinian Tradition*, Charles T. Matthews asserts that though he developed an Augustinian psychology to support his "Christian realism" in discussing our nature and destiny, Niebuhr has his own radical shift in understanding sin and evil, as he takes the "original sin" outside the literal understanding of the biblical event of Adam's fall. Niebuhr opposes all kinds of "simple" and "one-sided" understandings of human existence, which defines humans either as wholly "natural," so subject to scientific manipulation and reconstruction, or a wholly "free" as if humans are able to escape from all tragic conflict of the history. In contrast, Niebuhr's realism defines humans as both natural and free, which he calls "finite freedom."[23] In the first volume of *Nature and Destiny of Man*, Niebuhr begins his theology with critiquing modern anthropology, which is much too optimistic as it focuses only on the progress and the perfectibility of human. For him, modernity fails to realize that every growth of human freedom may have evil as well as good consequences. Human, he argues, was created with two aspects in tension, "nature and spirit." While nature is finite, limited, and bounded, spirit is infinite, unlimited, and free. Consequentially, a constant tension between the two is inevitable. Niebuhr calls this tension "anxiety of freedom." This anxiety, he says, is not itself a sin, but rather a precondition of sin. Because of this tension, sin is *inevitable* but it is *not necessary* at the same time. For Niebuhr, this anxiety, however, can lead to all creativity if human finds his security and satisfaction in God's love by faith, while it can lead to temptation of sin if human puts his security in exalting and loving the self. Therefore, Adam's story is not the cause or the origin of our sin, but a symbol of the human condition and tension.[24]

While the classical account of sin failed because it denies our history, denies our responsibility of sin, and insists that sin was necessary for our existence; Niebuhr argues, the modern account also failed because it denies our nature, affirms our responsibility of sin, and ignores the fact that we, ourselves, cannot overcome our wickedness. Then, Niebuhr goes further to define sin, in its basic form, as pride. While human, argues Niebuhr, was created to be in relationship with God and to make God the true center of man's life, man abused freedom that was given by the gracious God and, because of anxiety, lack of trust in God, and lack of security, wanted to establish the self as a center of life. In short, Niebuhr believes sin is the claim of self-sufficiency

23. Mathewes, *Evil and Augustinian Tradition*, 107.
24. Ibid., 110.

with no need for the divine, which means that replacing God with the human self is to break the first command, "to love God," while its consequence is to break the second command, "to love neighbor."[25]

The form of sin as the pride against God creates other forms of pride. First, the pride of power means that man attempts to make himself God. This form can be represented in two manifestations. The first manifestation is that man does not recognize human weakness; therefore, man trusts himself more than God. In this manifestation, man's ego involves injustice and seeks a security beyond the limits and human finiteness. The second manifestation of the pride of power is that man wants to have power in order to overcome a recognized weakness, which shows his lack of security. He says, "It is the sin of those, who knowing themselves to be insecure, seek sufficient power to guarantee their security, inevitably of course at the expense of other life."[26] Niebuhr attributes to the two forms of the pride of power to a basic sense of insecurity as one reason of the problem, he states, "Thus man seeks to make himself God because he is betrayed both by his greatness and his weakness, and there is no level of greatness in which the lash of fear is not at least one stand in the whip of ambition."[27]

The second form of pride for Niebuhr is intellectual pride or the pride of knowledge. It, for him, is the pride of reason "which forgets that it is involved in a temporal process and imagines itself in complete transcendence over history. In this, man attempts to be more than what he is. While he realizes that both mind and knowledge are finite, he always tries to deny the finiteness of human mind and makes knowledge infinite and ultimate. Again, says Niebuhr, it is a feeling of insecurity that lies as a foundation of this form of pride. Indeed, all assertions of the final knowledge and ultimate truth are challenged by the uneasy feeling that the truth is not final and blended with interests of the ego. Intellectual pride however, reveals the freedom that man has been given, "If man were not a free spirit who transcends every situation in which he is involved he would have no concern for unconditioned truth and he would not be tempted to claim absolute validity for his partial perspectives."[28]

The third form of sin as pride, for Niebuhr, is the pride of virtue or moral pride, which is "the pretension of finite man that his highly conditioned virtue is the final righteousness and that his very relative moral

---

25. Ibid., 112.
26. Ibid., 190.
27. Ibid., 194.
28. Ibid., 197.

standards are absolute."²⁹ In this man trusts his righteousness as the same standards of the righteousness of God, denying that he is sinner. The virtue, then, which should be good, is made the very vehicle of sin. For Niebuhr, the moral sin of self-righteousness is the final sin. "The whole history of racial, national, religious and other social struggles is a community on the objective wickedness and social miseries which result from self-righteousness."³⁰ In this, Niebuhr builds on Luther's definition of moral pride as the "final form of pride" and the gateway of spiritual pride. In *The Moral Man and Immoral Society*, Niebuhr insists on the necessity of the political governing authority because of the sinful human nature, which is "egotism" and self-centered of individuals or groups. He refuses to reduce sin to just sensuality and insists that it is pride that impacts the entire behavior of the human, while sensuality is one aspect of it. For him, Jesus' ethics is the solution of the problem of the pride because he is the pure embodied form of God's love—Jesus is the "impossible possibility."³¹

Therefore, through combing the anthropological "basic insecurity of human existence" with the notion of sin, Niebuhr claims for the Christian faith a more realistic outlook on the social world than can be found in modern thinkers, including John Dewey. He clearly writes,

> Professor Dewey has a toughing faith in the possibility of achieving the same results in the field of social relations which intelligence achieved in the mastery of nature. The fact that man constitutionally corrupts his purest visions of disinterested justice in his actual actions seems never to occur to him—The solution at which professor Dewey arrives is therefore an incredibly naïve answer to a much more ultimate and perplexing problems than he realizes.³²

And this is; indeed, because:

> The belief that man could solve his problem either by escape from history or by the historical process itself is a mistake which is partly prompted by the most universal of al "ideological" taints: the pride, not of particular men and cultures, but of man as man. A more adequate analysis of human destiny must therefore be based on the Christian faith, which has disavowed

---

29. Ibid.
30. Ibid.
31. Ibid.
32. Ibid., 110.

human pride in principle, even if it will not be able to exhibit in fact what it has so disavowed.[33]

In contrary, Dewey does not attack Niebuhr. Indeed, all religious works that Dewey wrote are two primary sources; an early talk he gave in 1880s titled, "The Obligation of Knowledge of God," and *A Common Faith*. However, in a short essay, titled "Unity and Progress," Dewey attempts to view Niebuhr's position in "After Capitalism—What?" He thinks that Niebuhr subscribes to a philosophy of history that is made impossible after the breakdown of the traditional European philosophies of history, which since Augustine have been of the nature of theodicies. These kinds of philosophies leave no room for considering the real life of the recent societies. Dewey, however, scorns what Niebuhr calls a "somewhat theological view of collective egotism and natural depravity of human nature."[34] One year later, in his article "Intelligence and Power," Dewey continues reflecting on Niebuhr's realism, hoping to correct Niebuhr's misunderstanding of his position, emphasizing that the main purpose of his new method is to have a right concept of human intelligence and its ability to incorporate action for problem solving. Quoting Niebuhr in *Moral Man and Immoral Society*: "The truest visions of religion are illusions which may be partially realised by being resolutely believed," Dewey adds "even if it be an illusion, exaltation of intelligence and experimental method is worth a trial."[35]

Niebuhr, on the other hand, insists that Dewey's rationality is not the answer of the world's problems. Dualism, for example, is not just one dualism, but many; yet, whether it is one or many, it is approximately the real facts of life. It is difficult, however, to do full justice to these two facts by any set of symbols or definitions.

> What is needed is a philosophy and a religion which will do justice both to the purpose and to the frustration which purpose meets in the inertia of the concrete world, both to the ideal which fashions the real and to the real which defeats the ideals, both to the essential harmony and to the inevitable conflict in the cosmos and in the soul. In a sense there is not a single dualism in life; rather there are many of them. In his own life, man may experience a conflict between his moral will and the anarchic desires with which nature has endowed him; or he may experience a conflict between his cherished values and the caprices of nature which know nothing of the economy of values in human

---

33. Niebuhr, *Nature and Destiny of Man*, 331.
34. Dewey, *Later Works of John Dewey*, 9:72–73.
35. Ibid., 9:108.

life. In his cosmic order the conflict is between creativity and the resistance which frustrate creative purpose. Whether the dualism is defined as one of mind and matter, or thought and extension, or force and inertia, or God and the devil, it approximates the real facts of life. it may be impossible to do full justice to the two types of facts by any set of symbols or definitions; but life gives the lie to any attempt by which one is explained completely in the terms of the other.[36]

Only philosophy, then, cannot be the answer; but rather a philosophy and religion which can do justice; as he puts it, "A philosophy for an Ethical Religion." Religion and religion alone could provide reasons for avoiding moral enervation. Religion was our one and only source for believing that we inhabit "a universe in which the human spirit is guaranteed security against the forces of nature which always seem to reduce it to a mere effervescence unable to outlast the collection of forces which produces it."[37] For Niebuhr, Dewey's naturalistic ethics cannot possess the power to change the human will or self-interest, which clearly reflects the need for a power that is beyond human nature in order to lift the man above nature. He states,

A purely naturalistic ethics will not only be overcome by a sense of frustration and sink into despair, but it will lack the force to restrain the self-will and self-interest of men and of nations. If life cannot be centered in something beyond nature, it will not be possible to lift men above the brute struggle for survival.[38]

In his 1934 "Terry Lectures" at Yale, which were published in the same year as *A Common Faith*, Dewey argues back and turns directly to the philosophy of religion, demonstrating that there is "religion" and there the "religious." Religion has to do with dogmas, institutions, and all related while religious points to certain experiences. While the distinction as such is well-known by the churches, what Dewey wants to do is point to "the difference between belief that is a conviction that some end should be supreme over conduct, and belief that some object or being exists as truth for the intellect."[39] Dewey accepts the first belief and rejects the other. For "There is but one sure road of access of truth—the road of patient, cooperative inquiry operating by means of experiment, record and controlled reflection."[40]

36. Ibid., 9:4-5.
37. Ibid.
38. Ibid., 9:5.
39. Dewey, *Common Faith*, 20.
40. Ibid., 32.

Truth and ideals are true only when "They are made out of the hard stuff of the world of physical and social experience."[41]

Obviously referring to Niebuhr's *Moral Man and Immoral Society*, Dewey insists that "Society is convicted of being "immoral" by evoking all the evils of institutions as they now exist, and the unexpressed premise is that the institutions as they exist are normal expressions of social relations in their own nature."[42] In a different perspective from Niebuhr, Dewey points to the lack of using the intelligence method as the main factor of the immorality of society. Social evils are accidental evils, Dewey believes, and by examining them carefully, it will be possible to find means to correct them. Those, such as Niebuhr, who reject the accidental nature of the evils in society, are forced to bring in references to sin and self-love. In Dewey's words,

> Vested interests, interests vested with power, are powerfully on the side of the *status quo*, and therefore they are especially powerful in hindering the growth and application of the method of natural intelligence. Just because these interests are so powerful, it is the more necessary to fight for recognition of the method of intelligence in action. But one of the greatest obstacles in conducting this combat is the tendency to dispose of social evils in terms of general moral causes. The sinfulness of man, the corruption of his heart, his self-love and love of power, when referred to as causes are precisely of the same nature as was the appeal to abstract powers.[43]

Dewey's insistency on the naturalistic method; however, could not convince Niebuhr, who insists that Dewey's appeal to the method of intelligence is just another example of "the faith of modern rationalism in the ability of reason to transcend the partial perspectives of the natural world in which reason is rooted."[44] Or, "part of an entire conception of the relation of time to eternity, and progressively devours its own finiteness."[45] While Dewey believes that most of the traditions are the main obstacle of the progress, Niebuhr insists that the real obstacle is not traditions and not habits, but egotism: the power hungry, predatory self-interest.

I would, indeed, agree with Niebuhr's theological critique of Dewey's philosophy of education on the issue of sin. Dewey is much too dependent on science, too optimistic, and too anthropocentric, giving too much credit

---

41. Ibid., 49.
42. Ibid., 75.
43. Ibid., 79.
44. Niebuhr and Santurri, *Interpretation of Christian Ethics*, 138.
45. Niebuhr, *Nature and Destiny of Man*, 246.

to the human experience while ignoring the reality of its intensive selfish attitudes and destructive consequences. Dewey's problem-solving model presupposes that humans live, think, and act in complete freedom, ignoring the power of the sinful human nature and its control over human behavior. If experience is the only way of justifying human action and thought in the world, this may maximize the individualism and evil attitudes in the world. Dewey's theory of thinking, including democracy, experience, and growth, was well developed and practiced at the beginning of the twentieth century, when humanity was challenged with, WW1 and WW2 and when the faculty of human reason and intelligence never succeeded to overcome the problem of the evil in the world. Likewise, we may see the attempt of the modern intelligence to solve the problem of terrorism by using violence. Also, what is called the "Arabic Spring," which was turned to be an "Arabic Fall" and nightmares when all good aims of the Arabic revolutions are turned into selfish and destructive goals.

Niebuhr suggests that Deweyans have an overly optimistic view of education, not realizing that for it to be transformative, it must have a sense of what he calls morale—a motivating energy that incites transformation. When he begins to identify a "moral simplicity in Protestantism which is closely related to its individualism," Niebuhr anticipates that the major theme of *Moral Man* is that "all human groups tend to be more predatory than the individuals which compose them."[46] Yes, Dewey is very useful for having a comprehensive understanding of life problems by using critical thinking and providing a scientific framework for more advanced and successful education. Yet, he failed to solve the problem of evil either individual or social, which required more than a science theory.

Although, on one hand, I appreciate Niebuhr's concerns about the inevitable negative influences of sin on human behavior, which, in many cases is represented in selfishness and violence, on the other hand, I agree with Dewey that human sin is existent any way, whether humans use traditional principles and fixed norms or progressive scientific theory, we are still sinful. Our ways of thinking and acting will neither worsen nor solve the problem of sin. This means that a struggle with sin must be the concern of human being during our entire life either using fixed norms or learning from life experience. To control human sin is to take it seriously, treating it in the light of God's grace by the power of the Holy Spirit. This, of course, does not hinder Dewey's essential method or general universal principles as prior knowledge.

---

46. Rice, *Reinhold Niebuhr and John Dewey*, 246.

I also disagree with Niebuhr and the conservative scripture-centered Christians on critiquing Dewey for creating an education model that is not based on fixed norms or general universal principles as prior knowledge, insisting on the Bible as the only fixed norm for life and practice. Dewey would defend that the main problem of using fixed norms is its incapability to cope with the uncertainty and dramatic changing of the contemporary world. Neither traditional norms, Dewey argues, nor traditional universal principles, are up to the task of coping with the problems raised by the dramatic changes in the present world. Inquiry and experience means a giant diversity of norms and principle. Only Inquiry and experience can create a giant diversity of norms and principle. He argues back,

> While all thinking is result in knowledge, ultimately the value of knowledge is subordinate to its use in thinking. For we live not in a settled and finished world, but in one, which is going on, and where our main task is prospective, and where retrospective—and all knowledge as distinct from thought is retrospective.[47]

Dewey asserts that he does not reject previous knowledge and norms; rather, he believes that they would enrich the process of inquiry. However, he would confirm that he rejects the bodies of beliefs that need only to be taught and learned as true, and he rejects the rigid forms of authoritative religious dogmas that people take as ultimate truth without examination. He would also argue that he is not only against any set of religious doctrines, but also against any scientific dogma that were taken from existence apart from the present experience and needs, agreeing with using past knowledge and norms that would be relevant to our contemporary experience.[48]

Indeed, I appreciate Dewey in rejecting the dogmatic understanding of what is called an ultimate truth. This fundamental perspective, indeed, has a high tendency to exclude and reject the other. I appreciate the Bible as the Word of God; however, this Word, according to Karl Barth is a living dynamic Word.[49] It is flexible and comprehensive enough to illuminate and address our present problematic situation. The Bible, as living knowledge of God, is not static conceptions but rather a dynamic transformative word. This reflects the dynamic divine-human relationship, where the Holy Spirit creatively guides the human being according to the nature of each problematic situation. The Bible, indeed, involve a vast variety of the human experience of God's action in the world. This means that we need to contex-

---

47. Ibid., 1, 100.
48. Dewey, *A Common Faith*, 39.
49. Barth, *Church Dogmatics*, 457.

tualize these incident texts to cope with our contemporary problems. This is extremely convenient to Dewey's insistency on using human experience as a source of teaching and knowing.

Third, Dewey was strongly criticized for his educational-end-goal (*telos*). Indeed, most of the Christian theologians, orthodox reformed in particular, believe that Christian life is directed to a specific end, as Jesus Christ is the *telos* of life. Having a good life is impossible without Jesus Christ who gives the meaning to life. Christian *telos*, then, is not to achieve a good life here on the earth; but rather, achieve the eternal life in Jesus Christ. Calvin puts all consideration on Jesus as the only end goal of life. It is clear, then, that every Christian practice moves toward a goal and nothing is aimless. God has a *telos* to transform God's people into the likeness of Jesus. Paul illustrates God *telos* for us: "Till we all come in the unity of the faith, and of the knowledge of the Son of God, unto a perfect [*teleion*] man."[50]

Dewey would argue that he is not philosophizing conceptual thoughts, or a priori knowledge as Kant, who attempted to escape from the challenges of the real life problems to a world of conceptual static ideas. He would rather be concerned to clarify that his philosophy is a scientific method to solve problems and his main goal for individuals is to have good life, while there is no fixed truth, nor one way of achieving flourishing of life. Therefore, every fact or knowledge must be examined in a process of inquiry in an actual life experience and all knowledge that is resulted in developing and improving human life is accepted as true knowledge. Christian beliefs must be submitted to the process as past experiences that stated in the Bible in order to improve and develop the present reality.

In a practical theological viewpoint, I would agree that Dewey was not a theologian. His approach, instead, is a problem solving of life, which never conflicts with Christian *telos*. When we believe in Jesus we are still in the world, facing problems, and going through multiple perplexing situations every day that we need to deal with in the best way. Dewey's theory of problem solving is needed to facilitate the life and ministry of individuals and church. The dynamic developing life that Dewey seeks is relevant to the protestant understanding of the kingdom of God as here and now, in which Jesus promises us better life, *eudemonia*.

Indeed, I do agree with Dewey's defense against Niebuhr's understanding of human being as a totally disabled being. Niebuhr believes that, because of sin, humans can think and do nothing. And while I agree with his account on the negative impact of sin on the human ability to have the right truth, about God, I disagree with his view that human being is nothing.

50. Eph 4:3, NIV.

With Paul Ricoeur, I refuse traditions that highly "exalt" human self, such as Descartes, Kant, and Husserl, in the meantime; however, I rejects traditions that "humiliate" the human self to the point of its disappearance, such as Nietzsche, Marx and Freud. In a Deweyan viewpoint, I see that Niebuhr's approach has fallen in the problem of *divisions and dualism* that most of the modern thinkers have fallen in and Dewey kept fighting for decades. This division that is putting the power of God in a conflict with human agency; faith in a conflict with reason; and Christian and philosophy in a conflict with secular and theology. Dewey rejects Niebuhr's account that whoever does not praise God is praising man, emphasizing that some of those who praise God praise themselves and all who are not praising God do not necessarily praise man. Moreover, I believe that sin is there in every case: either following Christian traditions or liberal thinking.

Feminist theology, on the other hand, rejects Niebuhr's account of sin, suggesting that an understanding of sin needs to be gender specific. In her 1960 essay "The Human Situation: A Feminine View," while Valerie Saiving agrees with Niebuhr on viewing sin as a "tension of freedom" between spirit and nature, she rejects Niebuhr's insistence on setting it as a general principle that equally applied on both man and woman. Saiving points to the natural biological and psychological differences between male and woman, which clearly distinguishes female's from male's experience and the kind of knowledge that results from it. Saiving writes,

> There are significant differences between masculine and feminine experience and that feminine experience reveals in a more emphatic fashion certain in the experience of the human situation, which are present, but less obvious in the experience of man.[51]

For Saiving, Niebuhr, indeed, has constructed his position towards sin primarily upon the basis of masculine experience and thus view the human condition from male standpoint. Consequentially, this doctrine "do not provide an adequate interpretation of the situation of women—nor, for that matter, of men, especially in view of certain fundamental changes now taking place in our own society." She argues that psychological observations, noting that, whereas little girls learn that they will grow up, just by waiting, to be women, boys on the other hand learn that to be men they must "do something about it. Mere waiting is not enough; to be a man, a boy must prove himself and go on proving himself."[52] While "Man knows that

---

51. Saiving, "Human Situation," 27.
52. Ibid.

CRITICAL THINKING IN THE CHRISTIAN TRADITIONS   145

he is merely a part of the whole but he tries to convince himself and others that he *is* the whole."[53] For this, female's sin is different from male's sin, for female's sin is the

Saving rejects Niebuhr understanding of sin as it humiliates human nature, "represent a widespread tendency in contemporary theology to describe man's predicament as rising from his separateness and anxiety occasioned by it and to identify sin with self—assertion and love with selflessness."[54] I am aware, says Saiving, that there is a structure of experience common to both men and women, so that we may legitimately speak of the "human situation" without reference to sexual identity. The only question, she argues, is whether we have described the human situation correctly by taking account of the experiences of both sexes and whether we longer make any distinctions between the potentialities of men and women as such. What actually signifies woman experience more than man experience, Saiving insists, is the ability of getting birth and mother child relationship, "The close relationship between mother and infant plays the first and perhaps the most important role in the formation of masculine and feminine character, for it means that the person with whom the child originally identifies himself is a woman. Both male and female children must learn to overcome this initial identification by differentiating themselves from the mother."[55] However, the male is permitted far greater freedom than the girl. Since the girl knows that she will like her mother, she does not go through any challengeable freedom to anything else while the boy knows that he has to do something to be a man. For female, then, self-differentiation and self-development is a journey through nature while male struggle between nature and spirit continues. In the *Creating Woman Theology*, Helen Tallon Russel agrees with Saiving, "when Niebuhr speaks out of his experience about the human situation, he assumes that he is speaking for all persons. Feminist theology has demonstrated that he is not."[56]

From a feminist theological viewpoint, Saiving sees that woman is more closely bound to nature than is man. This has advantages and disadvantages for her as a human being. The advantages lie in her greater degree of natural security and the lesser degree of anxiety to which she is subject, both of which make it easier, all other things being equal, for her to enter into loving relationships in which self-concern is at a minimum. Consequentially, woman's sin is different, it is "triviality, distractibility, and

53. Ibid.
54. Ibid., 26.
55. Ibid., 36.
56. Coleman, Howell and Russell, *Creating Women's Theology*, 10.

diffuseness; lack of an organizing center or focus; dependence on others for one's self-definition; tolerance at the expense of standards of excellence . . . in short, underdevelopment or negation of the self."[57]

Feminist theology is not my concern here, but rather the beautiful link Saiving makes between woman's closeness to her nature and the diminish of the "tension of freedom." In this, Saiving would agree with Dewey's naturalistic rationalism, which not only centralizes human existence in nature, and situates knowledge and truth in the personal experiential interaction between human being and environment, but also considers the natural human abilities to construct the own knowledge. Unlike Niebuhr's view of the human being as totally sinful and incapable of controlling spirit-nature tension, with Dewey, Saiving assures us that reconciling people with their human nature, trusting their natural capacities will leads more not to sin but rather, creativity and true knowledge. I believe, therefore, that Dewey's critical thinking theory is a useful framework, which would help to reconcile the divisions and dualism of Presbyterian education in Egypt. Instead of conflict, Dewey would help the Presbyterians in Egypt to see the harmony and integrity of the divine with the human; body with soul; reason with faith; philosophy with theology; and secular with Christian.

Human Reason and Knowing God John Calvin[58]

Humanism, Reason, and Rationality—Calvin and Logic

Having the doctrine of original sin and predestination back in mind, a crucial question that has always been raised is "what is, if there is any, the relationship

---

57. Ibid., 37.

58. John Calvin (1509–64) was born in Noyon, received a private education with the children of a Nobel family in the same city. Having distinguished himself at an early age, Calvin was deemed worthy of receiving the support of a benefice, a church-granted stipend, at the age of 12, so as to support him in his studies. At age 14, Calvin was enrolled at the College de la Marche in the University of Paris, though he quickly transferred to the College de Montaigu.

In Paris, Calvin first came into contact with the new humanistic learning while preparing for a career as a priest, where he earned his master's degree at the age of 18. However, he did not proceed with his original plan to prepare for a clerical career, as his father ordered his him to enroll instead at Orleans in the law faculty. Calvin obeyed, and applied himself, finishing his doctorate in law in 1532. In that same year, his first published book appeared a commentary on Seneca's *De Clementia*. Around 1533, Calvin experienced a *"subita conversione,"* a sudden conversion. As he fled Paris, on 1534 while he appeared in Noyon, and surrendered his clerical benefices. From that point on, Calvin no longer had a personal attachment to the Church of Rome.

In 1536, Calvin finished the first edition of his *Institutes of the Christian Religion*. It

between John Calvin and human reason and critical thinking?" Indeed, the impression that Calvin's theology, which is deeply scripture-centered, humiliates the human reason and its role in knowing God to the extent of "nothing" was reputedly raised by some scholars, both Presbyterian and non-Presbyterian along centuries. In his article, "John Calvin's Understanding of Human Reason in His *Institutes*," Jung S. Rhee states that "Whether Calvin is a rationalist became controversial in our century."[59] While John P. Le Coq in his article, "Was Calvin a Philosopher," answers his own question negatively, severely criticizing Calvin's lack of rationality,[60] many scholars agree with the positive understanding of Robert H. Ayers who, in his article, "Language, Logic, and Reason in Calvin *Institutes*," identifies Calvin's rationality and view of reason with Augustine and Aquinas: "In short, there is as high regard for reason in Calvin as there is in the Augustine and Aquinas."[61] While their epistemology is commonly characterized with in the famous expression, "We

---

enjoyed a wide popular demand, and the original supply was exhausted within a year. Instead of simply reprinting it, Calvin revised it, and the edition of 1539 expanded substantially the original work. This would be Calvin's pattern throughout the subsequent Latin editions of 1543, 1550, and 1559. French editions were printed in 1545 and 1560, and Calvin's French is easily as influential as Luther's German for the formation of the modern vernacular. Each Latin edition was a rearrangement of earlier material, as well as the addition of new components. Calvin also wrote commentaries on almost every book of the Bible, issued numerous tracts, and preached almost every day in Geneva.

In 1536, Guillaume Farrell shamed Calvin into sharing the leadership of Geneva. This period of Calvin's life lasted until the city council threw him out in April of 1538, when he settled in Strasbourg, and pastored a congregation. It was here that he began his other life work: commenting upon the books of the Bible. Beginning with the Romans commentary, written at least partially and published in Strasbourg in 1540, Calvin would comment upon most of the books of the scripture. However, Geneva called him back in 1541. Believing that Geneva was his particular call, he returned and alternately supporting and berating the council, until his death in 1564. It was in this period that Calvin made his other great contribution to the Church, preparing, and then forcing the city council to ratify, his Ecclesiastical Ordinances of the Church of Geneva. In this, all the principles of Reformed polity are found. In 1564, debilitated by a series of illnesses, Calvin died in Geneva. By the terms of his will, he was buried in an unmarked grave, so as to avoid any possibility of idolatry.

59. Calvin's thought is marked by a constant dialectic between the perspective of a wholly pure and good creator (God) and the corrupted created being (humanity). His anthropology and soteriology shows his dependence on Augustine, with the will being somewhat limited in human application, and powerless to effect change in its status vis-à-vis salvation. However, Calvin balances that with a hearty emphasis on human response to God's love and mercy in the created order, by correct action both in the human world and the world of nature. Rhee, "John Calvin's Understanding."

60. Le Coq, "Was Calvin a Philosopher?," 254, 256.

61. Ayers, "Language, Logic, and Reason," 285.

believe in order to know,"⁶² the three of them agree that no man is without the light of reason. And while they believe that reason is not the master of faith but its servant, they also believe that reason has an indispensable role to play in the task of faith seeking understanding.⁶³

Indeed, I believe that Calvin's high regard of reason and rationality is rooted in his early humanistic education. Quirinus Breen points to this fact by stating that Calvin converted to Protestantism after his "mental set" was already framed, "rather later in life."⁶⁴ Calvin, Breen says, had entirely committed to the humanistic studies until his twenty-fourth year when he "a seasoned humanist,"⁶⁵ while he had never shaken off the "mind set" and "had never got away from his humanistic inheritance."⁶⁶ Even though he was not slavishly adherent to his humanistic background in all its aspects, says Breen, his scholastic methodology and appeal to the "common sense" and reason was clearly rooted in his humanistic spirit.⁶⁷

While it is notably known that Calvin is a theologian whose thoughts are founded on the principle "sola Scriptura," some of the scholars believe that reason and rationality are the main method of Calvin's theology. In his article, "Calvin's Theological Method and the Ambiguity in His Theology," John H. Leith states that "Calvin's theological methodology was formally Biblicism but really rationalism."⁶⁸ Leith makes it clear that Calvin's "implicit confidence in the competence of reason to theologize on the basis of the biblical materials" was a crucial foundation of his theology. Leith states,

> Reason did become a source of his theology through speculation about and organization of the biblical materials. Calvin betrays little doubt as to the full competence of reason in the systematization and rational elaboration of the biblical materials . . . On the basis of the presupposition that the Bible supplies infallible material for theology and that reason is competent to manipulate and theologize about those materials, Calvin was convinced that he possessed the truth.⁶⁹

Leith continues, "While he avows the greatest loyalty to Scripture, he actually goes beyond Scripture as a result of an almost irresistible tendency to

---

62. Ibid., 284.
63. Ibid., 285.
64. Breen and McNeill, *John Calvin*, 146.
65. Ibid.
66. Ibid.
67. Ibid., 147.
68. Leith, "Calvin's Theological Method," 112.
69. Ibid., 112–13.

extrapolate rationally the scriptural data."[70] It is widely known that Calvin was the master of logic, as Breen calls his logic "an iron logic."[71] Breen adds, "There is a logic in the *Institutes*. In fact, it is 'full of logic.'"[72] While some attempt to figure out the kind of logic of Calvin, Breen insists that it is not a main concern here, but the real concern is that Calvin uses logic, "full of logic."[73]

Using a "full logic" is not actually the highest regard for Calvin, but using this logic to reconcile Biblicism with rationalism, which is more crucial in his theology. Herman Bauke sees three characteristics in Calvin's theology which would make all the diverse and contradictory interpretation of Calvin possible: rationalism, Biblicism, and *complexion oppositorum*.[74] Yet, the most significant discovery of Bauke is *complexion oppositorum*, which reconciles the other two contradictable motifs, Biblicism and rationalism. John H. Leith states,

> Calvin's theological method is not the deduction of a system from one or two central doctrines. He does not seek to find some *Diagonale* or *Stammlehre* or central doctrine or material principle from which individual dogmatic teachings can be deduced and developed. On the contrary, he seeks to bind existing individual dogmatic teachings, which are even in logical and metaphysical contradiction into a systematic coherence.[75]

It is clear, then, that those who believe in Calvin's rationality and use of reason are many in comparison with those who think that Calvin was not rational to the extent that some think that Calvin is too rational. He is well educated in human sciences, philosophy and anthropology in particular. In his doctoral dissertation published later, "John Calvin's Teaching on Human Reason," Leroy Nixon concludes, "Contrary to the popular opinion, Calvin *overemphasized* the ability of human reason," and he "*underemphasized* the limits of human reason." However, Jung S. Rhee disagrees with this, thinking that Calvin has neither over nor under emphasized human reason, but Calvin distinguishes human reason into different kinds: "reason of flesh" and "reason of the redeemed," "corrupted reason," and "restored reason," or "carnal reason" and "right reason." And as he rejects the former to take the later, Calvin is a perfect rationalist and his theology is a "rational theology."[76]

70. Ibid., 110.
71. Breen, "Calvin and Rhetorical Tradition," 13.
72. Breen and McNeill, *John Calvin*, 13.
73. Ibid.
74. Leith, "Calvin's Theological Method," 106-7.
75. Ibid., 107.
76. Rhee, "John Calvin's Understanding," 57.

Plato, Aristotle, Epicureans, and Stoic
—Calvin and Philosophy

It is commonly known that the influence of Greek philosophy on the Christian theology is more obvious and significant only on Thomas Aquinas[77] and Philip Melanchthon.[78] It is doubtless, however, that John Calvin, as a Christian humanist, highly appreciates classical philosophy. And despite this, he is influenced both directly and indirectly with classical philosophy, giving more attention to studying his direct citations of philosophical insights and providing a clearer view of his relation to this philosophy than the attempt to grasp "common themes" from the large scope of his indirect use of it. Indeed, Calvin does not attempt to synthesize classical philosophy and Christian doctrine; yet, he does give enough attention to certain doctrines of Plato, Aristotle, the Epicureans, and the Stoics. Calvin's relationship with these philosophies is manifested in different ways, as he commends some

---

77. Thomas Aquinas (1225–74) was a Catholic Priest in the Dominican Order and one of the most important medieval philosophers and theologians. He was immensely influenced by scholasticism and Aristotle and known for his synthesis of the two aforementioned traditions. Although he wrote many works of philosophy and theology throughout his life, his most influential work is the *Summa Theologica*, which consists of three parts. The first part is on God. In it, he gives five proofs for God's existence as well as an explication of His attributes. He argues for the actuality and in corporeality of God as the unmoved mover and describes how God moves through His thinking and willing. The second part is on Ethics. Thomas argues for a variation of the Aristotelian Virtue Ethics. However, unlike Aristotle, he argues for a connection between the virtuous man and God by explaining how the virtuous act is one towards the blessedness of the Beatific Vision (*beata visio*). The last part of the *Summa* is on Christ and was unfinished when Thomas died. In it, he shows how Christ not only offers salvation, but represents and protects humanity on Earth and in Heaven. This part also briefly discusses the sacraments and eschatology. The *Summa* remains the most influential of Thomas's works and is mostly what will be discussed in this overview of his philosophy.

78. Philipp Melanchthon (1497–1560), was a German reformer, collaborator with Martin Luther the first systematic theologian of the Protestant Reformation, intellectual leader of the Lutheran Reformation and an influential designer of educational systems. He stands next to Luther and Calvin as a reformer, theologian, and molder of Protestantism. Along with Luther, he is the primary founder of Lutheranism Melanchthon made the distinction between law and gospel the central formula for Lutheran evangelical insight. By the "law," he meant God's requirements both in Old and New Testament; the "gospel" meant the free gift of grace through faith in Jesus Christ. He started from Scholasticism; but with the contempt of an enthusiastic Humanist he turned away from it and came to Wittenberg with the plan of editing the complete works of Aristotle. Under the dominating religious influence of Luther his interest abated for a time, but in 1519 he edited the "Rhetoric" and in 1520 the "Dialectic." The relation of philosophy to theology is characterized, according to him, by the distinction between law and Gospel. The former, as a light of nature, is innate; it also contains the elements of the natural knowledge of God, which, however, have been obscured and weakened by sin.

of their insights, condemns others, and simply ignores others. References to classical philosophy, indeed, occupy an instrumental place in Calvin's theology, but his use of them is made incidentally as he develops his own "Christian philosophy."[79] The *Internet Encyclopedia of Philosophy* beautifully illustrates the issue:

> Given Calvin's occasional antipathy for philosophers, it is all too tempting to dismiss him as someone who knew very little philosophy, striking out at that which he did not know. However, tempting that may be, it simply is untrue. In the *Institutes*, his treatises, and the commentaries, Calvin continually demonstrates a familiarity with both general and specific philosophical knowledge, which seems to have been gained through his own study of their writings. What seems most significant about Calvin's use of philosophy is that in general, he refuses to accept a philosophical system. Instead, he considers philosophy as the history of human wisdom's attempt to search out answers to the questions of human existence. Thus, philosophers and their theories become paradigms for consideration, rather than structures for the organization of thought.[80]

Calvin's use of classical philosophy in forming important theological themes however is elective and unsystematic. While the classical philosophy, for instance, gives a good deal of attention to the principles that govern the universe, as the Epicureans think that the universe is ruled by chance and the Stoics argue that it is governed with the fate, Calvin opposes both positions, insisting that everything is governed by the providence of God. Calvin is also influenced by the Greek philosophers' understanding of God as a supreme being, the distinction between form and matter, the four causes and Aristotle's contribution to a subject-predicate logic and substance-attribute metaphysics.[81]

In his article, "Philosophical and Theological Influences in John Calvin's Thought: Reviewing Some Research Results," B.J. van der Walt points to the necessity of dealing with the question of Calvin's attitude towards classical philosophy and how he employs it. In van der Walt's viewpoint, Calvin neither appreciates nor condemns the classical philosophies, he clearly knows, uses, and transforms them for a deeper understanding of faith. And since he does not regard these philosophies as a source of truth, they do not actually

---

79. Partee, *Calvin and Classical Philosophy*, 27.

80. Internet Encyclopedia of Philosophy, "John Calvin," http://www.iep.utm.edu/calvin.

81. Aristotle, *Aristotle's Metaphysics*, VI, 1026 a 19f.

determine his thought, but contribute to it. Thus Calvin's use of philosophy was elective and unsystematic. In short, the influence of Calvin's knowledge of classical philosophies cannot be denied.[82] Partee concludes,

> Without doubt Calvin's knowledge of classical philosophy influenced his thinking. It would be a mistake, therefore, to dismiss Calvin's references to philosophy as an inconsequential residue of his early humanistic training . . . But it is important recognize that Calvin's use of philosophy is historical rather that systematic. Thus looks to philosophy for illustration of the truth rather than as a guide to it.[83]

In his book, *Calvin's Theology: A Study of Its Sources in Classical Antiquity*, Victor Nuovo came to the same conclusion, as he thinks that Calvin's attitude towards Greek and Roman antiquity can be summarized in both the concepts of rejection and dependence. Calvin's attempt to synthesize the Bible and antiquity, says van der Walt, is illustrated by Nuovo by means of specific themes from Calvin's thought. It is also indicated further that, to a large extent, Calvin's style is derived from antiquity and more specifically from stoic thought,[84]

> Hence, Calvin's effort at using philosophy must be understood as part of his humanism, rather than a tool of the coherence of systematization of his thought. Calvin placed logic in the curriculum of the Genevan Academy. He could illustrate faith with the four-fold causality of Aristotle. He can use the thoughts of the philosophers as aids to training the mind, and believed that not many pastors, and certainly no doctor of the church could be ignorant of philosophy. However, that respect lived in constant tension with his irritation at the efforts of philosophy (and philosophers) at exceeding their proper place.[85]

Calvin and Plato: In his book, *Speculation in Pre-Christian Philosophy*, Richard Kroner states that Plato is often thought to occupy a kind of middle ground between Christianity and pagan antiquity.[86] In *Calvin and Classical Philosophy*, Charles Partee offers a historical view that clearly illustrates the deep influence of Plato's philosophy, not only on some of the Christian

---

82. Van der Walt, "Philosophical and Theological Influences," 13, 75, 91.

83. Ibid., 146.

84. Nuovo, *Calvin's Theology*, 78.

85. Internet Encyclopedia of Philosophy, "John Calvin" http://www.iep.utm.edu/calvin.

86. Kroner, *Speculation in Pre-Christian Philosophy*, 71.

doctrines such as, Trinity, providence of God, opposition of materialism, and in favor of the immortal soul's quest for divine and eternal realm, but also on a punch of significant Christian thinkers, such as Philo, Plotinus, Origen and Augustine. Partee also refers to a quote from Solmsen's *Plato's Theology* saying, "It would be difficult to name a later theological system that is not in some way or order, directly or indirectly indebted to Plato."[87]

Among the Christian thinkers who are greatly influenced with Plato's philosophy is Calvin. Partee clearly states "Calvin views Plato not merely as one of the sounder philosophers, but as the most religious and sober of the philosophers.[88] And though Calvin insists that Plato is not a source of his theology, he admits that Plato knows something about holiness. Although it is not clear whether Calvin's philosophical knowledge is derived from his direct reading of the philosophers or mediated from secondary sources, "Calvin is certainly influenced by the various philosophical currents of his time, especially Platonism and Stoicism."[89] Referring to Boisset, Partee continues his emphasis on the impact of Plato's thoughts on Calvin's theology, "If Augustine is the theologian to whom Calvin refers most of frequently, Plato is the philosopher that most often cited and nearly always with favor."[90] For Partee, "One can say that for Calvin Plato is, as a philosopher, what Augustine is as a theologian."[91]

As Partee continues viewing the significant influence of Platonism on Calvin's different theological doctrines, he emphasizes that despite his method by which he seeks to identify common themes being questionable, Boisset is quite helpful in his identification of these themes of Calvin's Platonism. For him, Platonic influence on Calvin's doctrine of soul is quite firm, as Calvin cites Plato on the immorality of soul; the doctrine of the two worlds; and the contemplation of God. Boisset also claims the Platonic view of the sensible and intelligible realms may be applied to Calvin's doctrine of the visible and invisible church, and that Plato's doctrine of participation may be applied to Calvin's doctrine of the church and sacraments.[92] In his book, *John Calvin, the Church, and the Eucharist*, Kilian McDonell asserts, "Plato's concept of participation is to be seen with even greater clarity in Calvin's doctrine of the sacraments."[93]

87. Solmsen, *Plato's Theology*, 177.
88. Partee, *Calvin and Classical Philosophy*, 110.
89. Ibid., 111.
90. Boisset, *Sagesse et Saintese dans la Pensee de Jean Calvin*, 281.
91. Ibid., 221.
92. Ibid., 112.
93. McDonnell, *John Calvin, the Church*, 33.

Undoubtedly, Calvin is influenced by Plato both directly and through, Cicero, the early fathers, Augustine, and the Christian humanists. It is also evident that Calvin uses certain platonic insights and approves Plat's view of providence. Calvin states,

> We continue to live, so long as [God] sustains us by his power; but no sooner does he withdraw his lifegiving spirit than we die. Even Plato knew this, who so often teaches that, properly speaking, there is but one God, and that all things subsist, or have their being only in him. Nor do I doubt, that it is the will of God, by means of that heathen writer, to awaken all men to the knowledge that they derive their life from another source than themselves.[94]

Calvin and Aristotle: Doubtless, in an indirect way Calvin is influenced by Aristotle's view of God as a Supreme Being by the distinction between form and matter in substance, the four causes, and by Aristotle's contribution to logic, and metaphysics.[95] Despite his belief that theology is the highest branch of contemplation, Aristotle's understanding of God as Unmoved mover was not satisfactory for Calvin. And while Aristotle thinks that the world has a purpose, as he says, "God and nature create nothing that does not fulfill purpose,"[96] he does not believe that it is God's purpose, which is rejected by Calvin. Yet, Calvin, not only considers Aristotle's philosophy, but also appreciates him as a great philosopher. Therefore, while he insists that all philosophers who deny the providence of God are fools, Calvin clearly identifies Aristotle in a category of "the greatest of philosophers:"

> [W]e find that some of the greatest of the philosophers were so mischievous as to devote their talents to obscure and conceal the providence of God, and, entirely overlooking his agency, ascribed all to secondary causes. At the head of these was Aristotle, a man of genius and learning.[97]

In the meantime, while the *Institutes of Christian Relation* reveal that Calvin's use of Aristotle focuses mainly on the direct citation method, still on the basis of these references and others, it appears that Calvin knows Aristotle rather well, identifies him with the greatest philosophers, and uses his philosophy as a reference or as contrast to construct his Christian theology.[98]

---

94. Calvin, *Commentary on Psalms*, 102.
95. Partee, *Calvin and Classical Philosophy*, 97–98.
96. Aristotle, *Aristotle: On the Heavens*, 261 a 33.
97. Aristotle, *Aristotle's Metaphysics*, VI, 1026 a 19f.
98. Partee, *Calvin and Classical Philosophy*, 99.

Aristotelian faculty psychology, however, is the area where the deepest influence of Aristotle philosophy on Calvin's thoughts clearly appears. Following Aristotle's concept of the human soul as unified mind and will in a whole being, Calvin points to the superiority of reason and the inevitable unity of the mind and will in the human soul:

> Scripture is accustomed to divide the soul of man, as to its faculties, into two parts, the mind and the heart (*mentem et cor*). The mind means the intelligence (*intelligentiam*), while the heart denotes all the affections or wills (omnes affectus: aut voluntates). These two terms, therefore, include the entire soul (*totam animam*).[99]

Calvin and the Epicureans:[100] As man's "happiness" is its main concern through a serine and peaceful relation with the nature of things as they are, Epicureanism is called the philosophy of salvation. And though Epicureanism believes in the existence of the gods who live in the empty spaces between the material worlds, it insists that these gods are not entirely concerned with the creation or with human beings. Charles Partee thinks that the entire of Epicureanism is based on the atomism of Democritus that is expressed in Lucretius' comment that, "all nature as it is in itself is made of two things; for there are bodies and there is void, in which these bodies are and through which they move this way and that." According to Democritus, the universe is a purposeless interaction of atoms while Epicurus adds to this theory that the atoms have the capacity to spontaneously deviate from the straight line of fall. According to Epicurus, then, the nature of things is not made by the divine power, i.e., it is without divine cause and, moreover, without design. In living in a perfect happiness, the gods, according the Epicureanism, are never concerned with the mankind. Accordingly, some events happen in the world unpredictably by necessity and chance, which are out of man's control, while some events are within man's control. Man, then, is entirely alone in this world and all what this man can do is to seek happiness through doing the best to avoid pain. This pleasure

---

99. Calvin, *Commentary on Philippians*, 4:7.

100. According *Encyclopedia Britannica*, Epicureanism, in a strict sense, the philosophy taught by Epicurus (341-270 BCE). In a broad sense, it is a system of ethics embracing every conception or from of life that can be traced to the principles of his philosophy. In ancient polemics, as often since, the term was employed with an even more generic (and clearly erroneous) meaning as the equivalent of hedonism, the doctrine that pleasure or happiness is the chief good. In popular parlance, Epicureanism thus means devotion to pleasure, comfort, and high living, with a certain nicety of style. http://www.britannica.com/EBchecked/topic/189732/Epicureanism.

of avoiding pain is actually impossible unless this man uses the reason to hold pleasures against pain.[101]

Having deep understanding of the Epicurean philosophy, Calvin could object more strenuously to these views of God, creation, and providence. Determinedly, Calvin opposes and refutes the notion that God exists alone in the heaven apart from the creation. He says, "What good is it to profess with the Epicureans some sort of God who has cast aside the care of the world only to amuse himself in idleness? What help is it, in short, to know a God with who we have nothing to do?"[102] Further, Calvin continues his account against the Epicureans, "I say nothing of the Epicureans (a pestilence that has always filled the world) who imagine that God is idle and indolent . . . "[103] Then, he takes our attention to the logical fact that if there is a God, and this God is the one that has created the universe, it is quite logical that this God is the same one that preserves the works that he has made. Calvin says,

> Nobody seriously believes that the universe was made by God without being persuaded that he takes care of his works.[104] . . . The world was not created by God once, in such a way that afterwards he abandoned his works, but that it endures by his power, and that the same One who was once its creator is its perpetual ruler.[105] . . . Moreover, to make God a momentary Creator who once for all finished his work would be cold and barren, and we must differ from profane men, especially in that we see the presence of divine power as much in the continuing state of the universe as in its inception.[106]

Unlike the Epicureans, nature, for Calvin, is not neutral as it is the arena of God's activity toward man, "God himself has shown by the order of creation that he created all things for man's sake."[107] It does not seem that Calvin uses the principles of the Epicurean philosophy as a resource of his Christian theology. Yet, it is clear that he both knows it widely and knows how to argue against it. He writes,

---

101. Partee, *Calvin and Classical Philosophy*, 99–100.
102. Calvin, *Institutes*, (1559), I.ii.11.
103. Ibid., I.16.4.
104. Ibid., I.16.1.
105. Calvin, *Commentary Upon Acts*, 33.
106. Calvin, *Institutes*, I.16.1.
107. Ibid., I.14.22.

[The Epicurean] philosophy was to think that the sun is two feet wide, that the world was constructed out of atoms, and by trifling like that, to destroy the wonderful craftsmanship, which is seen in the fabric of the world. If they were refuted a hundred times, they had no more sense than dogs. Although, briefly, they admitted that there were gods, yet they imagined them to be idle in heaven and to be applying to magnificence of living, and that their blessing consisted in idleness alone. As they used to deny that the world was divinely created, as I have just said, so they supposed human affairs are turned by chance, and are not governed by the providence of heaven. To them the greatest good was pleasure, not obscene and unbridled pleasure indeed, but yet such as by its attractions more and more ruined men already naturally inclined to the indulgence of the flesh.[108]

It is clear, then, that Calvin is not against philosophy as a way of thinking, nor does he condemn its use even though he strongly stands against some philosophical thoughts, such as the Epicureans. But rather, he himself is, not only well educated in philosophy, but also has a well-trained philosophical mind, which enables him to argue back and creates his great doctrine of God's providence out of the Epicurean attack against the Christian faith.

Calvin and the Stoics:[109] As a whole, Stoic philosophy is a strict philosophical quest for salvation. For them, the final goal of life is a variety; God, Nature, Providence, Fate, or Necessity. While God is identified with nature, they also maintain that God knows, governs, loves mankind, and desires the human welfare. And, while they are concerned with the theoretical reason, which focuses on the nature of things, which should be in unity, governed with fate and necessity, and ruled with reason, the primary Stoic emphasis

---

108. Calvin, *Commentaries on Acts*, 17:28.

109. According to the *Internet Encyclopedia of Philosophy*, the term "Stoicism" derives from the Greek word "stoa," referring to a colonnade, such as those built outside or inside temples, around dwelling-houses, gymnasia, and market-places. They were also set up separately as ornaments of the streets and open places. The simplest form is that of a roofed colonnade, with a wall on one side, which was often decorated with paintings. Thus in the market-place at Athens the stoa poikile (Painted Colonnade) was decorated with Polygnotus's representations of the destruction of Troy, the fight of the Athenians with the Amazons, and the battles of Marathon and Oenoe. Zeno of Citium taught in the stoa poikile in Athens, and his adherents accordingly obtained the name of Stoics. Zeno was followed by Cleanthes, and then by Chrysippus, as leaders of the school. The school attracted many adherents, and flourished for centuries, not only in Greece, but also later in Rome, where the most thoughtful writers, such as Marcus Aurelius, Seneca, and Epictetus, counted themselves among its followers. See http://www.iep.utm.edu/stoicism.

is on practical reason, which is concerned with virtue for the sake of virtue itself and fulfilling the requirements of duty. And despite living accordingly nature is one of the main beliefs for the Stoics; they think that the world adopts the role of apathy, which means that the wise man should not be diverted from following the course of wisdom and truth.[110]

The Stoic doctrine, however, is divided into three parts: logic, physics, and ethics. In terms of the *logic* part, in addition to the logic of Aristotle, the Stoics add their theory of the origin of knowledge and the criterion of truth. They believe that all knowledge enters the mind, which is a blank state, through the senses, which clearly stands against Plato's idealism. According to this belief, truth is simply what corresponds to our impressions, to things while the criterion of this truth lies in sensation itself. Real things, the Stoics say, produce an intense feeling, or conviction, of their reality inside us. According to this perspective, there is no universal criterion of truth; it is based not on reason, but on feeling.[111] In terms of *physics*, the Stoics believe that "nothing incorporeal exists." If Plato places knowledge both in thought and reality, the Stoics place knowledge both in physical sensation and reality. In short, for them, what is known by the senses—is matter. Everything, they say, even the soul, even God himself, are material and nothing more than material. In the Stoics' perspective, there are two reasons for their conviction. First is their conviction of the unity of the world. Second is the conviction that soul and body, and God and world, are pairs that act and react upon one another, which is impossible to happen if both were not of the same substance. In terms of the Stoic *ethics*, their teaching is based upon two principles. First is that the universe is governed by absolute law, which admits of no exceptions. Second is that the essential nature of human is reason. These two principles, indeed, are summed in the famous Stoic maxim, "Live according to nature." In some sense, this actually means that the universe is governed, not only by the law, but also by the law of reason.[112]

Of all the classical philosophers, says Partee, the Stoics have the most developed consciousness of providence. As Edwyn Bevan states, "It was for faith in providence above all else that the Stoic stood in the ancient world."[113] Partee confirms that the Stoic doctrine of providence has a significant influence on the Christian doctrine since Paul to the reformers, "It is not surprising, then, that Calvin agrees with certain Stoic doctrines, such as the existence and sovereignty of God, their praise of nature, and their

---

110. Partee, *Calvin and Classical Philosophy*, 116.
111. http://www.iep.utm.edu/stoicism.
112. Ibid.
113. Bevan, *Stoics and Skeptics*, 44.

view of man's rational and social nature."[114] Partee also emphasizes that all of Calvin's teachings on the providence of God resemble the Stoic doctrine.[115] Not only parsing Stoicism that revels Calvin's clear awareness of this philosophy, but also criticizing its doctrine of fate,

> Those who wish to cast odium upon this doctrine defame it as the stoics' dogma of fate . . . We do not, with the Stoics, contrive a necessity out of a perpetual connection and intimately related series of causes, which is contained in nature; but we make God the ruler and governor of all things.[116]

Calvin believes that his view is sufficiently different from the Stoic view of fate by the fact that man interacts directly with God as revealed in Jesus Christ and not with God as a causative principle. However, despite Calvin's insistence that Stoics' fate and his predestination are not the same, as he believed that fate is a term that the Stoics gave to their doctrine of necessity while predestination is God's free counsel, by which he governs all things by his incomprehensible wisdom and justice, I think that the idea of fate has a clear influence on Calvin's understanding and conviction of predestination.

Philosophy itself, indeed, is not my intention of presenting this section, but rather the active and intimate relationship of Calvin with philosophy. It is might be easier to go with the common belief and say that Calvin uses philosophy as a framework of his theology. Yet, my conviction is that Calvin was a son of his contextual time and place, including language, science, philosophy, and everything. Having a significant critical mind and analytic skills, Calvin humbly made himself an active partner in the real life around him, selecting everything that would help make his Christian mission more understandable and more effective for all people in his age, Christian and non-Christian. Philosophy, then, is not only a way of thinking for Calvin, nor is it a frame work of his theology, but also a source of knowledge that helped him to construct his truth about God and reality in the clearest way he could.

Human as a Rational Being—Calvin and Anthropology

Deeply influenced with the Aristotelian "faculty psychology," Calvin embodies Aristotle's understanding that human soul (*anima*) could be

---

114. Partee, *Calvin and Classical Philosophy*, 120.

115. Ibid.

116. Calvin, *Institutes*, I.16.8. In his commentary on the 2 Thess 1:5, Calvin also writes, "Opposing to blasphemers, we leave control to God."

distinguished into the faculties or parts (*partes*) of intellect (*intellectus*) and will (*voluntas*) and could be viewed as the seat of the affection of the will.[117] Describing this, Calvin states that the "whole person" (*totus homo*) was fallen and that sin affected both parts of the soul, intellect and will.[118] In his initial statement of the 1539 *Institutes*, Calvin's emphasis on the problem of sin clearly illustrates his influence with Aristotle's belief of man as a rational being:

> The human soul consists of two faculties . . . Intellect and will. Let the office, moreover, of the intellect be to distinguish between objects, as each seems worthy of approval or disapproval; while that of the will, to choose and follow what the intellect pronounces good: but to reject and flee what it disapproves . . . Let it be enough for us, that the intellect is as it were the leader and governor of the soul. The will depends on its command (*nutum*) and in its own desires awaits its [i.e., the intellect's] judgment.[119]

Referring to Aristotle, Calvin continues his discussion by noting; "the mind has no motion in itself, but it moved by choice," which he calls the *intellectus appetitivus*, the appetitive intellect. Muller thinks that, Calvin does believe that there is no "power of soul" beyond intellect and will; that the inclination toward concupiscence or desire comes from sense and the inclination toward good from the intellect; and that when the will follows the intellect it will be regarded as the "affection of the intellect."[120] This is why Calvin adds a line of definition to the 1559 *Institutes* indicating that the faculties are located in the "mind and heart."[121] For this, reason has an aspect of social order, as "some seed of political order has been implanted in all men," which clearly proves that "no man is to be found who does not understand that every sort of human organization must be regulated by laws, and who does not comprehend the principles of these laws."[122] Reason enables man "To perceive more clearly how far the mind can proceed in any mater according the degree of its ability."[123]

---

117. Calvin, *Institutes* (1959), I.xv.7; II.ii.2; cf. Calvin's commentaries on 1Thess. 5:23.

118. Calvin, *Institutes* (1959), II.i.8-9; iii. 1; and cf. the commentary on Psalm 119:37.

119. Calvin, *Institutes* (1539), II, fol. 23

120. Muller, *Unaccommodated Calvin*, 165.

121. Calvin, *Institutes*, (1559), II.ii.2.

122. Ibid.

123. Ibid.

Describing the nature of the human as a rational being in Calvin's perspective, Leroy Nixon focuses on the abilities of reason to guide human conduct for it is competent to study, understand, make progress of all life aspects.[124] Nixon quotes Calvin,

> Since man is by nature a social animal, he is disposed, from natural instinct, to cherish and preserve society; and accordingly, we see that the minds of all men have impressions of civil order and honesty. Hence it is that every individual understands how human societies must be regulated by laws, and also is able to comprehend the principles of these laws. Hence the universal agreement in regarded to such subjects, both among nations and individuals, the seed of them being implanted in the breast of all without a teacher or lawgiver. The truth of this fact is not affected by wars and dissensions.[125]

In his distinction between the kingdom of God and the kingdom of the world, Calvin set forth a distinction between "things below" or "earthly things" and "things above" or "heavenly things."[126] Calvin points to the ability of human reason "before sin" to understand both heavenly and earthily things and, despite reason becoming unable to understand "heavenly things" "after sin," it still continues to have the ability to understand the "earthily things," He says,

> Hence, with good reason we are compelled to confess that its beginning is inborn in human nature. Therefore, this evidence clearly testifies to a universal apprehension of reason and understanding by nature implanted in men. Yet so universal is this good that every man ought to recognize for himself in it the peculiar grace of God. The creator of nature himself abundantly arouses this gratitude in us when he creates imbeciles. Through them he shows the endowments that the human soul would enjoy unpervaded by his light, a light so natural to all that it is certainty a free gift of his beneficence to each![127]

Following Augustine as his theological reference, Calvin makes another distinction between the supernatural and natural gifts of the human being.[128] While "faith, love of God, charity toward neighbor, and zeal for

---

124. Nixon, *John Calvin's Teachings*, 53.
125. Ibid., III.314.
126. Ibid., II.ii.13.
127. Ibid., II.ii.14.
128. Ibid., II.ii.12.

holiness and righteousness,"[129] are among the former, "soundness of mind and uprightness of heart"[130] are among the later. "Therefore, since reason, by which man discerns between good and evil, and by which he understands and judges, is a natural gift, it could not be entirely destroyed; but being partly weakened and partly corrupted, a shapeless ruin is all that remains"[131] However, it is important "that in the perverted and degenerate nature of man there are still some sparks which show that he is a rational animal, and differs from the brutes, inasmuch as he is endued with intelligence."[132] Calvin summarizes, "We see all mankind that reason is proper to our nature; it distinguishes us from brute beasts." It is, indeed, "the general grace of God," even after man's fall, "some traces of the image of God, which distinguish the entire human race from the other creatures."[133]

In short, Calvin's deep conviction that a human is a soul-oriented being, while a soul is reason-oriented is quite certain. And while "Soul consists of two faculties, understanding and will," the activity of this soul is decided in the interaction of these two faculties. And while he understands that "spirit" is a synonym of "soul," he believes that it is immortal but created essence, in which our intelligence lies, for understanding surely goes beyond the sense of body, and with our intelligence we receive the invisible God and the angels.[134] While Calvin believes that soul is "divinity in man,"[135] or "the divine nature within us,"[136] or the proper seat of "*imago Dei*,"[137] he almost identifies soul with reason, "Hence more anyone endeavors to approach to God, the more he proves himself endowed with reason."[138] Calvin regards understanding as "the leader and governor of the soul,"[139] even when he changes the term "reason as guide" or "the guidance of the reason," he uses the terms "understanding" and "reason" interchangeably. Calvin makes a clear statement about humans as rational beings in definition,

> For we see implanted in human nature some sort of desire to search out the truth to which man would not at all aspire if he

---

129. Ibid.
130. Ibid.
131. Ibid.
132. Ibid.
133. Ibid., II.ii.17.
134. Ibid.
135. Calvin, *Institutes*, I.v.5.
136. Ibid., I.v.6.
137. Ibid., I.xv.3.
138. Ibid.
139. Ibid., I.xv.7.

had not already savored it. Human understanding then possesses some power of perception, since it is by nature capitated by love of truth.[140]

In short, Calvin says, "nor does reason or intelligence belong to the body merely because man is called a 'rational animal.'"[141]

Human Reason and Knowing God
—Calvin and Pure Reason

The fact that some mystical superstition about the original ability of human reason is prevalent among Christians and theologians cannot be denied. For instance, the *natural limitation* of human reason at creation tends to be confused with the *corrupted limitation* because of the sinful fall. Yet, Calvin is clear in this regard without confusing the original ability of the human reason that was given to man by God in creation. For Calvin, God is God, and man is but a man despite the limitation of the human being in quality and quantity, and despite our immortal soul not being totally free from the limitation of the flesh. Man was created in the image of God, which makes it possible to personally communicate one's feeling, reason, and will with God.

For Calvin, although "his (God's) essence is incomprehensible; hence, his divineness far escapes all human perception,"[142] the limited human soul is still immortal and transcendental, and the pure reason is given to the human being in order to contemplate the divine "Truth." Though man is not enabled to know God directly, God, in his grace, gives another way to know him, for "upon his individual works he has engraved unmistakable marks of his glory, so clear and so prominent that even unlettered and stupid folks cannot plead the excuse of ignorance."[143] The most vast and beautiful system and skillful ordering of the universe is for us "a sort of mirror in which we can contemplate God."[144]

Contemplating God's glory in the creation would not actually be possible without the awareness of divinity that is naturally implanted within the human mind, he says,

---

140. Ibid., II.ii.12.
141. Ibid.
142. Ibid., I.v.1.
143. Ibid.
144. Ibid.

> There is within the human mind, and indeed by natural instinct, an awareness of divinity. This we take to be beyond controversy. To prevent anyone from taking refuge in the pretense of ignorance, God himself has implanted in all men a certain understanding of his divine majesty. Ever renewing its memory, he repeatedly sheds fresh drops.[145]

Therefore, the connection of human reason and the seed of religion is quite significant in Calvin's theology. The fact that God has created the human as a rational being as God's providence drives us to contemplate God clearly reveals the fact that reason and religion are inseparably united. "This of necessity happens to all men."[146] For Calvin, whether they are willing or not, all men are compelled to know that they are the "sign of divinity," and all the "seed of divinity" is a basic foundation of the human nature.[147] It is by natural instinct that this "awareness of divinity" existing within the mind of every man. It is a real gift from grace that

> To prevent anyone from taking refuge in the pretense of ignorance, God himself has implanted in all men a certain understanding of his divine majesty . . . Therefore, since from the beginning of the world there has been no region, no city, in short, no household, that could do without religion, there lies in this a tactic confession of a sense of deity instructed in the hearts of all.[148]

For Calvin, "no man is without the light of reason;"[149] religion is essential in human reason and reason and religion are the marks of "*imago Dei*." If reason enables man to fully understand and organize all aspect of life on the earth according to the will of the divine, the "seed of religion" identifies man from brutes and savages and leads man to worship God, for "it is worship of God alone that renders men higher than the brutes, and through it alone they aspire to immortality."[150] For Calvin, this is the "original ability that was given to man to contemplate and discern the truth and reach the right knowledge of man self and God," so that he has faith in God.

> Yet God would not have us forget our original ability, which he had bestowed upon our father Adam, and which ought truly to

---

145. Nixon, *John Calvin's Teachings*, 53.
146. Ibid., I.v.11.
147. Ibid., I.vi.1.
148. Ibid., I.iii.1.
149. Ibid., II.ii.13.
150. Ibid., I.iii.3.

> arouse in us a zeal for righteousness and goodness. For we cannot think upon either our first condition or to what purpose we were formed without being prompted to mediate upon immortality, and to yearn after kingdom of God. That recognition, however, far from encouraging pride in us, discourages us and cast us into humanity.[151]

Therefore, Calvin calls all men to seriously and faithfully search for the knowledge of God the Creator through contemplating God's works in creation,

> There is no doubt that the Lord would have us uninterruptedly occupied in this holy meditation; that, while we contemplate in all creatures, as in mirrors, those immense riches of his wisdom, justice, goodness, and power, we should not merely run over them cursorily, and, so to speak, with a fleeting glance; but we should ponder them at length, turn them over in our minds seriously and faithfully, and recollect them repeatedly.[152]

Nixon and Belford emphasize that Calvin is quite confident in the ability of reason to deduce the attributes of God through contemplating God's works in the universe. So, Calvin enthusiastically encourages all sciences, which obtain knowledge through "the closer observation of which astronomy, medicine, and all natural sciences are intended."[153] In the *Reformer for the 21st Century*, William Stacy Johnson emphasizes that according to scripture, Calvin believes that human beings are created in the image of God (Gen 1:26–28).[154] While this image separates human beings from the rest of creation, the divine image consists of natural God-given capacities, such as reason and freedom, and spiritual capacities, such as worshiping and honoring God. Being in this image ultimately means that human beings are called to reflect God's goodness on the earth. While this indeed, cannot happen except through faith, pure human reason was designed for a significant role to play in having this faith. According to Johnson, Calvin believes that Adam and Eve were living in a state of "original righteousness" before they sinned, for God created the first human with *a pure reason* in order to discern the ultimate truth and choose God, while the purpose of the first command was to test the willingness of this man to choose and obey God.

---

151. Ibid., II.1.3.
152. Ibid., I.xiv.21.
153. Johnson, *John Calvin*, 63.
154. Ibid., 63.

Indeed, Calvin's interest in "the study of humanities" is one of the important factors that shape his understanding of the great value of man as a rational being who is able to know God through the gift of pure reason. As he agrees with some philosophers that man is a "microcosm," Calvin thinks that man can comprehend God by studying the wide cosmos as well as concentrating on man, who is, not only the bearer of "*imago Dei*," but is also like a microcosm in his nature. Therefore, studies of human mind, reason, conscience, sense, behavior, history, relationship, and even language, is a significant way of discerning and understanding God through studying liberal arts education and developments.[155]

Therefore, in a chapter titled "Participation in God's Ways," of the same book, Johnson argues that Calvin considers faith to be the primary vehicle through which man receives God's blessings. Yet, Johnson continues, "Faith is ultimately a firm and certain knowledge of God's benevolence toward us, founded upon the truth of the freely given promise in Christ, both revealed to our minds and sealed upon our hearts by the Holy Spirit."[156] Faith, for Calvin, is a form of knowledge—not an abstract, but an experiential knowing, i.e., it is an intimate and familiar knowledge. It is not a form of "blind faith," nor is content that merely to accept the beliefs of others without question, but rather seeks true understanding while it trusts its own direct knowledge of God.[157]

For Richard A. Muller, nearly all of the studies of Calvin's concept of faith have declared that Calvin could not conceive faith apart from knowledge.[158] While scholars, such as Schutzeichel, emphasized the association of faith "*fides*" with knowledge "*cognitio*," Muller demonstrates knowledge as essentially a synonym for faith in Calvin's thought and argues that the concept of "certainty" is the center of Calvin's teaching. In his work, *Calvin and English Calvinism to 1649*, R. T. Kendall draws on the cognitive aspect of Calvin's theology saying, "where Calvin was intellectualist in his doctrine of faith, his successors voluntarist and experiential."[159] Calvin's intellectualism means, not only giving a priority to intellect, but an emphasis on intellect to the virtual exclusion of the will in matters of faith. In this emphasis, Kendall points to some key words that Calvin uses such as, "science," "recognition," "illumination," and "knowledge" (*scientia, agnitio,*

---

155. Rhee, "John Calvin's Understanding."
156. Ibid.
157. Johnson, *John Calvin*, 63.
158. Miller, *Unaccommodated Calvin*, 159.
159. Kendall, *Calvin and English Calvinism*, 12.

illuminatio, and *cognitio*) in passage that explain faith and declare that reason is highly appreciated as God's gift to man.[160]

In his book *The Knowledge of God in Calvin's Theology,* Edward A. Dowey, Jr. makes a short and clear statement that "Calvin's thought has its whole existence within the realm of God as revealer and man as knower."[161] Because of this, Dowey says, "One of the most common rebukes leveled against Calvin is that he over-intellectualized the Christian faith."[162] The meaning of the word "knowledge" for Calvin is fundamentally important, as he begins his two volumes of the Institutes with the statement, "without knowledge of self—there is no knowledge of God."[163] Calvin, indeed, believes that "the knowledge of God and that of ourselves are connected" and "joined by many bonds . . . which one proceeds and brings forth the other is not easy to discern."[164] Calvin is persuaded that the "true and sound wisdom" for man is to use human intellectuality to discern God, for "in the first place, no one can look upon himself without immediately turning his thoughts to the contemplation of God, in whom he "lives and moves."[165] Calvin's trust that the ability of human reason was not entirely destroyed by sin but corrupted reflects the possibility of using human rationality for a deeper understanding of faith. Looking carefully to Calvin's theology of human reason, and the link of faith and rationality, makes it clear that "intelligent faith" is the faith that Calvin deeply believes in.

Human Reason's Disability of Knowing God —Calvin and Sinful Reason

While God created the first human with pure reason in order to discern the ultimate truth and choose God, Calvin argues, the first man failed to choose God and fell in rebellion, pride and disobedience. Therefore, the state of the "original righteousness" utterly lost and converted to a "state of corruption," and the "original righteousness" is replaced with the "original sin."[166] Calvin calls this "total depravity." For him, "total" means that sin affects the whole person, heart, mind, body, and soul, i.e., the effect of sin is total in its extent,

160. Ibid.
161. Dowey, *Knowledge of God*, 3.
162. Ibid.
163. Johnson, *John Calvin*, 3.
164. Calvin, *Institutes*, I.1.1.
165. Ibid.
166. Johnson, *John Calvin*, 63.

as the whole human life is infected with sin; but not in its degree, as we have not turned to be without any degree of goodness.

> Here, I want to suggest briefly that the whole man is overwhelmed—as by a deluge—from head to foot, so that no part is immune from sin and all that proceeds from him is to be imputed to sin. As Paul says, all turnings of the thoughts to the flesh are enmities against God.[167]

Consequentially, after describing mankind as rational beings where there is no man without the light of reason and intelligence, Calvin immediately follows, "yet, that this light is so smothered by clouds of darkness that it cannot shine forth."[168] In Calvin's words,

> He shows that man's soul is so illuminated by the spark of God's light as never to be without some light flame or at least a spark of it; but that even with this illumination it does not comprehend God. Why is this? Because man's keenness of mind is mere blindness as far as the knowledge of God is concerned. For when the spirit calls men "darkness," he at once denies them any ability of spiritual understanding.[169]

Sin, he argues, has made a barrier to the free choice of truth. And even though this barrier has not totally destroyed the ability of human reason to mediate, think, and analyze, it has disabled reason to get the right path towards the divine truth and instead of taking human heart to humility, it takes the whole man to the wrong image about self and God, which leads to pride,

> For what is that origin? It is that from which we have fallen. What is that end of our creation? It is that from which we have been completely estranged, so that sick of our miserable lot we groan, and in growing we sigh for that lost worthiness. But when we say that man ought to see nothing in himself to cause elation, we mean that he has nothing to rely on to make himself proud.[170]

---

167. Ibid., II.1.9.
168. Ibid., II.ii.12.
169. Ibid., II.ii.19.
170. Ibid., II.1.3.

Therefore, says Calvin, humility is the urgent need for man, "So, if you ask me concerning the precepts of the Christian religion, first, second, third, and always, I would answer, "Humility."[171]

However, in contrary to those who think that Calvin just condemns human mind and reason, Richard A. Muller thinks that Calvin's real attempt is to balance mind and heart, which is so characteristic of the 1539 stream of the *Institutes*. For Calvin, while the Word ought to be "amply sufficient to engender faith," human mind in its perversity "is always blind to the light of God's truth." Likewise, Calvin sees philosophers who possess great mind and reason as great thinkers in everything rather than as receivers of the divine "truth." To the divine truth, not only their minds turn to be blind, but also their reason turns to be foolish because of sin. Calvin clearly states, "How volubly has the whole tribe of philosophers shown their stupidity and silliness! For even though we may excuse the others (who act like utter fools), Plato, the most religious of all and the most circumspect, also vanishes in his round globe."[172] Even the wisest philosophers and those who have attained the intellectual first rank, says Calvin, with their normal minds and reason cannot be compared to the "sacred reading," which has within itself the power to move the very heart of the reader.[173] In his words,

> When we so condemn human understanding for its perpetual blindness as to leave it no perception of any object whatever, we not only go against God's word, but also run counter to the experience of common sense... Indeed, man's mind, because of its dullness, cannot hold to the right path, but wonders through various errors and stumbles repeatedly, as if it were groping in darkness, until it strays away and finally disappears. Thus it betrays how incapable it is of seeking and finding truth.[174]... Paul, however, having expressly entered this discussion, speaks more clearly than all [1 Cor 1:18]. 'After condemning the stupidity and vanity of all human wisdom and utterly reducing it to nothing [cf. 1 Cor 1:13], he concludes: "The natural man cannot receive the things of the Spirit of God, for they are folly to him, and he is not able to understanding them because they are spiritually discerned" [1 Cor 2: 14].[175]

---

171. Ibid., II.ii.11.
172. Ibid., I.v.11.
173. Ibid., I. viii.1.
174. Ibid., II.ii.12.
175. Ibid., II.i.20.

Therefore, "If we want to measure our reason by God's law, the pattern of perfect righteousness, we shall find in how many respects it is blind! Surely it does not at all comply with the principal points of the first table."[176] Our sinful reason, indeed, will not be able to guide us in God's path, but rather in deceptions and illusions. "For we know all too well by experience how often we fall despite our good intention. Our reason is overwhelmed by so many forms of deceptions, is subject to so many difficulties, that it is far from directing us a right."[177] Moreover, Calvin states, "All ecclesiastical writers have recognized both that the soundness of reason in man is gravely wounded through sin, and that the will has been very much enslaved by evil desires."[178] And "Despite this, many of them have come far too close to the philosophers" and "strove to harmonize the doctrine of Scripture halfway with the beliefs of the philosophers,"[179] since they think that "man was commonly thought to be corrupted only in his sensual part and to have a perfectly unblemished reason and a will also largely unimpaired,"

> Thus it is pointless and foolish to restrict the corruption that arises thence only to what are called the impulses of the senses; or to call it the "kindling wood" that attracts, arouses, and drags into sin only that part which they term "sensuality." . . . Paul removes all doubt when he teaches that corruption subsists not in one part only, but that none of the soul remains pure or untouched by that mortal disease. For in his discussion of a corrupt nature Paul not only condemns the inordinate impulses of the appetites that are seen, but especially contends the mind is given to blindness and the heart to depravity.[180]

The point that Calvin rightly raises here is not an attempt to deny the gift of reason that was given to human beings by our gracious God, nor deny its natural ability to discern and know; but rather, to clearly point to the new reality that human sin was brought to human life and to the fact that human reason is not on the same page of God's spiritual reality because of its new sinful nature. Calvin says, "We are so vitiated and perverted in every part of our nature that by this great corruption we stand justly condemned and convicted before God, to whom nothing is acceptable but righteousness, innocence, and purity."[181] In *John Calvin, Reformer for the 21st Century*,

---

176. Ibid., II.i.24.
177. Ibid., II.i.25.
178. II.ii.4.
179. Ibid.
180. Ibid., II.i.9.
181. Ibid., II.e.8.

Johnson says that Calvin is persuaded that the first man failed to choose God and fall in rebellion, pride and disobedience. Pure reason, which was able to discern "truth," has become corrupted and unable to find the truth despite it is able to make truth about natural things.[182]

For Calvin, however, the disability of human reason is manifested in five aspects: simplicity, diversity, privacy, independency, and immorality. First, after sin, reason lost its ability to dig deeper in the divine matters, became limited to understand only the simple, and became a slave of logic. While the divine truth, Calvin argues, is complex, interrelated, and sometimes paradoxical, the corrupted reason cannot comprehend the truth beyond simple logic. Calvin is aware that sinful reason "forbids us to transfer the peculiar qualities of the one to the other"[183] and cannot subscribe what logic could not comprehend, accordingly, it rejects any paradox or mystery. Second, sinful reason is unable to achieve the unity of conclusion. Dichotomy, says Calvin, is an ample proof that reason cannot be a sole guide of the human life after it was corrupted. Not only "the rude and untutored crowd", but also "among the philosophers who have tried with reason and learning to penetrate into heaven, how shameful is the diversity!"[184] It is a clear fact that "men were taught only by nature, they would hold to nothing certain or solid or clear cut," and "this very confused diversity."[185] Calvin is deeply convinced "that motion of reason has been perverted, so that now reason is at variance with itself."[186] In short, there is "nothing firm" in man's reasoning.[187]

The third aspect that manifests the corruption of reason for Calvin is the selfishness and misuse of it for one's own justification. As it is clearly seen in Rom 1:21, all mortals "became vain in their reasonings" for all people reason according to their own authority, judgment, tradition or "their own way."[188] Indeed, Calvin intelligently comes to the fact that "the intellect is very rarely deceived in general definition or in the essence of the thing; but that it is illusory when it goes farther, that is, applies the principle to particular cases."[189] For instance,

---

182. Johnson, *John Calvin*, 63.
183. Calvin, *Institutes*, III.xi.6.
184. Ibid., I.v.12.
185. Ibid.
186. Ibid., II.,ii.12.
187. Ibid., I.xv.6.
188. Ibid., I.v.13-14.
189. Ibid., II.ii.23.

> Every man will affirm that murder is evil. But he who is plotting the death of an enemy contemplates murder as something good. The adulterer will condemn adultery in general, but will privately flatter himself in his own adultery . . . when he comes to a particular case, he forgets the general principle" and try to reasonably justify his own case.[190]

Fourth, as sin in its very nature is pride, the corrupted human reason does not depend on God, but rather judges God. Going against God's will, corrupted reason proclaims its independence from piety, religion or worship of God. "For they . . . wish nothing to be lawful for God beyond what their own reason prescribes for themselves,"[191] which they think more objective and dependable.[192] Fifth, corrupted reason, indeed, is unable to comprehend "love" as its major principle, developing, instead, some ethics that are conformable to the flesh. As Paul confirms in Rom 2: 14–15, "There is nothing more common than for a man to be sufficiently instructed in a right standard of conduct by natural law."[193]

Building on Calvin, Barth believes that human beings cannot have a right image of the divine because of two reasons, the first is human limitation and the second is human sin. In *Epistle to the Romans*, Barth frankly explains that our knowledge about God is not true knowledge. Sin destructed our ability to know God rightly. In other words, sin stands there between us and God, serves as a barrier that hinders us to see and encounter the true God: "We know that God is the one whom we do not know and this not-knowing is the problem and the origin of our knowing . . . What are God's works in their absolute riddleness other than questions without an answer."[194] Sin of man, Barth argues, will push him to reduce God to a *human notion* that serves man's personal needs, even if we desire to cooperate with God in noble actions, we turn God into a mere notion, a projection of our own needs.[195]

Like Calvin, sin, for Niebuhr, in its basic form is pride. Man was created to be in relationship with God, where this relation makes his humanity. God intended man to make God the true center of his life. In the contrary, man abused freedom because of his anxiety and wanted to establish the self as a center of his life, because of his lack of trust in God and lack of security.

---

190. Ibid.
191. Ibid., I.xvii.2.
192. Ibid., III.xxii.1.
193. Ibid., II.ii.22.
194. Ibid., 35.
195. Ibid.

Sin, for Niebuhr, then, is the claim of self-sufficiency and of no need for the divine. Replacing God with self is the breaking of the first command, to love God, while its consequence is the breaking of second, to love neighbor. This form of the sin as the pride against God is manifested in many forms, the pride of power, moral pride, and the pride of knowledge. In this, man attempts to be more than what he is. While man realizes that both mind and knowledge are finite, he always tries to deny the finiteness of mind and make knowledge infinite and ultimate.[196]

Corruption of mind and reason as well as the entire human being by sin, indeed, is clear and evident. So that Calvin wonders, "what could men's mind produce but all carnal and fatuous things?"[197] And he answers, we are "deprived of all credit for our wisdom and virtue,"[198] not only will and sensuality but also reason and understanding. The fact is that we have fallen from our original condition where we have been endowed with reason and understanding.[199] Then, Calvin concludes, "Human reason, therefore, neither approaches, nor strives toward, nor even takes a straight aim at, this truth: to understand who the true God is or what sort of God he wishes to be toward us."[200] For sin has brought man into a new reality as "we lack the natural ability to mount up unto the pure and clear knowledge of God."[201] So that, Calvin believes, man *ought* to proceed from knowledge of a god to knowledge of God, but cannot because of the noetic effects of sin. In short, after sin, Calvin insists, human reason, "which we count the most precious gift of all," has become radically named "empty reason."[202]

Restoring Human Reason Ability of Knowing God —Calvin and Redeemed Reason

Calvin believes that the natural limitation of human being to discern the divine truth before sin was balanced by the natural pure reason, which was able to contemplate God's knowledge. Yet, after human sin, a new reality was established, as contemplating God's knowledge has become beyond the ability of the corrupted human mind. Now, the incomprehensibility of God has become not possible, not only because of the ontological limitation of

196. Niebuhr, *The Nature and Destiny of Man*, 46.
197. Calvin, *Institutes*, IV.x.24.
198. Ibid., II.ii.1.
199. Ibid.
200. Ibid., II.ii.18.
201. Ibid., I.v.15.
202. Ibid., II.ii.25.

human being but also because of the human sin, which has deviated human reason from the divine truth. Therefore, Calvin is deeply convinced that until human being is transformed to conform the eternity, human reason cannot comprehend God face to face.[203]

For Calvin, however, it is entirely impossible for this transformation to take place without the power of the Holy Spirit. It is the work of the Holy Spirit to apply the redemption achieved by Christ to us and restores our soul to the original "*imago Dei*." "As long as Christ remains outside of us, and we are separated from him, all that he has suffered and done for the salvation of the human race remains useless and of no value for us," it is only by the Holy Spirit that "we come to enjoy Christ and all his benefits" for "the Holy Spirit is the bond by which Christ effectually unites us to himself."[204] For "man's understanding is pierced by a heavy spear when all the thoughts that proceed from him are mocked as stupid, frivolous, insane, and perverse,"[205] it needs to be healed by the grace of God, so that it must remain "a mere chaos of confusion."[206]

Only when the Spirit illuminates "the mind and seat of feeling" are we "drawn beyond our understanding" to the truth of God in Christ.[207] With the disability status of the mind, the Word, Calvin believes, has no effect "apart from the illumination of the Holy Spirit" nor this illumination restricted to the mind, as "the heart" must "also be strengthened and supported." After the regeneration of our nature, Calvin perfectly proclaims God "accommodates the knowledge of him to our slight capacity"[208] and the Spirit "accommodates the utterance to the measure of our understanding."[209] As Muller emphasizes, Calvin explicitly refers to this distinction between the "sinful" brain, which cannot apprehend the word of God and the true "knowledge of God" that is rooted in the heart.[210] Yet, Calvin is aware of the wide meanings of the term "heart" in the Old Testament when he states that "heart" often "includes mind," particularly when used in connection with "soul."[211] When the great commandment urges us to love God with all our heart and soul, we have to understand that the love of God involves a devotion to God with all

---

203. Ibid.
204. Ibid., III.i.l.
205. Ibid., II.iii.l.
206. Ibid., II.ii.18.
207. Muller, *Unaccommodated Calvin*, 167.
208. Calvin, *Institutes*, I.xiii.1.
209. Ibid., III.xxiv.9.
210. Calvin, *Institutes* (1559) I.v.9.
211. Calvin, *Commentary on Deuteronomy*, 6:4–9.

of our powers, while the form of the same commandment in Mathew, which adds the devotion of the mind to heart and soul, points towards "the higher seat of reason from which all purposes and thoughts proceed."[212] Therefore, in the Greek New Testament, heart and mind are frequently contrasted as representing different faculties of the soul.

In his *Commentary on Ephesians* (1548), Calvin offers a similar language where he speaks of a "twofold effect of the spirit on faith" that is directly related to the "two principal parts of faith," as the Spirit both "illuminates the mind" and "confirms the seat of our feelings."[213] For Calvin, the whole human being receives the benefits of this illumination—for faith resides both higher and deeper than understanding, "the Word of God is not received by faith if it flits about in the top of the brain, but when it takes root in the depth of the heart."[214] It is crucial here to recognize Calvin's holistic understanding of both the corruption by human sin and the regeneration by the divine spirit. In the restoration, "which we obtain through Christ," we have a renewal of soul consisting of reason and will, where Christ restores us "to true and complete integrity."[215] Just as man was totally depraved his restoration and renewal must be total and perfect, "Now the soul is not reborn if merely a part of it is reformed, but only when it is wholly renewed."[216] This regeneration should begin with regeneration of reason, for reason is the highest part of the soul, representing the image of God for which restoration is oriented.[217]

It is clear that Calvin's anthropological understanding is influenced by the Aristotelian faculty psychology of human soul as mind and heart, which both are included with the entire being in human corruption as well as in God's regeneration:

> Scripture is accustomed to divide the soul of man, as to its faculties, into two parts, the mind and the heart (*mentem et cor*). The mind means the intelligence (*intelligentiam*), while the heart denotes all the affections or wills (*omnes affectus: aut voluntates*). These two terms, therefore, include the entire soul (*totam animam*).[218]

---

212. Calvin, *Commentary on Matthew*, 22:37.
213. Calvin, *Commentary on Ephesians*, 22:37; 1:13 in (CO 51, col. 153).
214. Calvin, *Institutes* (1539) II, fol. 106.
215. Ibid., I.xv.4.
216. Ibid., II.iii.1.
217. Ibid.
218. Calvin, *Commentary on Phil.* 4:7 (CO 52, col. 61-62).

It is clear for Calvin, then, that linking mind and heart in faith appears to be a statement concerning the necessity of involving the whole person, intellect and will, in faith. Therefore, he states that the Word,

> Is not indeed a doctrine of the tongue, but of life; nor is it, like other disciplines, apprehended by memory and understanding alone, but it is received only when it is possessed by the *entire soul* and finds a seat and a refuge in the most profound affection of the heart.[219]

However, Calvin follow with a clear statement that "It therefore remains for us to understand that the way to the kingdom of God is open only to him whose mind has been made new by the illumination of the Holy Spirit."[220]

Making the mind new and restoring human reason to its original pure status, indeed, is not the only benefit of Holy Spirit regeneration of man, but so too is the accommodation of the Word of God to cope with the capacity of the understanding of this new mind. For Calvin, the revelations of God "have been accommodated to our capacity that we may better understand how miserable and ruinous our condition is apart from Christ."[221] God "describes God for us in human terms. For because our weakness does not attain to his exalted state, the description of him that is given to us must be accommodated to our capacity so that we may understand it."[222] Moreover, the image of God, Calvin continues, in the state of accommodation is not the reality of God itself but a seemingness of God to us, "Now the mode of accommodation is for him to represent himself to us not as he is in himself, but as he seems to us."[223] God, not only regenerates our mind and reason to be able to discern the truth, but also accommodates every means in which God reveals God, including the words of the Scripture for "matching the measure of our comprehension."[224] Calvin teaches us: "What, then, our mind does not comprehend, let faith conceive: that the Spirit truly unites things separated in space."[225]

If the regeneration of the whole human being is inevitably necessary, if this regeneration is impossible without the work of the Holy Spirit, if

---

219. Calvin, *Institutes (1539)*, XVII, col. 416.
220. Calvin's *Institutes (1559)*, II.i.20.
221. Ibid., II.xvi.2.
222. Ibid.
223. Ibid., I.xvii.13.
224. Ibid., I.xiv.8.
225. Ibid., IV.xvii.lo.

this regeneration must involve the entire being, mind and reason in particular, and if this regeneration accommodates God's revelation to the capacity of human understanding, faith is the only way for man to have it as a true reality in life. In Calvin's theological definition, faith is "the spirit of understanding."[226] Also, "understanding is joined with faith."[227] Faith is the "light of understanding,"[228] which heals our "defect of understanding."[229] "Until human reason is subjected to the obedience of faith," we cannot understand the creation of the world by God,[230] but "by faith we *understand* that the universe was created by the word of God."[231] Thus, the redeemed reason does not contradict the Word, but rather delights with the Truth because it is the believing reason restored by the Holy Spirit. Calvin's deep conviction is that faith is the precondition for the right reasoning.[232]

It clear, then, that Calvin agrees with Augustine on that when God restores our soul by the Holy Spirit through regeneration, it means that God creates a "new reason" as well as "new will."[233] Since regeneration presupposes death of man's corrupted nature on the cross with Christ, the restoration of human reason pre-requires giving up the corrupted reason and being united with the reason of God. Calvin continues arguing, "We are not our own: let not our reason nor our will, therefore, sway our plans and deeds . . . Conversely, we are God's . . . let his wisdom and will therefore rule all our actions."[234] This, indeed, is the difference between the corrupted reason and its philosophers from one side and the redeemed reason and its philosophies from the other. Calvin's distinction is that "they (unbelieving philosophers) set up *reason alone* as the ruling principle in man, and think that it alone should be listened to; to it alone," "But the Christian philosophy bids reason give way to, submit and subject itself to, the Holy Spirit so that the man himself may no longer lie but bear Christ living and reigning with him."[235]

226. Ibid., II.xii.5.
227. ibid., III..ii.3.
228. ibid., III.ix.5.
229. Ibid., II.iii.2.
230. ibid., I.xiv.2.
231. Ibid., I.xvi.l.
232. Ibid., III.ii.6.
233. ibid., II.v.15.
234. Ibid., III.vii.l.
235. Ibid.

John Calvin and Christian Education of the Presbyterian Church in Egypt: A New Theological Norm

First, Calvin's theological anthropology is deeply needed to help the Egyptian Presbyterians change their understanding of the nature of the image of God "Imago Dei," in which human being is created. As scripture-centered Christians, the presbyteries in Egypt emphatically believe that human being is created in the image of God. Their understanding of this image of God; however, is problematic and leads to division and dualism. For them, humbleness, love, mercy, honesty, self-denial and all the "spiritual attributes" are what make the true image of God in human being, while reason, will, freedom, creativity and all the "natural gifts" are earthly things, which must not be used in the spiritual life. In my reading of the Egyptian history since Islam in the seventh century, I think the insistency of the Egyptian Christians to deny the natural part of a Christian "believer" is rooted in their strive to exalt the divinity of Jesus over humanity as a defense against Muslim's attacks against incarnation theology. Being marginalized and a persecuted minority also played a central role in shaping the Christians' rejection of all kinds of limitations that they have to admit to accepting the natural "limited" part of this image while focusing on the spiritual part, giving them a sense of power and superiority, which they cannot achieve in reality. In contrast to the Egyptian view, indeed, Calvin beautifully portrays the human mind as a primary seat of the glory of the image of God,

> By the term "image of God" is denoted the integrity with which Adam was endued when his intellect was clear, his affections subordinated to reason, all his senses duly regulated, and when he truly ascribed all his excellence to the admirable gifts of his maker. And though the primary seat of the divine image was in the mind and the heart, or in the soul and its powers, there was no part even of the body in which some rays of glory did not shine . . . at the beginning the image of God was manifested by light of intellect, rectitude of heart, and soundness every part.[236]

Even though I disagree with the dualistic view of human being as a superior soul and inferior body that could reveal the impact of the classical philosophy, Plato, and Augustine on Calvin's theological anthropology, I still appreciate Calvin's high regards of human mind and reason as fundamentally divine gifts. Based on his study of Scripture, Calvin believes that man was created to be a servant-ruler under God; this why he was

236. Calvin, *Institutes*, I.xv.3–4.

endowed with the gift of reason, in order to be able to fulfill God's will in ruling the creation. Therefore, man cannot understand manhood who is created in the image of God as a rational being apart from his relationship to his Creator. Indeed, Calvin's high regard of all natural components of the human being, such as mind, reason, and will, as gifts from God helps the Egyptian Presbyterians to correct their understanding of God's image to include, not only spiritual, but also natural attributes of God. *Second, Calvin can help the Presbyterians in Egypt to reconcile Christian faith with human reason.* The fact that Christian faith is a real need to intelligently relay on the power of human reason to guide the Presbyterian conduct for a more effective ministry in Egypt has become a proved reality during the past few years. As Charles Partee says, the importance of necessity of integrating the work of human reason with faith comes from the fact that reason has many definitions, all of which are rooted in its functions. Partee says,

> Reason moving about its natural habitat has many definitions. They include connecting ideas, consciously, coherently, and purposely. Reason is the mind's rational, discursive activity of passing from propositions known or assumed to be true to other truths distinct from them but following logically from them. Over the centuries a substantial consensus developed that placed great confidence in reason.[237]

In light of this understanding, I have a deep conviction that while lack of this reasonable coherence was the main reason of the Egyptians' suffering under different dictator regimes throughout centuries, it, was also the main reason of the failure of the January 25th Revolution, and jumping of both Muslim brotherhood and the Military over the whole situation in Egypt. It is the same exact reason of the growth of superstations, seeking supernatural works, and divorce reading among the majority of the Egyptian society. Partee states that Robert Wilken, in his work *The Spirit of Early Christian Thought*, correctly places reason in service of faith and love.[238]

In contrary to the common understanding, Calvin is not anti-philosophical, nor is he anti-philosophers or philosophy in general. If so, would he have required logic in the Genevan Academy? Rather, his purpose is to turn the question of wisdom and philosophy clearly towards obedience to Christ. In the *Commentary on I Corinthians*, Calvin writes, "For whatever knowledge and understanding a man has counts for nothing unless it rests upon true wisdom."[239]

---

237. Partee, *Theology of John Calvin*, 306.
238. Ibid., 207.
239. Calvin, *Commentary on Epistles of Paul*, 80.

For him, the phrase "true wisdom" (*vera sapientia*) hearkens immediately to the beginning sentence of the *Institutes*. It was that basis of "true and sound wisdom" (*vera ac solida sapientia*),[240] which Calvin was seeking, in which all epistemologies should be rooted. Calvin, indeed, believes that reason and its fruits have their place in Christian faith and theology, yet, this place does not command a privilege over revealed wisdom.[241] In his *Commentary on 1 Corinthians*, Calvin argues that he is not against human reason; rather, his intention is to subject reason to God if one is willing to make right choices in life and follow God's will, "The apostle does not ask us to make a total surrender of the wisdom which is either innate or acquired by long experience. He only asks that we subjugate it to God, so that all our wisdom might be derived from His Word."[242]

Leroy Nixon and Lee A. Belford in *John Calvin's Teachings on Human Reason and Their Implications for Theory of Reformed Protestant Christian Education*, offer a comprehensive account on Calvin's understanding of the nature and usefulness of human reason for the Christian faith. According to them, Calvin believes that reason is able to guide human conduct and to understand the necessity for law and civil order, trusting that the universal reason and intelligence that is naturally implanted, is a special gift from God to man. The spirit of God confers excellent gifts even upon pagans for the common benefits of mankind.[243] However, Calvin urges us to remember that since natural reason is possessed only through the mercy of Almighty God, it should be entirely guided by the Spirit of God.[244]

Third, Calvin might help Presbyterian education in Egypt to reconcile rationalism with Biblicism and reason with the Bible, i.e., Calvin is necessary for a theological reading of the Bible. Like Calvin, the Presbyterians in Egypt are very scripture-oriented. However, unlike Calvin, one of the serious problems of the education and formation in the Presbyterian Church in Egypt is focusing on the literal reading of the bible. In the light of his long series of the *Commentary* of the bible and his *Institutes* as well, we clearly recognize Calvin's deep philosophical and theological ways of reading the Bible. This, indeed, is the reason that makes Calvin's theology strongly coherent and integrated. For Calvin, the Scriptures never lack reason; therefore, "so far as human reason goes, sufficiently firm proofs are at hand

---

240. Calvin, *Institutes*, I.i.1.
241. Internet Encyclopedia of Philosophy, "John Calvin (1509–64)."
242. Calvin, *Commentary on 1 Corinthians*, 3.18.
243. Nixon, *Calvin's Teachings on Human Reason*, 53.
244. Calvin, *Institutes*, III.iv.8.

to establish the credibility of Scripture."[245] With the guidance of the Holy Spirit, Calvin recommends, "Indeed, these human testimonies which exist to confirm it will not be vain if, as secondary aids to our feebleness, they follow that chief and highest testimony."[246]

In Nixon and Belford's understanding, Calvin is convinced that reason can serve faith through critical reading of the scriptures. His rational theology begins with the concept of Scripture as rational as he understands that the Scripture is full of "reasoning:" God is reasoning, Jesus is reasoning, Paul is reasoning, and every author is reasoning.[247] So, for Calvin, the whole Scripture is rational, even though some of the biblical texts are not comprehensible to the natural reason. In his interpretations, in order to get its deepest meaning, Calvin subjects the Scripture to literary criticism. It is evidenced by his zeal to restore the true meaning of Scripture, his respectful mention of the critical works of others, and his hermeneutical principle to understand the Scripture as real messages to actual historical situations, instead of taking verses and words out of their real context. Refraining from the traditional method of searching for hidden "deeper" meanings, it is stated in the *Presbyterian and Reformed Review*,

> Calvin is the founder of modern grammatico exegesis. He affirmed and carried out the sound and hermeneutical principle that the Biblical authors, like all sensible writers, wished to convey to their readers one definite thought in words which they could understand.[248]

Calvin himself has sought that his thoughts are reasonable interpretation contextual exegesis. He also has been angry with the scriptures' unreasonable interpretation, he says, "But we must not allow Christ's enemies to twist Scripture into an alien meaning to defend their evil case."[249] In the meantime, Calvin uses the logic of natural reason to construct his theology by deduction, analysis, synthesis, and argument of the Scripture while he appeals to the natural and universal reason to attack false doctrines and theology. Indeed, Calvin's understanding of human reason as a gift from God that helps to have an understanding faith is very useful to help the Egyptian Presbyterian in understanding the serious theological problems that they bring to the Christian

---

245. Ibid., I.viii.
246. Ibid., I.viii.13.
247. Ibid., II.iii.1. III.xxiv.16. II.iii.2.
248. Warfield et al., "Historical Theology," 466.
249. Calvin, *Institutes*, IV.viii.11.

faith by taking the bible literally and standing against the works of human reason for a deeper understanding of the holy text.

Fourth, Calvin is useful to help the Presbyterian education in Egypt to have a holistic approach to the source of knowledge, unifying Christian with unchristian. Indeed, dualism is a real problem both in the process of public and Christian education in Egypt. For no reason, people create a serious conflict between things that should be in a harmony and integrity. As a trusted theologian and founder of the Presbyterian Church, Calvin is useful to bring these divisions together in a harmonious and integrative approach for more effective education and productive life. Calvin not only relays and refers deeply to philosophy and human reason in constructing his theology, but also offers a great theological account on the value and usefulness of these resources for Christian theology. And while Calvin gives all respect to the Bible as the main source of the divine knowledge, he gives much attention to the necessity of the liberal arts and music as divine gifts to reveal God's glory. In contrast to the common belief of many, arts were not opposed by Calvin but encouraged and even recommended. Reflecting on the first appearance of arts by Jubal who invented the harp and organ in the Old Testament, Calvin emphatically says that this text reveals the "excellent gifts of the Holy Spirit." Calvin continues to explain that in the artistic instinct, God has enriched Jubal with rare endowments, believing that the power of arts prove most evident testimonies of the divine bounty.[250] More emphatically, in his *Commentaries on Exodus*, Calvin declares, "all the arts come from God and are to be respected as Divine inventions."[251] For Calvin, the Holy Ghost is the only source of these precious gifts. According to Kuyper, the arts are given to us for our comfort in our depressed state of life, as they react against the corruption of life and nature by the curse.[252] Kuyper assures us that Calvin sees arts as, "one of the richest gifts of God to mankind."[253]

Calvin helps Presbyterian education in Egypt not only by reconciling theology with philosophy and Christian education with music and arts, but also in reconciling the Christian resources (the Bible) with the unchristian "secular" recourses of education. For Calvin, this belief is rooted in his belief that human reason is God's gift to both believers and unbelievers. In his book *John Calvin's Teachings on Human Reason and Their Implications for Theory of Reformed Protestant Christian Education*, Nixon and Belford offer a notable account on Calvin's belief that both believers

---

250. Kuyper, *Lectures on Calvinism*, 92.
251. Ibid., 153.
252. Ibid., 92.
253. Ibid., 143.

and unbelievers receive the gift of reason from God. Even though fallen, the human mind still retains admirable gifts of God, which must not be despised. The spirit of God confers excellent gifts even upon pagans for the common benefits of mankind.[254]

Calvin's conviction of the unity of any truth is rooted in his conviction that all truth has only one source—God, who is the Truth. Even though Calvin distinguishes the natural reason from redeemed reason for a positive purpose, which is to save reason's ability in the "things below," Calvin clearly rejects any dichotomy in human knowledge of truth as well as any division of the holy truth from secular truth. Moreover, he believes that those two reasons do not exclude each other but rather share a "common" natural desire of yearning for the Divine Truth or "God." Accordingly, he recognizes inseparable unity between reason and revelation for both are *God—given* truths.[255] While condemning liberal arts and secular resources of knowledge by the church resulted in many serious problems, such as division and dualism and separating education from life, unifying the educational sources by Calvin helps construct a holistic approach to the Presbyterian education and formation in Egypt.

Fifth, Calvin might help unify theory and practice and reason and life experience in the education process of the Presbyterian Church in Egypt. For centuries, it was thought that reason is the master ruler of experience, where experience is evaluated and judged by reason. In the contemporary understanding, the reverse is being argued by both philosophers and theologians. Following the former ideal, there is almost no place for daily life experience in the process of both public and Christian education in Egypt. Teaching the biblical stories, memorizing bible verses, learning some Christian values and principles, and commanding learners to apply them in their life has been the main education pedagogy in the Egyptian church for decades. As it was discussed in the first chapter, this pedagogy resulted in multiple serious problems, such as separating education from life, thought from action, and theory from practice.

Unlike the Egyptian education, throughout his life, Calvin followed his distinctive belief that theology must be pious, experiential, and rational, insisting, "The knowledge of God does not rest in cold speculation, but carries with it the honoring of him."[256] Piety is requisite for the knowledge of

---

254. Nixon, *John Calvin's Teachings*, 53.
255. Ibid.
256. Calvin, *Institutes*, I.xii.1.

God and God is not known where there is no piety and obedience, which is a "reverence joined with love of God,"[257]

> For it is a doctrine of the tongue but of life. It is not apprehended by the understanding and memory alone, as other disciplines are, but it is received only when it possesses the whole soul, and finds a seat and resting place in the inmost affection of the heart . . . it must enter our heart and pass into our daily living, and so transform us into itself that it may not be unfruitful for us . . . its efficacy out to penetrate the inmost affection of the heart, take its seat in the soul, and affect the whole man a hundred times more deeply that the old exhortation of the philosophers.[258]

Reflecting on Calvin's deep conviction that knowledge of God in its very nature is experiential knowledge, William Stacy Johnson states,

> First, *faith* is a form of knowledge—not an abstract, bookish sort of knowledge but a personal knowledge similar to the way we know a close family member or a trusted friend. It is an intimate and familiar knowledge. Thus the faith Calvin is talking about is very different from "blind faith." True faith is not content merely to accept what others say without question. It trusts its own direct acquaintance with God's ways.[259]

It is clear for Calvin, then, that what the pious mind perceives is the "practical knowledge" which is doubtless more certain and firmer than any idle speculation.[260] The true knowledge of God is an "experience" of Christ in life.[261] It is a testimony of Spirit gained through a life of religious piety and only through this testimony is certainty about one's beliefs obtained, as "nothing other than what each believer experiences within himself— though my words fall far beneath a just explanation of the matter." And "While there is a logic of concepts, there is also a logic of life, of reality."[262] In light of this, Calvin is quite useful to help place experience as fundamental elements of constructing the divine truth in the Presbyterian education and formation process in Egypt.

Finally, Calvin is necessarily useful to help the Presbyterian education in Egypt to understand what democracy and freedom truly mean. It is

---

257. Ibid., I.vi.2.
258. Ibid., III.vi.4.
259. Johnson, *John Calvin*, 63.
260. Calvin, *Institutes*, I.xiii.13.
261. Ibid., I.ii.1-2.
262. Ibid.

actually known by many that John Calvin was one of the significant fathers of modern democracy—a seed or starting point of a developing democratic system that has unfolded later into the liberal western democracies of the modern era. In his book *Christianity and Democracy: A Theology for a Just World Order*, John W. de Gruchy writes that although Calvin was a second-generation reformer, his humanistic, legal training, and his context, has led to a significantly different reforming principle which succeeded to bridge the gap between the medieval and modern life in terms of natural rights, fundamental law, and consent of people. It was noted by many, indeed, 'the striking correlation, both in time and place, between the spread of Calvinist Protestantism and the rise of democracy. And despite the critiques' claim that the connection between Calvin's theology and modern democracy is accidental rather than rational, economic and social rather than theological, representative forms of democratic governments were established and flourished in those countries in proportion to developing and growing of Calvinism or Reformed traditions.[263] Emil Doumergue thinks that modern democracies were founded on Calvin's belief that a sovereign God secures and gives authority to a sovereign community, which means that Calvin is the founder of modern democracy.[264]

In his article, "Calvin the Lawyer,"[265] John Witte, Jr. believes that Calvin learned a lot about rights and liberties as a young French law student in the 1520s. It is not surprising, then, that Calvin opens his first major theological publication, the 1536 edition of the *Institutes of the Christian Religion*, with a clear call for freedom: freedom of conscience, freedom of exercise, freedom assembly, freedom of worship, freedom of the church, and attendant public, penal, and procedural rights for church members. Later on, in his same 1536 Institutes, Calvin called for the freedom not just of Protestants, but also of all peaceable believers,

> [W]e ought to strive by whatever means we can . . . that they may turn to a more virtuous life and may return to the society and unity of the church. And not only are excommunicants to be so treated, but also Turks and Saracens, and other enemies of religion Far be it from us to approve those methods by which many until now have tried to force them to our faith, when they forbid them the use of fire and water and the common elements,

---

263. De Gruchy, *Christianity and Democracy*, 76.
264. Ibid.
265. Witte, "Calvin the Lawyer," 1-23.

when they deny them to all offices of humanity, when they pursue them with sword and arms.²⁶⁶

Over the next twenty-five years, Calvin continued to build his case for freedom by offering a series of lectures, sermons, and commentaries of the biblical text that are concerned with freedom, such as,

> "For freedom, Christ has set us free." "You were called to freedom." "Where the Spirit of the Lord is, there is freedom." "For the law of the Spirit of life in Christ has set [you] free from the law of sin and death." "You will know the truth, and the truth will make you free." "You will be free indeed." You all have been given "the law of freedom" in Christ, "the glorious liberty of the children of God."²⁶⁷

When considering these lectures, sermons and commentaries of these biblical passages, John Witte, Jr. states some of the significant talks of Calvin that clearly illustrate Calvin's deep conviction and the high regard that Calvin gives to liberty and freedom: "There is nothing more desirable than liberty," Calvin writes, liberty is "an inestimable good," "a singular benefit and treasure that cannot be prized enough," something that is worth "more than half of life." "There is nothing more desirable than liberty." Liberty is "an inestimable good," "a singular benefit and treasure that cannot be prized enough," something that is worth "more than half of life." "How great a benefit liberty is, when God has bestowed it on someone." Calvin emphasizes the importance of the "right to vote," he once said, is the "best way to preserve liberty." "Let those whom God has given liberty and the franchise use it." "[T]he reason why tyrannies have come into the world, why people everywhere have lost their liberty . . . is that people who had elections abused the privilege." "[T[here is no kind of government more salutary than one in which liberty is properly exercised with becoming moderation and properly constituted on a durable basis."²⁶⁸

In his later years, John Witte, Jr. assures us that Calvin was concerned with the subjective "rights" of individuals, and their "liberties" or "freedoms." Sometimes, Calvin uses general phrases as "the common rights of mankind," the "natural rights" of persons, the "rights of a common nature," or the "the equal rights and liberties."²⁶⁹ Yet, in Calvin's concept, rights are

---

266. Calvin, *Institutes*, II.26.

267. Zondervan, *NIV Church Bible*.

268. Calvin, *Institutes*, 20.7.

269. Comm. Gen. 4:13; *Comm. Harm. Law Num.* 3:5-10, 18-22, Deut. 5:19; Comm. Ps. 7:6-8; Lect. Jer. 22:1-3, 22:13- 14; Lect. Ezek. 8:17; Comm. I Cor. 7:37.

never apart from duties and the entire purpose of having rights and liberties is to enable a person to practice the duties and responsibilities of the faith. He says, "we obtain liberty in order that we may more promptly and more readily obey God in all things."[270]

A crucial point for this research, indeed, is Calvin's understanding of freedom and liberty as the inner freedom or "freedom of conscience." In some instances, he describes this as a natural order, an order of nature, or an order of creation. While in other instances, he uses more anthropological language, saying, our human conscience, the inner voice, our natural sense of right and wrong. More often, he describes freedom as a divine, spiritual, moral, or natural law. What he basically means by these terms, Witte, Jr. believes, is to make a set of norms that transcend and legitimize the positive laws of human authorities as a responsible moral being, as God, Calvin believes, has written this natural law on the hearts and consciences of all people since creation and rewritten it in the pages of Scripture.[271]

Conclusion

Constructing a theological norm of critical thinking was the main purpose of this chapter. To do so, a theological criticism of Dewey's scientific theory of critical theory was offered in the first section. For this, I found Niebuhr's theological account of sin relevant approach to balance Dewey's optimism. While I briefly called a feminist psychologist and theologian Valerie Saiving into this debate, through which an interdisciplinary dialogue as an approach to the Presbyterian education in Egypt has become inevitably required. In the second section, John Calvin's theology of human reason and rational thinking was offered. Calvin's understanding of the theological anthropology, human as a rational being who is created in the image of God and his relation with classic philosophy, all were explained in more details. Then, I introduced three kinds of reason according Calvin's belief: a natural pure reason, a corrupted sinful reason, and redeemed sanctioned reason.[272]

In the third section of this chapter, in six aspects, I found Calvin's theological understanding of human reason and rationality useful to illuminate and address the educational problematic reality of the lack of critical thinking in the Egyptian context. It has become clear for me that Calvin's work would help the Egyptian Presbyterians to theologically consider human

---

270. Cavlin, *Commentary on 1 Peter* 2:16; *Institutes* (1559), 3.17.1-2; 3.19.14-16; 4.10.5.

271. Witte, "Calvin the Lawyer."

272. Partee, *Theology of John Calvin*, 305.

nature as a rational being, helping them to reconcile faith with reason and read the Bible Theologically Instead of literally. In meantime, Calvin helps the Egyptian Presbyterians reconciling Christian with secular, theory with practice, and theology with philosophy, as Calvin helps reconciling creation theology with redemption theology. For Calvin, while sinful reason is disabled to discern the divine truth, the Holy Spirit, who creates a new mind and restores human wisdom to its original status before sin, guides the "redeemed" reason to return again to its ordinal wisdom, becoming able to discern the divine truth ability.

Indeed, I agree with Calvin's account, not only because it copes with the reality of all humans, but also because of it integrates with the rest of the reformed theology. The modern philosophy of the history, indeed, tells a lot about the damage and destruction that resulted from the self-confidence of the human mind to act alone without the help of God. Niebuhr's account of human sin as a pride, for instance, explains the egotism and self-centeredness of mankind after sin, which reflects the reason of division and separation Calvin sees the essential need for man to be helped, i.e., to be in unity.

CHAPTER 4

Teaching for Christian Wisdom

Toward A Holistic Approach to Christian Education in the Presbyterian Church in Egypt

Formation takes place when Christ takes shape in the way people relate to one another and practice the Christian way of life in their own community. People learn about forgiveness not simply hearing about it in the Sunday school, but by receiving forgiveness and forgiving one another. People learn about the healing power of God's grace when they are receiving a concert support and recovering in their congregation from alcohol abuse and failed marriage. Formation takes place when the leaders of the congregation reach out across racial lines in charge of reconciliation and they invite others in the congregation to join them and participating in the process . . . I think more important today, the programs we offer or the formal teaching on education we offer is the quality of relationships in the kind of the community we offer folks as they come back to the church and continue grow up in the church . . . I think education today is better thought of as teaching people to understand what they are already experiencing. THE Stories of the scripture tell our story; it is why we do things the way we do them. It means that educational today must be formational and not simple informational.[1]

Holistic Approach as A Resolution of Division and Dualism

Using Osmer's "four tasks of interpreting practical theology" as a framework of this research, the first chapter was organized to offer a thick ana-

1. Richard Osmer, Lutheran Theological Seminary, https://www.youtube.com/watch?v=PTrZkxyjbTU.

lytic description of the lack of critical thinking and the main factors and consequence that resulted from the division and dualism in the process of the Presbyterian education in Egypt. Through years as an educator in the context of the Egyptian church, I believe *dualism* has been a serious and fundamental problem for Christian education. As it was mentioned earlier, the Presbyterians in Egypt insist on putting things in conflict, as an either . . . or pattern: either divine authority or human agency, faith or reason, theology or philosophy, etc. consequentially, with lack of awareness, the Presbyterian Church in Egypt, puts itself in conflict with the world, refusing secular literature, arts, music, and drama, condemning the use of philosophy and reason, and rejecting all sources of education that are not Christian. This dualism, indeed, is a serious factor that both contributing to and resulting in the lack of critical thinking skills in the process of church education. For Dewey, this dualism works as a barrier that leads to absence of coherence and integrity both individually and socially.[2]

Reflecting on (Rom 12:2), "Do not conform to the pattern of this world, but be transformed by the renewing of your mind," Fayez Fares points clearly to the serious need of the church to adapt an approach of education that is able to include the work of the human mind as the greatest gift from God to man, giving much attention to the human mind and spark of reason that is given by God the creator to be the source of human enlightenment in this world. All the mysteries of the nature were hidden until God has shone the divine light in some human mind and they discovered some of these miseries. It was this divine spark that led Archimedes, Newton, Einstein, and others. It is a tragedy of the human begins, then, just ignore the gift as an evil, while the whole human being was created in the image of God.[3]

In his book, *Self-Awaking in Experiencing God: Enlightening Messages*, Fares continues his emphasis on the need of including reason as a fundamental partner in the process of the Presbyterian education in Egypt for a deeper understanding of the Christian faith and life. In a chapter entitled "Spirituality, Rationality, and Faith." Fares writes a clear statement that spirituality does not mean absence of mind, understanding, or awareness, and holding illusions and legendries, but rather exalting the spiritual and rational principles to guide our thinking and practice in the world. While rationality does not mean rigidity and mechanical life, but rather, using mind and reason in order to reach a deeper understanding of life experiences. It is unquestionable that God is Almighty enough to do miracles and supernatural things; yet these things are exceptional and very specific to certain

2. Dewey, *Experience and Education*, 18–21.
3. Fares, *Self-Awaking in Experiencing God*, 17–25.

situation and certain purposes, which cannot substitute for the natural laws and reasonable judgment that God has put to rule the universe.[4]

Recognizing how the Egyptian Presbyterians regard the Bible, Fares refers again to some biblical verses that confirm the need of the its education to adapt an intelligent approach, "By faith we understand that the universe was formed at God's command, so that what is seen was not made out of what was visible" (Heb 11:3). By faith we understand, it is clear here that "faith" is not in conflict with, but rather a source of "understanding." Fares also refers to Augustine's famous statement, "*credo ut intelligam*, "I believe in order to understand." Faith and reason, however, are never in conflict. Job rightly, states "But it is the spirit in a person, the breath of the Almighty, that gives them understanding" (Job 32:8). For fares in, in short, God is the mind of the universe and Jesus is the "*logos*," means the "divine mind."[5]

For Fares, If Jesus is the *logos* or the divine mind; he is also the "wisdom," "Out in the open wisdom calls aloud, she raises her voice in the public square . . . I will pour out my thoughts to you, I will make known to you my teachings" (Prov 1:20–23).[6] "For wisdom will enter your heart, and knowledge will be pleasant to your soul. Discretion will protect you, and understanding will guard you" (Pro 2:10–11). And Jesus himself "called the crowd to him and said, "Listen and understand." And, "If any of you lacks wisdom, you should ask God, who gives generously to all without finding fault, and it will be given to you" (Jas 1:5).

Living with faith, then, does not conflict with reason, and obeying God does not mean to think and act without understanding. God, who made the whole creation and set natural laws, is the one who has given people mind to understand them, and God who leads humans to the light of faith is the one that gives them a reason to understand their experience with God in the journey of life. More importantly for Fares is that the spark of light of mind and reason is not exclusive to scientific and natural innovation, but rather to enlighten all dimensions of the human life of seeking the truth. This fact, Fares argues, reflects clearly the need for a different approach to the Presbyterian education, such an approach that is able to overcome the problem of division, unifying divine with human, faith with reason, and Christian and unchristian. Such an approach that is able to guide learners to develop analytical thinking in the process of education, freeing their intelligence and thoughts in reaching the truth.[7]

4. Ibid., 35–38.
5. Ibid., 39–42.
6. NIV translation.
7. Fares, *Self-Awaking in Experiencing God*, 17–25.

Like Fares, Makrm Naguib points to the urgent necessity for a different approach to the Presbyterian today, an approach that gives enough room for using mind and reasonable thinking. In his book *Conservative or Liberal*, Naguib offers strong emphasis of the meaning of freedom in the reformation theology as of the freedom conscience. An individual finds herself or himself at a "fork" of different choices in everyday life where s/he is to choose one way. The difficulty of making such a decision has increasingly become more complicated in the light of the constant changes and complexity of the contemporary life. This difficulty, indeed, is rooted in our fixed Christian norms, which are distinguished from the norms of our society. Such situations, argues Naguib, could leads us either to hypocrisy and false virtues or alienation and withdrawing from our social context and lose their mission in the world. The only way for us in this tragedy, say Naguib, is to grow in Christian wisdom and develop critical minds. Educating people in freedom, then, is the way to create a Christian with real wisdom and hearty commitment to the Christian faith. "It is for freedom that Christ has set us free. Stand firm, then, and do not let yourselves be burdened again by a yoke of slavery"[8] Practicing this freedom of mind and conscience creates some sort of tensional struggle; yet, practicing freedom as an approach to truth, is the way for a Christian to grow as an independent wise Christian, trust the Holy Spirit to guide the whole process.[9] So, the church has to create new pedagogies, approaches, and goals, offering church education enough freedom, allowing learners to reflect on their actual practice.[10]

For Ikram Lamay, it is hard to believe that God intends for God's kingdom to have the same form of thoughts and practice year after year. Referring to Jesus words in Mark 2:22, "no one pours new wine into old wineskins. Otherwise, the wine will burst the skins, and both the wine and the wineskins will be ruined. No, they pour new wine into new wineskins," Lamay emphasizes that as well as the message of the Gospel is new everyday, our approaches of conveying and teaching this message requires to be renewed constantly to be relevant to our time and context. It is clear in the Christian theology, says Lamay, that the kingdom of God always takes the shape of the contextual culture, which is a form of the incarnation.[11]

In the introduction to his last book *The Focus*, Awsam Wasfy[12] beautifully illustrates this urgent need for a different approach to the Christian life

---

8. Gal 5:1, NIV.
9. Naguib, *Conservative or Liberal*, 43.
10. Ibid., 53.
11. Lamay, *Interview*.
12. Awsam Wasfy is a psychiatry and psychotherapist, earned his MDiv from the

in Egypt. Wasfy is convicted that the real need of the church in Egypt is to find the focus of our Christian life, which cannot be approached without deep reflective insights instead of the superficial and direct looking to the reality. It is true that Christianity, in its deep essence, is not a doctrine or a system of laws that one has to obey and wait for a reward; rather, it is an invitation to grow in the new creature that Christ offers to the world. A life of constant spiritual and ethical formation and transformation throw discerning God in each experience of our life. This kind of life requires a new approach church education, an approach that unifies the divisions of thoughts. Theology, Wasfy concludes, should find a way to cooperate with its contemporary partners, such as philosophy, anthropology, psychology, sociology, activists in human rights, and artists in order to reach the depth, purpose, and process of the Christian faith.[13]

In his article "Christian Education in Egypt: Past, Present, and Future," Maurice Assad argues that a real reform of the Presbyterian education in Egypt should begin with a reform of its approaches. While philosophers, theologians, and educators in the world try to formulate new conceptions in an attempt towards bringing the human race to its true self-consciousness and self-awareness as full beings, the Egyptian education suffers alienations, contradiction, and division. Like John Calvin, Assad believes that knowing God always begins with knowing ourselves while knowing ourselves is not possible without an understanding of our true contextual life experience. Therefore, man gains true knowledge of self and God only when he considers "experience" as a main source to this knowledge. Indeed, theory is always born in the course of practice, which means, "The quality of spiritual life can be seen as the continuous growth towards becoming mature persons. This growth towards maturity is a dynamic process of becoming "whole" and "holy." The Christians are alienated in the Egyptian context, which they live in since it alienates itself from the contemporary literature, art, drama, and music.[14]

Division and dualism, then, reveal the urgent need to a holistic approach to Christian education in the Presbyterian Church in Egypt, such an approach that is able to bring things together in harmonious dialogue,

---

ETSC in 2005. He is the author and founder of "Life" Association for support, recovery, and Life-Skill Training Instead of being ordained as a pastor, he put all his interest in group therapy of marginalized and wounded groups, such as homosexual, widows, and abused children. Wasfy published about twenty-five books in the field of psychotherapy and spiritual growth. He is also one of the well-known Christian speakers and lecturer in the ETSC in Egypt.

13. Wasfy, *The Focus*, 105.
14. Ibid., 55.

unifying them in a coherent process of constructing truth. A constructivism approach to Christian education, I believe, can help the Presbyterian educators in Egypt reconcile faith with reason, theology with philosophy, theory with practice, Christian with secular, spiritual with physical, and Bible with literature, arts, music, and other non-Christian resources for education. In short, it would help Egyptians to educate a whole being for full freedom, full understanding of their everyday life experience, and for creating critical thinkers that able to achieve a better faith, life, and ministry.

Osmer's Practical Theology and Christian Education

While Richard Osmer is a professor of Christian education; his deep understanding and awareness of the nature of this field as theology, guided him to see the task of Christian education within the wider realm of practical theology. Practical theology, for Osmer, is a threefold discipline: the practical moral reasoning an individual practices when is involved in a social issue, the interpretation of a particular situation of individuals for discerning what God requires them to do or to be, and a concrete response to the different situations.[15] In order to achieve its goals, practical theology includes empirical research and its own theoretical foundation, which it forms in dialogue with other theological disciplines, such as systemic theology, church history, and biblical studies, and with nontheological disciplines, such as philosophy, psychology, sociology, and anthropology. In addition of being practical in its very nature, it has increasingly become a clear fact that practical theology is inherently interdisciplinary in character.

In "Teaching as Practical Theology," while Osmer surmises the historical development of practical theology as a science in seven phases since sixteenth century to the recent time, in the final stage, which is the most important one for Osmer, he confirms that theology was influenced by two trends. First, the rise in popularity of "praxis epistemologies" and second, the realization that practical theology is not done simply by specialists and experts, but by every Christian and by the church. Illustrating practical theology as a practice of the church clearly defines practical theology as a hermeneutical discipline.[16] In short, if I have to choose some key words of Osmer's version of practical theology, I would say practical theology for Osmer is: contextual—congregational, praxis, empirical research, practical reason, reflective analysis, theology, sciences, cross-

15. Ibid.
16. Osmer, "Teaching as Practical Theology."

disciplinary, hermeneutical circle, constructive, and new practice-guiding theories. However, for the purpose of this research, I point to particular dimensions of Osmer's understanding of Christian education as practical theology, describing them with my own titles, which I use as a preparatory stage for creating my own approach to education as practical theology by adopting and employing Osmer's approach.

Christian First—Education as Practical Theology

In contrast to schools of education that focus on curriculum and method, through years of teaching Christian education, Osmer has developed a distinctively Reformed theologically orientated school of Christian education. What really characterizes Osmer's school of Christian education is the fact that he always takes his theological heritage seriously. It is not accident, then, that Osmer's publishing extensively focuses on "practical theology" and not just "Christian education," which identifies that, for Osmer, education finds its orientation within the larger field of practical theology. This, indeed, comes from a deep understanding that Christian education is first Christian and therefore must deal with foundational questions as revelation and theological anthropology before proceeding to any other question. Christian education, then, is primarily a theological task, which takes place in a particular congregation and particular context. It is the reason that prevented Osmer from reducing Christian education to just curriculum or method.

However, while he clearly has deep roots in the reformed theology, Osmer does not have a certain preference of theology, nor is he exclusively committed to a particular theologian, rather, Osmer is always attracted to the broader theological traditions. The main concern for Osmer is to find a theological foundation of the teaching ministry in the broader heritage of Evangelical theology, including reformed. In his book, *A Teachable Spirit*,[17] Osmer clearly wants the three offices of Christ that are recognized by reformed theology to be the teaching office of the church. In *The Teaching Ministry of Congregations*,[18] he spends the first part explaining Pauline theological understanding, intending to appropriate Pauline themes of catechesis, exhortation, and discernment to the task of education. In *Practical Theology: An Introduction*,[19] Osmer points to the fact that God provided Israel with leaders over the course of its unfolding covenant relationship. He

17. Osmer, *Teachable Spirit*.
18. Osmer, *Teaching Ministry of Congregations*.
19. Browning, *Fundamental Practical Theology*.

refers to the leaders appointed by God in the Old Testament to teach Israel, lead them to repent, and protect them as the reference, as those on which the New Testament and reformed theology was built. Reformed theology, says Osmer, reflects on these teachings, and links them with the threefold office of Jesus. Osmer says,

> God provides Israel with leaders, anointed with the Spirit of God, to help it live with covenant fidelity. Priests play a special role in Israel's worship of God, overseeing the cult of offering sacrifices to God on the people's behalf. Judges, sages, and kings provide leadership in the organization of the covenant community, offering wise teachings, settling disputes guiding its political affairs, and protecting it against external threats. Prophets speak God's word to Israel, announcing divine judgment when it strays from covenant fidelity, calling it to repent, and offering hope if it returns back to God.[20]

For Osmer, in short, theology is, profoundly, the very basic foundation of Christian education. Yet, the vast verity of theologians that he refers to and adopts, the threefold office unity that he seriously points to, and the unity of teaching with practice, where theories are actually born out of faith community praxis, all embody Osmer's comprehensive approach to Christian education as practical theology.

Cross-disciplinary—An Inevitable Dialogue of Theology with Sciences

Locating Christian education in the realm of practical theology, for Osmer, if education is first "Christian," meaning theology, and it is second "education," means educational theories, a cross-disciplinary relationship of theology and human sciences is quite inevitable. Indeed, educational theory itself includes a wide verity of fields, such as philosophy, psychology, sociology, and anthropology, all of which exist in a cross-disciplinary relationship, which

> Refers to the way practical theologian engages other branches of theology and other fields of knowledge such as the social sciences, the arts, natural sciences, and so forth. I see cross-disciplinary work as quite complex and as including interdisciplinary,

---

20. Osmer, *Practical Theology*, 27–28.

interdisciplinary, multidisciplinary, and metadisciplinary dimensions.[21]

For Osmer, the importance of the cross-disciplinary work comes from being necessarily methodological decisions of practicing education as practical theology,

> It is easiest to illustrate the importance of methodological decisions about cross-disciplinary work by focusing on the interdisciplinary level. This has to do with the decisions a practical theologian makes about which fields are to be engaged and how their relationship to practical theology is conceptualized.[22]

Osmer, then, points to the families of the interdisciplinary work that emerged in recent years according to the method that theologians use to relate theology with the other sciences, assuring us that these families resemble one another in certain ways. First is the *correlational family*. It hopes to bring theology in an equal influential conversation with other sciences and includes Paul Tillich's method of correlation, David Tracy and Don Browning's revised correlational methods, and Rebecca Chopp's and Mathew Lamb's revised praxis correlational methods. Second is the *transformational family*. It intends to give theology the final word to transform the other dialogue partner within a practical theological perspective, and includes the Chalcedonian paradigm of James Loder and Deborah Hunsinger. Third is *transversal rationality*. It locates theology among other disciplines as in Calvin Schrage and Wentzel van Huyssten.[23]

For me, Osmer's approach to education and practical theology is a unifying and reconciling approach. It helps, not only reconciling the education process with theology, but also reconciling theology with nontheological disciplines. Believing that all goodness is from God, like Osmer I believe that every good means that helps human to understand his or her situated experience more fully and deeply is a spiritual means. And because faith practices are embedded in a network of factors studied by other disciplines, cross-disciplinary reflection is inevitable. Indeed, Osmer is to help useful unify the whole human experience with the spiritual experience.

---

21. Osmer, *Teaching Ministry of Congregations*, 307.
22. Ibid.
23. Ibid., 308.

Osmer and Howard Gardner—An Interdisciplinary Dialogue Model

In *The Teaching Ministry of Congregations*, especially in the chapter regarding Nassau Presbyterian Church, Osmer points to his use of Gardner as a scientific dialogue partner. He draws the attention to three case studies of congregations, where each congregation is framed by an interdisciplinary theory, empirical research methodology and practical theological interpretation. It is, indeed, easy to recognize that Osmer is not focusing on a particular kind of disciplinary dialogue partner, but rather he is comprehensive in drawing on as many scholars as he can, as he never satisfied with only one scholar. It is the dialogue itself more than any particular partner that Osmer is concerned with.[24] Indeed, Osmer's nine hundred sixty five pages dissertation with a detailed account of several educators is an evident. While Osmer offers about a hundred and some pages explaining John Dewey's philosophy, in order to make Dewey relevant to Christian education, he followed it with another great account on George Albert Coe. In Mikoski's term, Coe baptized Dewey.

However, it is not accident then that he uses Howard Gardner in particular. Gardner's multiple intelligences theory, in fact, sets the cognitive psychological understanding of "intelligence" into the practicality of the process of education. For Osmer, Gardner is especially important for education because of three aspects; Gardner is contextual, comprehensive, and teleological. First, for Gardner, rationality takes place in a context, where the current thoughts of this context should be taken into consideration. Gardner, thus, is as contextual as Osmer. Second, Gardner is also as comprehensive as Osmer. In his theory, an educator can find a consideration of different ages, different genders, and different intellectual capacities of different leaners. Gardner also embraces and comprehends previous research, uses, and adds to it. Third, like Osmer, Gardner focuses on end goals or end-states, so he is teleological, which means that Gardner is relevant to education because practices have an inherent teleological nature.[25]

Hermeneutical Circle—A Creative Method of Practicing Practical Theology

Practical theology as a hermeneutical discipline in its very nature is, indeed, one of the deep convictions for Osmer. According to Osmer, practical

---

24. Osmer, *Teaching Ministry of Congregations*, 113.
25. Gardner, *Multiple Intelligences*.

theology has been impacted by hermeneutical theory in two ways. First, he describes the theological task of every Christian as the "reflective dimension of piety—the attempt to understand God and the world in relation to God," which links theology to the lived experience. Just as hermetical theory views all human thoughts and actions as hermeneutical, practical theologians have realized that human experience should be submitted to a theologically interpretive task. This definition of the purpose and nature of practical theology gives it an advantage of engaging both academic theology by trained people and Christian congregations and individuals who reflect it in an ordinary human ways.[26]

The second way Osmer sees that hermeneutics have impacted practical theology is the hermeneutical circle. Osmer argues that at different modes of theological reflection, each moment (including biblical interpretation, historical interpretation, systematic interpretation, and practical action and reflection) can be viewed in terms of the hermeneutical circle as a part of larger whole. To prove his theory, Osmer explores teaching ministry as a hermeneutical activity at specific moments in which education takes place through reflective and interpretive methods. This process of teaching as a theological reflection and a hermeneutical interpretive mode, can be achieved, says Osmer, by focusing on: choosing subject matter; understanding the learners and their potentialities; interpreting the context in which teaching is done; deciding upon curriculum in relation to the values of the larger community; and the teaching approach taken to a particular teaching event.[27]

Building on his preceding practical theologians, Osmer continues to develop and expand his understanding of practical theology as a hermeneutical discipline. In *Developing A Public Faith: New Directions in Practical Theology*, Osmer and Friedrich Schweitzer identify the writings of James Fowler as significant contributions that helped redefine the field of practical theology. According to Osmer and Schweitzer, the works of Fowler not only provide a concrete example of what practical theology should be, but also redefine it as a hermeneutical circle. What Fowler attempts to do is to develop a systematic practical theology where human vocation and divine praxis are inseparably woven together. Fowler, Osmer, and Schweitzer provide four tasks of interpreting practical theology, which are viewed as a hermeneutical circle, each task mutually influencing the other: the descriptive-empirical, interpretive, normative, and pragmatic task. In other words, practical theology is concerned with what is going on, why it is going on, what forms

26. Ibid., 226.
27. Ibid., 228–29.

religious practice ought to take, and how they can be carried out in a particular situation. In light of their hermeneutical nature, these tasks of interpreting practical theology help practical theologians to construct action-guiding theories of contemporary religious practice.[28]

In *The Teaching Ministry for Congregations,* Osmer says, "practical theology is that branch of Christian theology that seeks to construct action-guiding theories of Christian praxis in particular social contexts."[29] Osmer then continues explaining in the introduction and epilogue of this book, the four tasks of theologically interpreting the praxis of Christian communities as a starting point for understanding practical theology in a contemporary mode. Finally, Osmer fully expands and develops his theory in his book, *Practical Theology: An Introduction.* Referring to contemporary hermenutes, such as Heidegger and Gadamer, Osmer makes it fully clear that practical theology must be hermeneutical in nature and function, and then he explains in more details the four tasks of interpretations of practical theology.[30] He states, "Much contemporary practical theology attends to four tasks along the lines of a hermeneutical circle or spiral."[31]

Because I'm using Osmer's thoughts as a framework for this research, in my introduction to this research, I offered a detailed discussion of the hermeneutical circle. However, I would here point to some notes about it. First, the tasks of the circle are not a linear manner, but they mutually feed each other in a circle or spiral way. It is a dynamic constant task of interpretation. Second, the main intention of practical theology for Osmer is to lean on the practical reason and the natural ability of an individual to observe, analyze, interpret, and criticize, so, it is a rational dialogue between practical theology and practical reason. Third, the comprehensiveness of Osmer's approach can be clearly detected through this circle. One can easily find theory and practice in a dialogue, theology and philosophy, faith and reason, personal observation and empirical research, theology and sciences, reflection and construction, revelation and experience, goal and method, etc. Fourth, while it is deep, comprehensive, and includes a vast verity of elements, this circle is as easily applied to practices as to all people, scholars and non-scholars, can successfully use it for better life and ministry.

---

28. Schweitzer and Osmer, *Developing a Public Faith.*
29. Osmer, *The Teaching Ministry of Congregations,* xiv.
30. Osmer, *Practical Theology,* 22.
31. Ibid., 17.

Praxis—From Practice to Theory

Osmer rejects the notion that practical theology is merely an application of some theories or thoughts of the other disciplines as systematic theology or biblical studies, but rather theology, in its very nature, is practical. It begins with careful reflection on the actual practice within the life of the faith community in a particular congregation and particular context. In their book, *Religious Education between Modernization and Globalization,* Richard Osmer and Friedrich Schweitzer start constructing a new understanding of practical theology by criticizing the modern view of practical theology as a field that should emerge from a pure rationality such as medicine, ethic, and rhetoric, reducing it to applications of theories and research emerging in "fully scientific" methods from the other theological disciplines. Osmer and Schweitzer affirm that this understanding has been called into question in light of contemporary philosophy and science since there is more than one model of theory-practice relationship such as neo-Aristotelian, critical social theory, and pragmatism. Classical and modern models of rationality that conceptualize knowledge as secured by following universal rules that can be transported one disciplinary context to another is strongly questioned too.[32] Osmer states in his book, *A Teachable Spirit: Recovering the Teaching Office in the Church,* that

> The heart of practical theology is reflection that takes place in the midst of unfolding situations emerging out of social practices in an attempt to shape actional responses that are appropriate to what can be discerned of God's purposes for the world as they are brought to bear on unique contexts of experience.[33]

Osmer's main focus is to emphasize that practical theology is "praxis," that is, a dynamic process of critical theological interpretation that goes from practice to reflection to theory to practice. The final goal is a view toward improving these practices through concrete proposals. This process is informed by cross-disciplinary reflection because faith practices are embedded in a network of factors studied by other disciplines. What is attempted here is to heal the split between theory and praxis and between the systematic and practical, believing that, "the old splits are both 'nontheological' and obsolete."[34] In this way, I see practical theology as relevant to our postmodern time with all its complexity, uncertainty, and fragmentation. Practical theologians, then, will need to be aware that what happens in the

32. Osmer and Schweitzer, *Religious Education,* 1–3.
33. Osmer, *Teachable Spirit,* 162.
34. Osmer, *Practical Theology,* 145.

ordinary lives of people and in the political and social structures of society is of great theological significance, both in the making of new theological theories and in the forming of visions of faithful action.

Sources of Justify Truth—Reconciling the Bible with Other Resources

Adopting the Wesleyan Quadrilateral sources of Justification, justifying our truth in a practical theological perspective is a fundamental component of Osmer's system of thoughts for interpreting practical theology. With much respect to scripture as the universal truth, Osmer believes that this truth is not only composed of many small truths, but also believes that this truth should be contextualized by certain people in a certain place and time. This, indeed, means that using human reason and personal experience of everyday life to justify this truth is inevitably required. In the meantime, as the interaction of scripture, reason, and experience of the fathers might help inspire us, reflecting on the Christian traditions is as important as using scripture, experience, and reason in justifying our knowledge and Christian truth in our journey with God in the recent time.

Osmer's attitude of reconciling all divisions and contradictions in the course of practicing Christian education as practical theology is clearly evident. It is in this circle as well as his hermetical circle of the four tasks that Osmer helps us to use a hermeneutical approach toward a deeper understandable faith, but also to develop a hermetical mind and well-trained reflective reason and critical thinking skills.

Teaching for Christian Wisdom: Toward a Holistic Approach to Christian Education in the Presbyterian Church in Egypt

In the light of the text, "All this is from God, who reconciled us to himself through Christ and gave us the ministry of reconciliation: that God was reconciling the world to himself in Christ, not counting people's sins against them. And he has committed to us the message of reconciliation"[35] reconciling the divided is my approach to Christian education of the Presbyterian Church in Egypt. Since the main purpose of this research is helping the Egyptian Presbyterians to construct critical thinking, I believe adapting Osmer's approach to Christian education as practical theology in order to

---

35. 2 Cor 5:18–19, NIV.

bring fragments and dualistic elements into a harmonious dialogue based on the understanding of the Kingdom of God as reconciliation, which was incarnated in Jesus helps to achieve this purpose. In Jesus, indeed, the heaven unified with the earth; the divine with human; spiritual with material; natural human with the redeemed Christian, and creation theology with redemption theology, "thy kingdom come, thy will be dome, on earth as it is in heaven."[36] Reflecting on Elaine Grahame's *Transforming Practice: Pastoral Theology in an Age of Uncertainty*,[37] Osmer says,

> One of the most prominent characteristics of our postmodern context is a lack of consensus over values . . . In *Transforming Practice*, Elaine Graham argues that practical theology much face up to the challenges of a postmodern context characterized by a high degree of pluralism, fragmentation, and skepticism, it is a context of uncertainty which it is no longer possible for theology to build on a consensus values in society. Nor can theology take for granted the authority of traditional sources and norms of the church. It must find new ways of developing truth claims and values that will be persuasive to a skeptical postmodern world.[38]

Indeed, I see Osmer's approach to practical theology as comprehensive as the reconciling message that we are given by Jesus Christ. Osmer's purpose is to reconcile faith with reason, theology with human sciences, theory and practice, the richness of the biblical text with hermeneutical understanding of its deep message, individual community, cognitive with spiritual, and systematic interpretation with creative pedagogy. The purpose of education has an eternal *telos* in Christ with goals of addressing real life problem that reflected by the everyday experience. In *Practical Theology: An Introduction*, Osmer explains that practical theology is a self-consciously hermeneutical enterprise,[39] which means that the main purpose of practical theologians is to get the holiness out of the parts and fragmentations.

Coherent unity of any approach to Christian education as practical theology in the light of the unity of the reign of God is clearly manifested in Gordon Mikoski's introduction to his "Neo-Protestant Practical Theology." While he views practical theology as Christological and Trinitarian tasks, Mikoski argues, Neo-Protestant practical theology should be the paradigm of unifying everything in a whole. He says,

36. Matt 6:9–1, NIV.
37. Graham, *Transforming Practice*.
38. Osmer, *Practical Theology*, 153-54.
39. Ibid., 4.

> As an enterprise focusing on the complex and multifaceted relationship between divine and human action, neo-Protestant practical theology sees the task of practical theology as Christological and Trinitarian in character. The paradigm for relating eternity and time, universal truth and contextually shaped particularities of experience, is the incarnation and work of Jesus Christ. Traditional Chalcedonian Christology—embraced by the vast majority of Christian traditions—affirms that the divine and the human natures of Christ's existence must be given their appropriate due, without confusion and without collapsing one reality into another. The divine and the human, the eternal and temporal comes together in harmonious, beautiful, and just order in person and work of Jesus Christ. Inasmuch as neo-Protestant practical theology seeks to relate complexities of human individual and social life to the reality of God and God's Reign on earth in history, it takes Chalcedonian Christology as its theological starting points and framework. Yet, it is not sufficient to focus only upon Jesus Christ as the core problematic of this approach to practical theology because Jesus Christ, as attested in scripture, is empowered by the Holy Spirit and works to the glory of the one who he called "Abba." The Christological problematic of neo-Protestant practical theology has, therefore, to be seen and situated within a larger Trinitarian framework.[40]

John Dewey, indeed, views the kingdom of God in a way that is quite close to the Christian view as unity and harmony of all people, practice, and thoughts. In his article "Christianity and Democracy," he views the kingdom of God as the full freedom of thought and practice, considering fellow humans in equality and "shared praxis," while freedom, for him, is the spiritual unification of humans together. Dewey says,

> The spiritual unification of humanity, the realization of the brotherhood of man, all that Christ called the kingdom of God is but the further expression of this freedom of truth. The truth is not fully free when it gets into some individual's consciousness, for him to delicate [i.e., enjoy] him with. It is freed only when it moves in and through this favored individual to his fellow; when the truth which comes to consciousness in one, extends and distributes itself to all so that it becomes the Common-wealth [hyphen in original]. The republic, the public affairs. The walls broken down by the freedom, which is democracy, are all the walls preventing the complete movement

---

40. Cahalan and Mikoski, *Opening the Field*, 174–75.

of truth. It is in the community of truth thus established that the brotherhood, which is democracy, has its being. The supposition that the ties which bind men together, that the forces which unify society, can be other than the very laws of God, can be other than the outworking of God in life, is a part of that same practical unbelief in the presence of God in the world which I have already mentioned.[41]

For Dewey, the beauty of life and existence that God has given the human being and the whole creation is the wholeness of the human being as well as the wholeness of the creation and everything, Dewey conclude his holistic understanding of education,

Surely to fuse into the social and religious motive, to break down the barriers of Pharisaism . . . which isolate religious thought and conduct from the common life of man, to realize the state as one Commonwealth of truth—surely this is a cause worth battling for.[42]

John Calvin, on the other hand, is deeply convinced with the unity and mutual interaction of both the kingdom of God and the kingdom of the world, believing that both are God's kingdoms. In the *Institutes of the Christian Religion*, Calvin emphasizes that the kingdom of the state is temporal, concerned with the present life in the physical world, and regulates the outward human behavior, while the kingdom of God is eternal, concerned the spiritual life, and resides in the deep mind and soul of humans. However, both civil order and church are part of the temporal kingdom as they deal with temporal laws and externals. The two kingdoms, nevertheless, are God's and they are legitimate and divinely ordained. God rules the civil kingdom as a creator and sustainer but rules the spiritual kingdom as a redeemer and Savior. These two kingdoms, and God's ways of ruling them, are never to be confused, but are clearly distinct. Unlike Augustine, for Calvin distinction between the two kingdoms is not antithesis; for him, the two kingdoms are not the kingdoms of God and Satan, instead, both are God's and God rules both. Calvin argues that another order is to be established to keep this authority and order of the world from deviation. This new order is the participation of all people in discussion and making decisions, which is the first seed for the democracy.[43]

---

41. Dewey, "Christianity and Democracy," 60.
42. Ibid.
43. Calvin, *Institutes*, II.xx.

Looking carefully to Calvin's account on the two kingdoms, indeed, reflects some important theological issues that are closely relevant to my approach to Christian education of the Presbyterian Church in Egypt. First, Calvin is concerned with reconciling "creation" theology with the "redemption" theology, which is one of the major factors that form splits and division in the church. Calvin's understanding of the sovereignty of God over all creation, assures us of the goodness of the whole creation because it is God's creation. This, indeed, helps reconcile Christian with secular, believing that all things are from God. Second, Calvin's conviction that both Christian and secular kingdoms exist together in a temporal state here on the earth, beautifully helps reconcile material and physical with spiritual. This indeed, is quite needed to help the Egyptian Presbyterian education to change its position towards unchristian resources, such as literature, arts, music, and drama. Third, the third way for Calvin is discussion among all people is a basic foundation of my approach, in which all dimensions are rooted. Participation of all people in discussion in order to find solutions and make decisions does open the door for a dialectical education in the Presbyterian Church in Egypt. For me, dialectical education, without doubt, is a convenient medium, in which a reconciliation of all divisions takes place.

Understanding the nature of the kingdom of God as unity and harmony of all division, will help the Presbyterian education in Egypt to bring all divisions and fragments together, which in turn will help reconciliation: the divine authority with the human agency; spiritual with material; Christian with secular; eternal with temporal; faith with reason; theology with philosophy; theory with practice; and the universal message of the bible with the contextual experience. My holistic approach, indeed, will, not only help reconciling divisions and fragmentations, resolve the problem of dualistic thinking, and transform a blind faith into an understanding faith, but also help discern the truth as a whole unified truth. It is also in the course of this process of reconciling dialogue that a learner will have enough freedom to reflect, analyze, and practice, which helps developing critical thinking.

Goal—Reconciling Education with Life

Borrowing Thomas Groome's expression about the reign of God, "here and now, but not yet," in a practical theological viewpoint, could be quite helpful in unifying the goal of Presbyterian education in Egypt. As it was discussed earlier, like public education, one of the processes of Presbyterian education and formation in Egypt is putting all the focus on preparing the children for the future. While this perspective, indeed, is rooted in the serious misunderstanding of the nature of the child as an incomplete human being, who is educated not to be a mature but a complete being in the future, its consequences are serious as well. A significant lack of participating in this kind of education as a joyful and interesting process comes on the top of these consequences. This indeed, alienates the learner from the process, giving him little or no interest to be engaged in active learning, turning him to be a passive receiver of some pre-made knowledge that is incapable of developing him as a critical thinker. Based on his anthropological awareness that a child is a whole human being in the process of maturation, Dewey, indeed, gives Egyptian Presbyterian education a new spark to make education a real life for learners, preparing the class to be joyful, without stress or fears. This gives the Christian education in Egypt the inspiration of designing new goals for leaners, practicing, enjoying their practice, reflecting on their experience, learning, and constructing their own knowledge. According to Csikszentmihalyi in his book *Creativity*, joy promotes understanding and creativity. It is simply a process of continuous growing through both living and learning in freedom. At the end of *My Pedagogic Creed*, Dewey clearly states,

> I believe that every teacher realizes the dignity of his calling; that is a social servant set apart from the maintenance of proper social order and securing of the right social growth." "I believe that in this way the teacher always is the prophet of the true God and the usherer in of the true kingdom of God."[44]

Calvin, on the other hand, agrees with Dewey in understanding man as rational being who was created in the image of God and should live and learn from experiencing his own faith here and now, Calvin helps the Egyptian to fill the gap that Dewey's pragmatic perspective leaves. Besides here and now, Calvin teaches the Egyptian Presbyterians to consider that one of the fundamental goals of Christian education is to prepare disciples of Jesus for the future ministry in the world. This holistic approach to the goal of education will help learners to recognize the continuity of their experience and to find a way to interpret it. Through a model of such an approach that I have tried in the ETSC in January 2013, one of the aims was to call learners to enjoy life through the process, and the feedback from all learners was positive.

---

44. Dewey, *My Pedagogic Creed*, 77–80.

Christian First—Reconciling Education with Theology

Lack of using a theological language, is one of the major problems of the lack of critical thinking skills in the course of Christian education in the Presbyterian Church in Egypt. While Christian education is first "Christian," meaning theology, for many reasons, the process of Presbyterian education in Egypt has put its entire attention in the Bible as the only source of knowledge; reading the Bible in a literal manner and creating some procedures for marital problems, Sunday school, and youth ministry. This, indeed, resulted in faithful scripture-centered Christians with a significant lack of theological understanding. It is expected, then, that while there are four areas under the name "practical theology department" in the ETSC: Christian education, pastoral care, homiletics, and Christian education, practical theology itself has been never known as a science or taught as a discipline.

Thinking theologically, Osmer argues, is the way, not only to understand, the reality of God and world, but also to understand how and why other people think and act and how and why a practical theologian works in certain ways. In his epilogue of *The Teaching Ministry of Congregations,* Osmer clearly points to this necessity of making *theological rational* a basic foundation of the teaching ministry,

> *Theological rational* points to an account of the central theological convictions that explain why a practical theologian works in certain ways. It links substantive claims about God and the world in relation to God to other methodological decisions. For example, the theological rational of James Loder and Deborah Hunsinger affirm a strong Christocentrism, building on the arguments of Soren Kierkegaard and Karl Barth, respectively. This is in turn is explicated in terms of the Chalcedonian paradigm, which provides key rules to guide thinking about the relationship between the human and divine. This theological rational is linked to other methodological decisions, such as their interdisciplinary method and their understanding of the epistemological status of knowledge emerging out of praxis. In contrast, the theological rational provided by many liberal and feminist practical theologians is based on an account of Christ as a liberator of the marginalized and oppressed, which informs their decisions to adopt a neo-Marxist understanding of the theory-praxis relationship and revised praxis correlation model of interdisciplinary work. The point to underscore is that methodological decisions in practical theology do not take place in vacuum; they presuppose a substantive theological rational that

underwrites some of the most important methodological decisions a practical theologian makes.[45]

While Don Browning portrays a beautiful picture of Christian education as practical theology, he offers a great account of the importance of locating Christian education in the wider field of practical theology by embracing the practical reason for creating critical and rational people who have enough Christian wisdom in order to have a deeper understanding of God and reality. In his book, *Fundamental Practical Theology*, Don Browning suggests a process by which "communities of memory" (such as churches) can better exhibit "practical reason" or practical wisdom. He calls this four-movement process, which he recommends for all theological inquiry and theological education, "fundamental practical theology."[46] In Browning's words,

> The structure of practical theology and the structure of Christian education are the same. Christian education, like fundamental practical theology, moves from descriptive theology backward to historical and systematic theology and forward to strategic practical theology. It does this in elementary ways for the young and immature in the faith; it does it in increasingly complex ways for the older and mature in the faith. All Christian education, like all practical theology, takes place in communities of faith, inquiry, and action. Like practical theology, Christian education should first describe the questions that emerge from the situated praxis of a Christian community and other communities with which it has dialogue. Christian education then takes these questions back to the classic sources of Christian ideals and norms. This sets up a *play* between question and text, a to-end-from process of questioning the text, listening to the text, and being questioned by the text. As the practical educational process becomes more serious (more like work), it tries to gain more systematic and critical grasp of both situated practice and text. Finally, the educational process returns to the concrete problems that stimulated the practical reflective process in he beginning. This last step is parallel to the moment I call strategic practical theology.[47]

I believe that a comprehensive approach to Christian education in the Presbyterian Church in Egypt should include theology as a fundamental

---

45. Groome, *Sharing Faith*, 14.
46. Browning, *Fundamental Practical Theology*, 2.
47. Ibid., 213.

part of the process both in the church and the ETSC. Locating education in the wider realm of practical theology doubtlessly will help the Presbyterian leaders, not only to resolve the problematic lack of creative pedagogy, but also to develop rational theological skills of reading the text and context, theory and practice, and social and spiritual experiences. This, indeed, clearly requires beginning with the ETSC as a strategic key place of theological education in Egypt.

Love of Wisdom[48]—Reconciling Education with Practical Reason

Since my major in Egyptian public education was not philosophy, from primary school to the end of my college study, I heard nothing about philosophy. Consequentially, I barely knew the names of Socrates, Plato, and Aristotle. Parallel to the public education in Egypt, I have grown up in the Presbyterian church of Egypt since I was six, where I used to spend hours in the Sunday school, among youth, in the church club every day until I graduated from college as a medical doctor. In contrast to public education that taught me nothing about philosophy, church education in the Presbyterian Church directly and strongly taught me that philosophy is a curse, which stands against Christian faith and obeying God. Sadly, this led me to view philosophy with hatred and disrespect. While this antipathy towards philosophy, indeed, was one of the major factors of lacking Christian wisdom for the majority of the Presbyterians in Egypt, it has also led the church isolating itself from the rich experience of huge number of philosophers.

A main concern for Don Browning is to put together a whole approach to practical theology, which includes the experiential and situational level, the reflective level and the orientation level. He places his way of doing practical theology within a tradition of practical philosophy, which he traces back to Aristotle's practical wisdom, "phreonesis." Not only Browning, but also most of the leaders that God has sent to God's people were greatly influenced with the ancient Greek philosophy and the philosophy of their age. Writing his gospel, John, for example, is influenced with Plato's Forms, which is clearly manifested in stating that Jesus is the "true" life, light, bread, water, and etc., So too were Paul, Augustine, Thomas Aquinas, and many others. More significantly, John Calvin, the founder of the Presbyterian Church, was deeply influenced by many of the classical philosophy.

48. According to Oxford Dictionaries, the word philosophy comes from the Middle English from the old French philosophie, via Latin from Greek philosophia "love of wisdom."

In his *Practical Theology: An Introduction*, Osmer calls this "sagely wisdom." What I intend to do, then, is to base my new approach to the Presbyterian education in Egypt on philosophy as the second foundation beside theology. This will help the Egyptian Presbyterians, to use the different philosophical methodologies to examine their religious thoughts and beliefs in the world. This also will help to understand that philosophy is not against faith, not a call against the existence of God, and not having faith in God, but rather is an examination of the way that people understand who God is, the way they understand the self and the way they think and act in the world. Indeed, I see philosophy as a very Christian way for many reasons. First, it does fulfill Jesus' call to examine ourselves, ways, thinking, and kind of knowledge we are taught by others. Second, since one of the dimensions of sin, for Calvin, Niebuhr, and others, is the pride of knowledge, using philosophy to reflect and examine our experience, thoughts, and belief, clearly fulfills Calvin's call for humility. Third, it copes with all philosophers and educators who deeply believe the way of thinking is a major problem of many today. And because many of these philosophers are Christians, it is evident that philosophy is not against Christian faith. In my comprehensive approach to Christian education philosophy should have a significant role to play in equipping learners with Christian wisdom for better faith, life, and mission in the world.

An Inevitable Dialogue—Reconciling Theology with Sciences

In his book, *Critical Thinking, What Every Person Needs to Survive*, after referring the roots of critical thinking to Socratic inquiry, Richard Paul argues that truth can best be sought after by means of dialogical thinking—"thinking that involves a dialogue or extended exchange between different points of view or frames of reference."[49] This kind of thinking allows one to challenge one's perceptions, suspend one's historical and cultural bias, and test the strengths and weaknesses of differing points of view.[50]

If God is good, so God is the source of all goodness in the world. All disciplines, then, that assist individuals to understand their experience more deeply and fully are from God. Indeed, I'm convinced that it is not only human sciences that are concerned with interpreting human experience and helping improve human lives, but also all innovations and creativity that upgrade human welfare and flourished life. Philosophers, psychologists,

---

49. Paul, *Critical Thinking*, 292.
50. Ibid., 293.

sociologist, anthropologist, and others scholars that are concerned with human development, indeed, are inspired by the Holy Spirit, which means that their continuation in improving Christian faith is necessary and useful. And since God is a sovereign and free God who can reveal the ultimate truth by any means, I have faith that nontheological disciplines should be considered as important source of constructing and understanding our truth.

In the Sunday morning service, March 27, 1892, Dewey delivered a talk entitled, "Christianity and Democracy." In this speech, which was published later in *Religious Thought at the University of Michigan*, Dewey wants to read Christian theology, and secularize Christian ethics into the politics of the world. Religion, for Dewey, is "an expression of the social relations of the community." In his article, "The New Psychology," he says,

> Thus modern psychology is intensely ethical in its tendencies. As it refuses to hypostatize [this word means 'to attribute real identity to'] abstractions into self-subsistent individuals, and as it insists upon the automatic spontaneous elements in man's life, it is making possible for the first time an adequate psychology of man's religious nature and experience. As it goes into the depths of man's nature it finds, as stone of its foundation, blood of its life, the instinctive tendencies of devotion, faith, and idealism which are the eternal substructure of all the struggles of the nations upon the alter stairs which slope up to God.[51]

This is why Jack L. Seymour and Carol A. Wehrheim link understanding with unifying pieces together in one coherent whole. In "Faith Seeking Understanding: Interpretation As a Task of Christian Education," they say, "To understand is to re-present and think clearly about the meaning and the coherence of the subject matter—the religious heritage. Clear thinking is the basis for evaluation and decision."[52] This coherence of an educational approach requires "Christian educators must seek to clarify the relationship of Christian education to the wider learning environment."[53] Another dimension of integrity for such an educational approach to be achieved is that "The foundational relationship of Christian education to both educational theory and theology must be explored continually."[54]

Believing that all sciences, thoughts, and disciplines are fallible, imperfect, and incomplete, cross-disciplinary work is essentially required for both practical theology and Christian education. This, indeed, is what

---

51. Dewey, "New Psychology," 60.
52. Seymour and Miller, *Contemporary Approaches*, 147.
53. Ibid., 159.
54. Ibid., 161.

profoundly guided Osmer to construct his belief in what he calls "transversal rational." Using the image of pickup sticks, he emphasizes that various forms of knowledge can intersect at particular points and have a relationship but not need to have a permanent relationship. In the epilogue to *Teaching Ministry of Congregations*, Osmer discusses what he means by "transversal rational," when he offers the image of permeable floating relational pods. For Osmer, any particular thing or issue always contracts and is constructed from within and from without. Individuals and congregations are not islands that can isolate themselves from outside influences. The evangelical distinction between "the world" and "the church" is nonsense as far as he is concerned. The same people who go to local public school go to Sunday morning worship in the local church. For Osmer, all institutions and people have boundaries but those boundaries are permeable. This fact reflects the necessity of a free and instigated dialogue between all sciences for a deeper understanding of human experience.[55]

The fact that interdisciplinary dialogue is properly about Christian education must be clearly established. It is my conviction that Christian education, at least in the modern age, is a meeting of at least two different scholarly domains: theology and educational theory. Educational theory in turn includes a wide variety of fields such as philosophy, psychology, sociology, anthropology, hermeneutical theory, and political science. In short, since I believe that there is no such thing as pure "Christian" or pure "education," but rather that the two mutually influence each other, it is inherent in the very nature of Christian education that any discussion of Christian education is a discussion between disciplines— "an inevitable dialogue."

Hermeneutical Task[56]—Reconciling Education with Interpretation

It has been known for long time that hermeneutics is the science of interpreting ancient text. Yet, today; practical theologians discovered its ability of interpreting other disciplines, human life and experience as well as the ancient texts. In the epilogue of *The Teaching Ministry of Congregations*, Osmer teaches the hermeneutical character of practical theology

> Hermeneutics is the art and science of interpretation. It focused originally on the interpretation of ancient texts. Over the course

55. Osmer, *Teaching Ministry*, 308.
56. I borrow the term "Hermeneutical Circle" from Osmer. In his latest book *Practical Theology: An Introduction*, Osmer describes his four task of interpreting practical theology as a hermeneutical circle.

of twentieth century, however, hermeneutics was broadened to include the interpretive dimension of all disciplines, resulting in a revision of the older view of science as completely objective and natural. Within this important and broad—reaching discussion of hermeneutics, some philosophers and theologians have reworked the older concept of a hermeneutical circle to describe the different tasks involved in a comprehensive process of interpretation. It is helpful to view the tasks of practical theology along these lines.[57]

Indeed, the reason of being serious about introducing the Egyptian Presbyterians to the hermetical nature of practical theology is the usefulness and necessity of the hermeneutical task for constructing critical thinkers in the process of education. Like Dewey's reflective thinking as the only educative thinking, Calvin gives much attention to human as a rational being and to the ability of the redeemed reason to reflect and construct the own knowledge by the help of the Holy Spirit. Within Osmer's framework of education as a comprehensive practical theology, I can see both Dewey's and Calvin's conviction as he writes in the *A Teachable Spirit*,

> The heart of practical theology is reflection that takes place in the midst of unfolding situations emerging out of social practices in an attempt to shape actional responses that are appropriate to what can be discerned of God's purposes for the world as they are brought to bear on unique contexts of experience.[58]

Charles Gerkin's hermeneutical approach to practical theology is a good example who, in his book *Living Human Document* develops a theory of pastoral counseling from an interdisciplinary dialogical perspective. He employs hermeneutical theory to relate theology and psychology in pastoral counseling. He views pastoral counseling as a "dialogical hermeneutical process" of helping the care-seekers interpret the stories of their life by using theological and psychological languages of human experience.[59] Gerkin writes that practical theology

> is the critical and constructive reflection on the life and work of Christians in all the varied contexts in which that life takes place with the intention of facilitating transformation of life in all its dimensions in accordance with the Christian gospel. Practical theology, seen from a narrative hermeneutical perspective,

---

57. Osmer, *Teaching Ministry of Congregations*, 304.
58. Osmer, *Teachable Spirit*, 162.
59. Gerkin, *Living Human Document*, 28.

involves a process of interpretative fusion of horizons of meaning embodied in the Christian narrative with other horizons that inform and shape perceptions in the various arenas of activity in which Christian participate.[60]

With Osmer, I have increasingly become aware of the deep need of the Presbyterian education in Egypt to adopt and employ hermeneutics, taking its functions seriously for a deeper and understandable faith. In this age of much complexity and uncertainty, the Egyptian Presbyterians should be more aware that it is not enough for Christian leaders to simply pass on the traditions and practices of the past, nor is it enough for the Egyptian theologians and teachers of the ETSC to simply hand on the Christian cultural heritage of the West without serious modification and contextualization. In both the church and academy, the challenge of developing new forms of Christian practice and good reasons to justify these practices by using hermeneutical minds is a real challenge.[61]

Dialectical—Reconciling Education with Creative Pedagogy

I am not up to set a list of pedagogies here for many reasons: first, because of the nature and scope of this research. Second, because I alone am not enough to change one of the major problems of education, both public and Christian in Egypt. The fundamental changes that I intend to recommend in the education process in Egypt are to guide all members to participate in setting everything of the teaching learning process. Third, because the main purpose of this research, indeed, is theoretical about developing and using critical thinking in the education in Egypt. In another word, the purpose of this research is to shape some principles of a new approach to education in Egypt as a preliminary theory of Christian education, which might encourage others to further build on and create other new approaches. Fourth, to be concerned with making a list of methods of education is to make myself a slave again to the traditional approach of education, which I already attempt to reform.

Yet, the aim of this part is to attract the Egyptian Presbyterian educators' attention to face the fact of the necessity of setting "dialogue" as the foundation of a creative pedagogy. Since there are vast cultural, educational, and social differences among the local Presbyterian churches in Egypt

---

60. Ibid., 61.
61. Osmer, "Practical Theology: A Current International Perspective."

between the countryside, suburban, and urban churches, what I attempt here is to construct some principles that might help the Presbyterian educators to construct their own creative pedagogy in each distinctive context. First, any creative pedagogy that would help create critical thinkers should design education as a dialectical in nature: a pedagogy that is rooted in free dialogue, not only between teacher and learners, but also between leaners and each other. Second, any creative pedagogy should help educators to discover and promote the natural capacities of learners towards continuous growth. Third, a creative pedagogy should be designed to meet and deal with the different kind of learners' intelligence and reflect different capacities of learning. Considering the diversity and pluralism of intelligence and the capacities of learning means an educator is required to use more than one method in the same class. Fourth, interdisciplinary methods are increasingly required for successful education in Egypt because of the increasing number of social, psychic, and educational problems of the Egyptian context due to poverty, lack of education, overpopulation, and the struggle between the Christian principles and value and the Islamic society. Fifth, all creative pedagogy, such as of Bloom, Groome, Osmer, and others, always begins with observation, analysis, criticism and ends with creating a new. Sixth, almost all—creative pedagogies of Christian education as practical theology are always rooted in the hermeneutical theory so that learners are to develop the ability to interpret both text and contextual practices. In fact, while nothing of my January 2013 class in the ETSC was not dialectical, the final evaluation by students was really positive.

Curriculum: Reconciling Education with Life Experience

Two problems are basic in making the curriculum of the Christian education in the Presbyterian Church in Egypt. First is the high focus on quantity over quality, which offers little or no space for reflection, analysis, or creativity. Second, most, if not all, of the curricula of Presbyterian education are imported from other places, and for large extent, are translated from a Western context, which always fails to interpret the contextual experiences and do not meet the actual needs of learners. As a basic element of my holistic approach to the Presbyterian in Egypt, I believe that fundamental changes are deeply required in the curriculum of its process. For this, I suggest that any innovation of this curriculum should follow some basic principles. First, like Dewey, Calvin, and Osmer, I intend to offer learners' experience a central place in the process of education. While the contemporary understanding of practical theology believes in beginning with practice of the faith community, both individual and congregational practice of the Egyptian Presbyterian Church is so rich that a vast number of valuable-content-curricula can be easily constructed. Second, I suggest that a good curriculum should consist of little number of subjects and small determined requirements, so that enough space for reflection, analysis, and criticism is allowed. For this, Osmer criticizes educators that insist to cover large amount of content in one subject, which works as a barrier to critical learning, as the pressure to process more data does not enable learners to take enough time to integrate what they have learned into thinking. Third, good curriculum, I suggest, should include case studies, critical incidence reports, and sharing personal experiences. According to Osmer, this allows leaners to be engaged in a scientific and theological interpretation of particular episodes, situations, and contexts.[62] Fourth, good curriculum should be able to educate for life. In other words, it should be able to link subject matter with real learners' life with its complexity and uncertainty. Indeed, reflecting and analyzing learners' experiences was a fundamental element of the curriculum that I have already taught in January 2013 in the ETSC. And while the teaching-learning process itself was quite enjoyable for both learners and myself, my students were deeply and enthusiastically engaged.

Learner-Centered—Reconciling Learner with Humanity

If lecturing, indoctrination, memorization, and written examination, as it was described in the first chapter, are the main elements of the teaching methods, it is expected, then, that the teacher-centered paradigm is mode of teaching in Presbyterian education as well as public education in Egypt. In a tribal sense, there are some figures that believe they know everything while others know nothing. These figures include, the father, the teacher, the pastor, the Christian educators, the older people, and so forth. The reasons for this are fundamentally political, cultural, and religious. This practice is the main reason of lack of critical thinking among the Egyptians in general. Transforming a teacher-centered into a leaner-centered paradigm of education is one of the main challenges of my holistic approach to Presbyterian education in Egypt.

To achieve this transformation is to focus on some principles. First, assisting educators and teachers to be aware of the potential natural capacities of the learning children, who are whole beings in the process of maturation.

---

62. Osmer, *Practical Theology*, 211.

Second, helping educators to construct a sense of their true identify as an educator whose main job is facilitating a successful educational process and guiding learners to choose. Third, reflecting on Paulo Freire's *A Pedagogy for the Oppressed*,[63] an educator should be taught about the dehumanization that always results from the teacher—centered style while reflecting on Palmer Barker' *The Courage to Teach*,[64] educators need to learn the equality of both teachers and leaners and the basic wright for everyone to have voice and to be an active partner in the process.

Multiple factors will contribute toward promoting a learner-centered paradigm. Teaching all members of the process about the real meaning of democracy as freedom of intelligence and freedom of thoughts, organizing creative method that rooted in dialogue, and organizing a limited number-classes will help. In the January 2013 class that I taught in the ETSC, while the time that I was allowed was two hours, I divided these two hours into six sections, fifteen minutes for each and while I was responsible for leading the final fifteen minutes-section, I allowed my leaners to lead the other five. While I led *lectio divina* in the first session of the class, I allowed my students to lead it in the rest of the eleven sessions, while I reflected of the required reading according Bloom's observe, analyze, criticize, and create, in the first session, they were required to lead this reflection during the rest of the course, while I offered an analytic case study according to Osmer's critical incidence report in the first session, they did the same during the rest of the course. My role during the five sections of the class that my students had to perform was guiding, clarifying, and facilitating. Indeed, the feedback from students and the objectives that they achieved was highly positive, especially as I taught Christian education as practical theology in light of what I have already leaned at PTS. My real joy from this experience of teaching was not only the positive feedback of my students and the high level of comprehension they reached, but also the hope that filled my heart that transforming Christian education in my church in Egypt is possible.

Democracy—Reconciling Learner with Freedom

If the extraordinarily changing circumstances in Egypt reflect something in the past four years, they reflect the Egyptians' deep yearning for freedom. Seeking a new flourished life, good president and government, dignity, and social justice, all have increasingly become basic goals for most of the Egyptians today. However, in my observation as an educator,

---

63. Freire and Macedo, *Pedagogy of Oppressed*.
64. Palmer, *Courage to Teach*.

for most of the Egyptians, including the Presbyterians, democracy is not more that getting rid of a dictator regime and having free elections to choose a good president and parliament.

Like Dewey, I deeply believe that democracy in its very nature is freedom while freedom is primarily a freedom of thoughts and intelligence. I also believe that democracy is a personal way of thinking, living, and participating in shared experiences. Democracy as freedom, then, is an individual matter that becomes social when all people learn how to think and practice as democratic characters. This indeed, reflects a crucial fact that "democracy as freedom" is not possible without a democracy of education. It is a fact that creating a democratic character begins with education, when learners are allowed, not only to learn, but also to practice actual democracy as freedom in the classroom.[65] Teaching about democracy and freedom in this way is not actually what I believe will develop such a mode of democracy, but in-class, actual practice of freedom is the way that will help developing them as democratic characters.

Dewey and Calvin, in fact, offer serious study of freedom, which is quite helpful in the course of practicing such a democracy in the Presbyterian Church in Egypt. While Dewey relies on the natural potentials and capacities of all human beings to grow continuously, calling democracy "freedom of intelligence," Calvin, on the other hand uses a similar term when he characterizes freedom as the "freedom of conscience," "one aspect is spiritual, whereby the conscience is instructed in piety and in reverencing God; the second is political, whereby man is educated for the duties of humanity and civil life that must be maintained among men."[66]

While Egyptians, including Presbyterians, have a real desire for freedom, the wrong image that they have about freedom as liberation from a dictator regime is really problematic and is more chaotic than freedom. What actually happened in some of the Presbyterian churches in Egypt during the past four years can easily portray this picture when the youth of these churches just stand in the Sunday service carrying big notes, saying to the pastor "Go!" Among those pastors indeed, were two of the most significant theologians and preachers in Egypt. Getting rid of the dictator regime of Mubarak and Muslim Brotherhood, indeed, allowed most of the people in Egypt, including the church people, to work on getting rid of all kind of authority, which was turned to chaos. Calvin wants to do is to wed faith with reason, which is really needed to realize freedom as personal

65. Dewey, *Democracy and Education*.
66. Calvin, *Institutes*, III.vi.13.

way of life that is based on a freedom of intelligence and true awareness of both rights and responsibilities.

The alternative that I suggest instead is not authoritarian or full freedom, but "authoritative" paradigm. While the authoritative model of education allows enough freedom, offering everyone a space for voice and experience, the teacher as a guide is responsible to lead the class, in love and freedom, towards fulfilling a particular vision. In other words, authoritative is a transitional middle stage between a submissive authoritarian and permissive education.

Source of Truth—Reconciling the Bible with Other Sources

Like most of the protestant churches, the Presbyterian Church in Egypt is scripture-centered church. This, indeed, is a real strength for a minor church in an Islamic society, especially when memorizing Qur'an is required by all students, including Christians, in all before collage stages. Literal words of the Bible, however, are the Egyptian way of justifying the truth by finding a biblical verse, story, or situation that is similar to their experience, trying to have a similar response, regardless of interpretation, understanding, or appropriation.

Reflecting on the Wesleyan Quadrilateral, Osmer points to four sources of justifying the truth: scripture, traditions, reason, and experience. For Osmer, the interplay between the four and the way we relate each of them to the others is subject to a wide verity of perspectives. Wesley himself has a deep conviction that scripture is the first and strongest measure of truth, then experience, then reason, then traditions. I believe that using reason to reflect on and analyze the living experience of theology and traditions is the way to develop Christian wisdom. For many reason, indeed, I believe that only the Bible is not enough, even though it is a basic and fundamental source of truth. First, believing that God is the source of every good material or means. Second, believing in the sovereignty of God over the whole creation, I believe that God is free to reveal God by any means. Third, living in a contextual time and place, interpreting spiritual experience cannot be actualized apart from intermitting the socio-cultural experience. Fourth, unlike other religions, which believe in the oral and written revelation, I believe that revelation in Christianity is a continuous, living and dynamic revelation because it exceeds the oral and written to an incarnated form of the living Word of God, Jesus. In short, theology cannot be fully apart from philosophy, Bible from arts literature music, and faith apart from reason.

From a practical theological viewpoint, I see this approach to justify truth as both holistic and reasonable. In reality, we do not really use any of them apart from the others—when we read the Bible for example, we need to use our mind to understand while only what we experience out of what we read in real life becomes a truth for us. We also always need to refer to the actual or written experience of the others to affirm our experience. The Bible itself is a mixture of God's revelation, human experience, human reasonable reflection and older Christian traditions.

For me, this conviction of referring to multiple sources of justifying our truth opens the door for reconciling Christian and non-Christian resources of learning. In addition to using the Bible in a dialogue with reason, experience, and traditions, we can also use it in a dialogue with secular arts, literature, music, drama, etc., thus giving us confidence while we are conversing theology with other sciences. Calvin rhetorically wonders,

> Shall we deny that the truth shone upon the ancient jurists who established civic order and discipline with such great equity? Shall we say that the philosophers were blind in their fine observation and artful description of nature? Shall we say that those men were devoid of understanding who conceived the art of disputation and taught us to speak reasonably? What shall we say of all the mathematical sciences? Shall we consider them the savings of madmen?[67]

Calvin's definite answer of his own question is "No." For he himself could not read those ancients' writings without "great admiration." For Calvin, if the Spirit of God is the sole source of truth, the works of human reason is the grace of the Holy Spirit. In this, Calvin disagrees with the common notion that the Holy Spirit does not work in unbelievers, but only works in the believers. He says, "for what is said as to the Spirit dwelling in believers only, is to be understood of the Spirit of holiness by which we are consecrated to God as temples."[68] While people think that "the statement that the Spirit of God dwells *only* in believers (Rom 8:9), Calvin, indeed, understands it as referring to the Spirit of sanctification." As "for the common benefit of mankind,"[69] the same Spirit, Calvin says, works also through the work and ministry of the ungodly. Therefore, Calvin refers every reasonable and rational activity to the works of the Holy Spirit whether these activities are practiced with believers or unbelievers, insisting, "if the Lord has been pleased to assist us by the work and ministry of the ungodly in physics,

67. Ibid., II.ii.15.
68. Ibid., II.ii.16.
69. Ibid.

dialectics, mathematics, and other similar sciences, let us avail ourselves of it, lest, by neglecting the gifts of God spontaneously offered to us, we be justly punished for our sloth."[70]

A New Name—Reconciling Education with Formation and Transformation

In the first session of her class "PT9008 Models of Adolescent Formation in Contemporary Christianity," Kenda Creasy Dean required all her students, including myself, to write a short unofficial paper defining three important key words in the field of Christian education: education, formation, and transformation. Then she led her students in a long discussion about the differences between these three. If, indeed, Dean's class was of a real value and usefulness for me, I believe that the first session's discussion on these terms was actually of a highest value among other sessions. Out of this useful discussion, the title "Christian education" has begun to be question for me. I had just started to be exposed to the title "religious education," which, in a conservative Egyptian background, was always a negative term, as people think it leads to loss the Christian identity of education. Along with all that I have learned at PTS, Dean's discussion has shaken the old title "Christian education," wondering whether it reflects what the process is really meant to be.

Indeed, I believe that the title "Christian education" is strong for some reasons. It points to the Christian identity of the kind of education we practice; it views education as a theological task; and it also embodies the interdisciplinary nature. However, the term, "Christian education," I believe, does not exactly explain what actually takes place in the process, which is really summarized by three of the terms that we discussed in Dean's class. If education is the information that we provide to the learner, and formation is what the faith community does to help the learner transform, transformation is what internally takes place in the entire life of the learner. Rejecting the old belief that these three go in a linear way from education to formation to transformation, through her class, Dean helped us to realize the fact that the three of them intertwine, overlap, and feed each other, which means that leaners are continually and alternatively are subject to the three of them.

In this regard, I adopt PTS' title "education and formation" to the Egyptian Presbyterian education in Egypt—a title that is able to include the main three principles of the actual process. However, because of the Islamic

70. Ibid.

context of the Presbyterian education in Egypt, I blend this title with the word Christian so that I call it "Christian education and formation."

Holistic Approach to Education and Formation in the Presbyterian Church in Egypt—What Is New?

While the main purpose of this research, was primarily to address the lack critical thinking in the process of Presbyterian education in Egypt, in light of the multiple educational and theological factors that formed this problem, other serious problems of the educational process have come to the surface, which reflected a clear need for a new approach that is able to address these problems. Adopting Osmer's comprehensive approach to practical theology I have come to the fact that a "reconciling dialogue," is strongly needed for unifying the process of the Presbyterian education in Egypt. While Osmer's comprehensive approach inspired and helped me to bring Dewey and Calvin in a dialogue, constructing what I call "a holistic approach" to Christian education, I see this approach useful to illuminate and address the problematic educational situation in the Presbyterian Church in Egypt in many ways:

First, the holistic approach to Christian education and formation in the Presbyterian Church in Egypt will work as a proper medium, in which critical thinking will be born and developed. In describing the problematic educational situation in the Presbyterian Church in Egypt, it has become quite evident to me that the lack of using a reconciling dialogue between conflicts and fragmentations is the main factor of significant lack of critical thinking in the education process. It is "dualism" and an either . . . or pattern of thinking that always results in accepting ready-made thoughts and beliefs by others without criticizing, understanding, or internalizing, which is hard to allow using the gift of human reason critically. Indeed, the main method that the Presbyterian educators dominate in Egypt could be described as "monologue." It is a speech that offers no space for learners to reflect, analyze, and create their own "truth." This is a dehumanizing way (according to Friere) that turns a learner from subject into an object with an inability to participate in the process as an active partner, but rather, as a dependent receiving learner that does not possess critical thinking skills. Given enough freedom and guidance, learners are called to be active partners in the process of thinking and reflecting through a mutual dialogue in a democratic environment where all members of the educational process, including the teacher, are equally subject to the process as learners. In this philosophical and theologically oriented class, all learners are invited and respectfully encouraged to use human reason in order to have a deeper understanding of the subject, which in turn, will help them to recognize their identity as genuine rational beings and transform them into critical thinkers.

Second, my holistic approach will introduce the Christian education and formation to the Egyptian church as practical theology. As it was mentioned earlier, it is ironic, indeed, to recognize that practical theology is merely known in Egypt. In the Evangelical Theological Seminary in Cairo (ETSC), practical theology as a discipline has never been taught since it was established about one hundred fifty years ago. With other eight scholars who are interested in linking theology with the practical ministry in the Presbyterian Church in Egypt, we created a group on the Facebook entitled the "Arab Seminar for Theological Research and Application" (ASTRA). Awsam Wasfy, the admin of the group is a significant Christian educator in the Presbyterian Church in Egypt. Wasfy is a psychiatrist who has studied theology at the ETSC, is strongly concerned with linking theology with psychology. Responding to his request to write a comment on his book *The Focus* before publishing it, I tried to locate the book in the interdisciplinary character of practical theology. Yet, Wasfy's response back to my comment was a real surprise, as he humbly admitted that he is practicing his ministry in the field of practical theology for about twenty years while he never knows it as a discipline. With having permission Wasfy's permission, I include here a translation of a part of his impressions:

> To be honest, Samy, your comment on "practical theology" awakened a continuous zeal and dialogue inside me about continuing my theological studies—an idea that kept burning my heart, but I kept saying it is too late and it is better to spend the rest of my life in the practical ministry, particularly, I'm the only one that started therapy program for homosexuals in the Middle East. My gratitude to you for guiding me to the field that I'm working for years and do not know its name "practical theology" or its character.[71]

Indeed, introducing Christian education and formation as practical theology to the Presbyterian Church in Egypt has increasingly become an essential need for me in order to achieve such reformation that I dream.

Third, the holistic approach to Christian education and formation will assist the Egyptian Presbyterians to construct their contextual theology. Since it is first establishment one hundred and fifty years ago in Egypt, the Presbyterian Church rooted its ministry on Western theology. *The Institutes of Christian Religion* of John Calvin are almost the main theological source for

---

71. Awsam Wasfy, https://www.facebook.com/groups/672504479525925/.

the Egyptian Presbyterian Church while most of the Egyptian Presbyterians barely know theologians rather than John Calvin, the entirety of the theological thoughts of the Presbyterian doctrines in Egypt were conveyed by the first American missionaries in Egypt and few people who studied theology in the West. While the English language stands as a barrier for most Christian learners in Egypt, there are few theological books that are translated into Arabic. The lack of using critical thinking in the process of Christian education and formation, however, resulted from poor philosophical and theological orientation and reflection on the actual life experience resulted in a significant lack of a contextual theology that is deeply rooted in the midst of everyday life problems of the faith community practice that is Egyptian nature. Consequentially, while the biblical texts are the main references for the Pastors and Christian leaders, most of the Presbyterians mostly depend on these pester for discerning their truth.

The cry for the need of a "Contextual Arabic Theology," however, was begun by Abdel Meseh Estafanos, in the commencement and graduation of the class 120, 1982. In a speech entitled, "Towards A Contemporary Egyptian Evangelical Theology," after a comprehensive introduction including the centrality of the cross, the multiple forms of the gospel, and the diversity of the theological schools in the church history, Estafanos offered a number of crucial questions: how could theology become Evangelical; how could the Evangelical theology become Egyptian; how could the evangelical Egyptian theology become contemporary? For Estafanos, since Arabic mentality is different from Western mentality, we have to find relevant Arabic theological language, which help us find answers of such crucial questions. A language, Estafanos continues, that sufficient to describe the Triune God in an Islamic context—a context where believing in one God is extremely fundamental. In the same way, we need an Arabic language that is relevant to introduce the incarnation theology, in a context where people can never imagine God in a place away from the highest heaven; salvation atonement; redemption; and others, all what we used to introduce through Syriac terms in an Egyptian context.

The cry for a contextual theology continued burning some Egyptian scholars' hearts until the Culture House, a publication house that belongs to the Presbyterian Church in Egypt, gathered eight researching papers in attempt to offer an interpretation of some theological issues in an Egyptian perspective, such as the identity and practice of the minority in Egypt, the Arabic-Israel struggle, and salvation in other religions. These papers were published in published a six hundred volume, entitled *Toward a Contemporary Arabic Theology*.[72]

With much attention to the usefulness of reflective interpretation of the practice of specific individuals, groups, or congregations in a certain context, Osmer draws from Browning understanding of the practice of the faith community as a "theory-laden-practice." Indeed, I see Osmer's contextual and congregational focus as a real help of creating contextual Egyptian theology. It is the constant reflection on their contextual experience that helps the Egyptian Presbyterians to recognize their real spiritual, social, cultural problems and helps them redefine these problems, constructing their new theological theories to guide these practices in the future. In short, the ability of solving contextual problems helps construct contextual theology. In the *Models of Contextual Theology*, Stephen Benvans argues that theology needs to be contextualized in order to be able to meet the needs of the church and society:

> A way of doing theology that takes into account, or we could say puts in a mutually critical dialogue, two realities. The first of these is the experience of the past, recorded in Scripture and preserved and defended in the church's tradition. The second is the experience of the present or a particular context, which consists of one or more of at least four elements: personal or communal experience, "secular" or "religious" culture, social location, and social change.[73]

Fourth, my holistic approach to Christian education and formation in Egypt will play a significant role in developing and practicing true democracy. In the light of Dewey's philosophy of education, it has become evident to me that democracy is not election or getting rid of a dictator regime, but rather a way of life. With Dewey, I believe that democracy is freedom—a freedom of thoughts and intelligence, and this freedom is the work of education. Freedom of thoughts and intelligence, therefore, are given enough space in the holistic approach to Christian education and formation in the Presbyterian Church in Egypt—a process that I attempt to transform from an one-direction monologue into a mutual dialogue in an environment of freedom and equality and learner-centered process. It is in this actual in-class practice of true freedom and equality that Egyptian Presbyterians can be transformed into democratic characters.

Fifth, the holistic approach to Christian education and formation in the Presbyterian Church in Egypt can work as a paradigm shift towards a

---

72. Zaki, *Towards Contemporary Arabic Theology*, 506.
73. Bevans, *Models of Contextual Theology*, 64.

new educational process. Instead of setting goals for preparing children for the future life, goals will be addressing real life in the present. Instead of indoctrination, memorizing, and written examination as a main method of teaching and learning, a creative pedagogy will be created, a pedagogy that is based on a free dialectic education where each individual will have a voice as an active partner in the process. Instead of ready-prepared-knowledge curriculum, everyday life experience will be considered as its main element. Such as lacking contextual theology, most of the curricula that are used in the educational process of the Presbyterian Church in Egypt are usually translated from Western curricula. Introducing Christian education as interdisciplinary dialogue, as praxis, and as a learner—centered paradigm to the Presbyterian Church in Egypt will, indeed, inspire the Presbyterian leaders to consider the richness of their contextual experience, use their reason to reflective critical on these experiences, and create their own goals, methods, and curricula.

Finally, the holistic approach to Christian education and formation in the Presbyterian Church in Egypt is useful to reconcile the divisions within the Egyptians as human beings. One of the real problems that were described in the first chapter is the insistence of the traditional education to drive the Egyptians into dualisms and divisions, which have led the Presbyterians in Egypt into much confusion and struggle. My holistic approach to Christian education and formation as practical theology is not only include other disciplines that help human beings to deeply understand spiritual experiences in a socio-cultural context, but also helps to bring these disciplines into a reconciling dialogue. This, indeed, not only reflects the wholeness and integration of the truth the individual constructs out of conversing all sciences together, but also reflects the wholeness and fullness of the human being, as it addresses all human dimensions, physical, social, psychological, intellectual, and sexual. It also helps guide human being in a full freedom, which, in Dewey's conviction, is the freedom of intelligence and freedom of thought, which in turn helps create critical thinking skills and intelligent judgment in all life situations.

Conclusion

IN THIS DISSERTATION, I have argued that using a new approach to the Christian education and formation in the Presbyterian Church in Egypt might help illuminate and address the significant lack of critical thinking in the process. Drawing from a philosopher, psychologist, and educator John Dewey and a theologian and reformer John Calvin within the understanding of Christian education as practical theology by practical theologian Richard Osmer as a framework, I philosophically explored and theologically evaluated the problem in its socio-cultural context in Egypt for a better and democratic approach to Christian education and faith formation among the Egyptian Protestants.[1] Along the course of my research, while Dewey helped me to illuminate the educational factors that formed the problem in its socio-cultural context and Calvin helped me to illuminate the theological factors in its congregational context in the Presbyterian Church, Osmer inspired with a holistic approach to Christian education and formation, an approach that might help address the problem in the Presbyterian church in Egypt.

In the course of my research, however, I realized that most of these factors, educational and theological, are deeply rooted in a ground of dualism—the insistency of the Presbyterian educators in Egypt on creating a conflict and division within the process of education, which clearly resulted in a significant lack of a dialectic education, and in turn, resulted in the lack of critical thinking. Following Osmer's four tasks of interpreting practical theology, I have begun this research with a thick analytic description of the problem through referring to many of the Egyptian writers, Christian and secular, applying a simple model of empirical research, and through my personal observation as an educator in Egypt. John Dewey in the second

1. It is important to make it clear that I do not intend to do a hermeneutical, but rather to carry practical theology with its hermeneutical function to the Presbyterian Church in Egypt in order to help its learners an educational project by focusing on the process that helps learners develop critical thinking skills and recognize that Christian education is not just techniques and procedures, but rather practical theology and practical reason.

chapter helped me to understand the problem in a deeper while his account on anthropology, democracy, human experience, and creative pedagogy, were of real help to recognize the roots of these problems in the Presbyterian education as a reflection of the public education in Egypt. In the third chapter, while I brought Reinhold Niebuhr and Valerie Saiving in a dialogue with John Dewey, John Calvin, the founder of the Presbyterian church, offered a real theological understanding, not only of the problem, but also of theological anthropology, value and necessity of using human reason, Calvin's account on human reason, the pure natural before Adam's sin, the corrupted because of sin, and redeemed reason by the work of Jesus, was a real help for me, which in turn, is of a clear help to the Presbyterian in Egypt.

In the fourth chapter, I adopted Osmer's approach to Christian education as practical theology to create my holistic approach to Christian education and formation in the Presbyterian Church in Egypt. Since Osmer's approach is a clear call for bringing all divisions into a harmonious dialogue, which helps both individuals and congregations to construct their own truth, it, indeed, inspired me to construct a holistic approach to the Christian education and formation in Egypt in the light of the theological understanding of the reign of God as reconciliation. Reconciling faith with reason, theology with philosophy, Christian with secular, the Bible with experience, all are rooted in reconciling God's authority with the human agency and creation theology with redemption theology, which is not possible without teaching Christian education and formation as practical theology. The hermeneutical nature of practical theology, indeed, will help to bring all divisions and conflict of the education of the Presbyterian Church in Egypt into a harmonious and integrating dialogue, which will help transform the whole process into *Teaching for Christian Wisdom: Towards A Holistic Approach to Christian Education and Formation in the Presbyterian Church in Egypt.*

APPENDIX I

Empirical Research—A Survey

A Study of the Current Status of Christian Education
In the Presbyterian Church of Egypt
May 2012

IN A SIMPLE MODEL of qualitative research applied on a considerable number of the Presbyterian leaders in Egypt, in May and June 2012, the fact a significant lack of critical thinking has become evident in many ways. This survey was applied on 52 of the Presbyterian educators in two different presbyteries, Cairo and Minya.[1] Survey involves, pastors that are ordained in the church during the past ten years; Christian education leaders, including Sunday school leaders, high school leaders, and youth leaders; and ETSC students of different years.

The survey included thirty-two questions organized in seven groups. The first group-included question 1, composed of five parts, and focus on personal information of each participant's church, ministry, education, etc. The second group includes the questions 2–4 and attempted to pay attention to the educators' understanding of Presbyterian education in Egypt. The third group included the questions 5–7 and shed light on the impact of public on Christian education in Egypt. The fourth group included the questions 8-14 and aimed to examine the main sources of knowledge for teachers and learners in the process of the Presbyterian education in Egypt. In particular, this focus on human reason and experience, in addition to human sciences and arts. The fifth five; was organized to examine the theological understanding of using human reason in the Christian education in light of John Calvin's theology of reason. The sixth group included the questions 17–24 and in more details aimed to examine the participants' knowledge

---

1. Choosing Cairo and Minya presbyteries has a reason. While Minya presbytery is almost the biggest among the eight presbyteries of the Presbyterian church in Egypt, Cairo presbytery involves among its members most of the leaders, administrative offices, and educational centers, such as ETSC, CEOSS, and Synod of the Nile.

of John Dewey's educational theory, with more focusing on democracy of education, experience, and teacher-learner relationship. In the last group, which includes the questions 25–32, gives more attention to the issue of critical thinking, its necessity and importance, and how the church understands and uses it in the process of education.

Group 1, Personal Information:

1. Personal Information:

    Name: _____ Age: _____

    Church: _____

    Ministry: _____ For how many years: _____

Group 2, Christian Education:

2. I know the term, "Christian Educations,"

    ☐ Yes   ☐ No

3. There is a specific ministry for Christian education in my church:

    ☐ Yes   ☐ No

4. In this ministry, the following are practiced:

    • _____

    • _____

    • _____

5. The following individuals practice the ministry of Christian Education:
    - A full time Christian Education pastor
    - Graduates from the faculty of arts in education
    - General college graduates
    - High School graduates
    - Uneducated

6. The goals of Christian Education in my church are:
    - Building Christian Faith
    - Formation of Christian disciples

- Political and Social education for learners
- All of the above

7. "The Teaching-Learning process in the Egyptian schools and universities depends mainly on indoctrination and as much memorization of knowledge as possible, which was imposed through teachers while learners have no role in gaining knowledge themselves"

    I agree with this statement _____ %

8. Christian Education in the Presbyterian Church was influenced _____ % by the public education in Egypt

9. The similarities between methods of Christian education in the Presbyterian Church and Public education in Egypt are:
    - Indoctrination
    - Memorization and remembering
    - Lectures
    - Both lectures and discussions
    - All of the above
    - Other methods

Group 3, Source of Truth:

10. The main source of knowledge in the Presbyterian Church:
    - The Bible
    - Christian traditions
    - Theology
    - Experience
    - All of the above
    - None of the above

11. Other sources of knowledge
    - Literature and poetry
    - Music and singing
    - Theatre and art
    - Painting and sculpting
    - All of the above

12. Theology is considered a basic foundation to Christian education in the western hemisphere. In your opinion, Christian education of the Presbyterian church of Egypt is based on theological understanding by _____ %

13. The human sciences (philosophy, physiology, sociology, etc.) are considered an important source of theological learning in the Western Hemisphere. These sciences are used as a source of theological learning for the Presbyterian education in Egypt _____ %

14. Human reason plays a crucial role in justifying the truth about the Christian education process in the Western Hemisphere. In your opinion, human reason is used for the same purpose in the Presbyterian education in Egypt _____ %.

15. Many Christian educators in the Arabic world believe that the use of human reason in the Christian Education process weakens faith and lessens obedience to God. From your perspective, _____ % of Christian educators of the Presbyterian church of Egypt follows this belief.

16. In your opinion, the reason for this belief is
    - The belief that human reason is evil because of sin
    - Limitation of human reason and inability to approach the truth
    - The deep link between reason and philosophy, which isn't a Christian science
    - The belief that the Bible includes all.

Group 4, John Dewey:

19. The American educator John Dewey sees that human being is born with four natural abilities: the ability to observe; reflect and examine; communicate; and create. For Dewey, good education for Dewey is the one that help learner to grow continuously in these abilities. While the role of the teacher is to create a proper educational environment, the teacher also confirms the strong link between the degree of education that allowed in the process and building and developing critical thin king skills and problem solving skills of everyday life. In your assessment of the Christian education process in the presbyteries church in Egypt, democracy is allowed in _____ % in the Presbyterian educational process:

    ☐ 0%   ☐ 25%   ☐ 50%   ☐ 100%

20. The role of the teacher in the knowledge the learner gain in the process represents:

    ☐ 0%   ☐ 25%   ☐ 50%   ☐ 100%

21. The role of the learner in the knowledge the learner gain in the process represents:

    ☐ 0%   ☐ 25%   ☐ 50%   ☐ 100%

22. The teaching-learning process of the Presbyterian Church in Egypt, the teacher always has the final work of judging the truth in:

    ☐ 0%   ☐ 25%   ☐ 50%   ☐ 100%

23. As an educator in the Egyptian church, I accept that both teacher and learner to be equal members in the educational process and in judging the truth in:

    ☐ 0%   ☐ 25%   ☐ 50%   ☐ 100%

24. For John Dewey, true knowledge is not possible away from personal experience while good education can not be practice without giving the learner enough freedom to share this personal experience, reflecting on and analyzing them so that learner can develop critical thinking skills and problem solving skills as well.

    ☐ Agree   ☐ Disagree

25. The education and formation process of the Presbyterian Church in Egypt depends _____ % everyday experience of the learner represents as a source of knowing.

    ☐ 0%   ☐ 25%   ☐ 50%   ☐ 100%

26. In your understanding, the lack of using experience as a source of knowing in the educational process of the Presbyterian Church in Egypt because of:

    - The belief of the church that personal experience cannot be generalized not be taught.
    - The belief of the church can lead to spiritual pride.
    - Some people use their experience to attract sympathy and gain personal benefits, emotionally and physically.
    - All above.
    - None of the above.

Group 5, John Calvin:

17. Reformer John Calvin believes that God gave human a "pure" and creative reason that is able to discern and know God. Calvin believes also that human sin changed this reason into a "corrupted" reason that is unable to discern or know God despite its ability to think creatively in all secular sciences. While the "redeemed" and righteous reason by the work of Jesus Christ becomes able again to discern and know God through reasonable thinking in God's revelations.

    ☐ Agree   ☐ Disagree

18. In your conviction, Christian educators of the Presbyterian Church in Egypt believe in Calvin's understanding of human reason.

    ☐ 0%   ☐ 25%   ☐ 50%   ☐ 100%

Group 6, Critical Thinking:

27. I know what is called critical thinking:

    ☐ Yes   ☐ No

28. In your viewpoint, the number of the Presbyterian educators that know critical thinking:

    ☐ 0%   ☐ 25%   ☐ 50%   ☐ 100%

29. Christian educators of the Presbyterian Church in Egypt understand "critical thinking" as:

    - The ability to see the weaknesses of others.
    - The ability to criticize others, declaring them in public.
    - Using human reason to analyze all what are heard and seen in the daily attempting to see both strengths and weaknesses, recognizing problems and the real factors that formed them.
    - All of above.
    - Non of the above.

30. 30. In your opinion, the methods of education of the Presbyterian Church in Egypt are able to create critical thinking minds:

    ☐ 0%   ☐ 25%   ☐ 50%   ☐ 100%

31. In your estimation, the main reason of the failure of the Christian education process in the Presbyterian Church in Egypt to create critical thinking:

    • _____

    • _____

    • _____

32. In order for the Christian education in the Presbyterian church in Egypt to be able to create critical thinking, I suggest:

    • _____

    • _____

    • _____

APPENDIX 2

Empirical Research—Focus Group Discussion

A Study of the Current Status of Christian Education In the Presbyterian Church of Egypt
May 2012

THREE FOCUS GROUPS WERE held in different places and dates. The first was in the Evangelical Theological Seminary in Cairo (ETSC) in May 26th, which included 6 people that are concerned of CE ministry in the Presbyterian Church in Egypt; two pastors and four leaders that were graduated from the ETSC evening M.Div. program. The second was in the in the CE department of the Synod of the PC in Egypt in June 1, 2012, with 7 leaders of the CE Council. The third was in Minya Presbytery in June 4, 2012 with 29 pastors and CE leaders.[1]

As "critical thinking" was the subject matter of the discussion, I tried my best to gather as much data as I can about the real status of the Christian education process of the Presbyterian Church in Egypt in relation to this subject. Therefore, the same groups of question in the appendix 1 were used. The discussion was led to reveal some real data about the current status of the issue of critical thinking; how do pastors and Christian education leaders understand critical thinking, for what percent does it exist, the degree of democracy that is allowed in the education process, using experience as a fundamental way of learning, the teacher-learner relationship, the methods of education and the effect of all of this on creating critical thinking skills.

---

1. Choosing Cairo and Minya Presbyteries because they are the two biggest two of the PC in Egypt.

APPENDIX 3

Empirical Research

*An Interview Studying
the Current Status of Education in the
Presbyterian Church of Egypt
May 2012*

Introduction to Project:

- Samy Estafanos, PhD candidate and Presbyterian minister at the ETSC, writing on the critical thinking in the process of Christian education of the church.
- Explain the important role that this interview will play in creating this project.
- Thank you for participating.

Primary research Question

What kind of pedagogical practice that helps learners of the Presbyterian Church in Egypt to create critical thinking skills?

Existence of Critical Thinking:

1. In your perspective, for what degree critical thinking is lack or absent from the Christian education process of the Presbyterian Church in Egypt.
2. In your perspective do Presbyterian educators in Egypt accept or refuse using the mind and reason in spiritual issues and why?

3. In your viewpoint, how much does the church need to use mind and reason in the Presbyterian education process in Egypt? And how much this is important for the mission of the church in the contemporary age?

Christian Education and Public education

4. What are the methods of education that are commonly used in the educational process of the Presbyterian Church in Egypt and what is your assessment of these methods?

5. For what extent that the Christian education process of the Presbyterian Church was influenced with the public education in Egypt, methods of education In particular, and what are the results of this?

Democracy of education and critical thinking

6. Is there any direct or indirect relationship between the degree of democracy that allowed in the educational process and the level of the critical thinking developed and used in the spiritual matters and why?

Experience and critical thinking

7. For how extent that the Presbyterian educational process depends upon using experience as a main source of education? And what is the relationship between this and developing critical thinking skills.

Source of justifications and critical thinking

8. Do you think that the Bible is the only source of knowing in the Christian education process of the Presbyterian Church in Egypt? And why? And to what extent is human reason used to understanding it?

9. Does the Presbyterian Church use other sources of education rather than the Bible? Is there a place for the human sciences (philosophy and reason, sociology, educational theory, and psychology)? And is there a place for arts and literature, music and poetry, drawing and sculpting, and drama and theater?

Closing Questions:

10. *What kind of pedagogical practice that helps learners of the Presbyterian Church in Egypt to create critical thinking skills?*

11. Is there what you want say?

Six Interviewed of the Presbyterian educators:

1. Onsi Anes:

    Medical doctor.

    Th.M. from UTS-PSCE

    Ordained pastor in the Presbyterian Church in Egypt.

    Director of the CE association of the Evangelical churches in the Middle East.

    Part-time- teacher of CE at the ETSC.

    One of the well-known leaders of CE in Egypt.

    A PhD candidate at Fuller Theological Seminary.

2. Yosri Elias:

    The founder of the middle school meeting of the PC in Egypt.

    Director of the middle school council of the Nile Synod for 25 years.

3. Shaher Luka:

    The head leader of the main committee of youth of the PC in Egypt.

4. Hani Jack:

    A young pastor who is concerned with making contextual CE curricula.

5. Sameh Hanser:

    Medical doctor. Director of leaders' training and coordinator Haggai Institute in the Middle East and North Africa. Gifted in creating methods.

6. Ikram Lamay:

    PC pastor for 40 years.

    A president of the ETSC 1990-2000.

    A professor of Comparative religions and scientific thinking at the ETSC.

    Published about 10 books.

APPENDIX 4

Empirical Research—Data Analysis

Survey:

Item	#		Notes
Pastor, educators, and ETSC students	52	40.4%	
Know "critical thinking"	46	88.5%	
Memorization is the main method of education	50	87.5%	
Bible is the only source of justification	50	96.2%	
Other sources (social sciences).	50	30%	
Theology	50	35%	
Human reason	50	15%	
Christian educators of the Presbyterian Church in Egypt believe that reason weakens faith and obedience to God	50	73.5%	– Reason is too limit – reason is sinful – the bible includes everything that a Christian need. – Human reason is linked to philosophy, which is unchristian science.
There is a lack of democracy in the education process in the Presbyterian Church in Egypt.	50	75%	
Role of the teacher in relation to the role of the student.	50	85%	

Item	#		Notes
There is a lack of using experience in Christian education	50	78.5%	– Experience leads to spiritual pride – people abuse experience to withdraw sympathy from others – experience could not be generalized.
I know what is called "critical thinking"	5	82.7%	17.5 of pastors and educators do not know critical thinking. Among these are, 2 members of the Christian education Council of the Synod of the Nile, 2 of ETSC students, and 6 of the Christian education leaders of the Church.
In your opinion, Christian educators in the Presbyterian Church in Egypt know critical thinking	50	16.5%	
Christian education leaders understand critical thinking as the ability of criticizing others and confronting them with their mistakes.	50	48.1%	
Critical thinking is need in the process of Christian education in the Presbyterian Crouch in Egypt for:			– Helps the church and individual to meet with the huge and constant changes of the society – allows for developing a contextual and realistic theology – create an environment that promotes creativity both in theory and practice.
Methods of education in the Presbyterian Church in Egypt helps create critical thinking	50	17.5%	Reasons of failure to create critical thinking: – misconception of "criticism" – dictatorship – lack of educated leaders – memorizing methods – Islamic theology-significant lack of reading skills and research methods in learning.

The survey revealed some important points.

- First, 90% of the applicants think that critical thinking is lacking in the Christian education process of the church in 85% because they believe that it weakens obedience to God and understood as declaring others' weaknesses.
- Second, Christian education was influenced with the public education in 85%, especially in using memorization as the main method, the domination of the teacher, lack of using experience in the process, and lack of democracy.
- Third, the failure of Christian education process to create critical thinking is because of, misunderstanding the term as proclaiming the weaknesses of others, lack of democracy, lack of trained educators, and lack of creative methods.
- Fourth, the lack of using human reason in the process of Christian education is because of the belief that reason is limited, sinful, and linked with philosophy, which is unchristian sconce. Also because of the conviction that the Bible includes everything one might needs in life.
- Finally, more than 90% of the applicants see the real need for developing and suing critical thinking in the process of the Christian education process in order to help the church and individuals to meet the huge and constant changes of the contemporary life, helps promotes creativity, and helps create a contextual theology.

Focus Group Discussion:

Three groups of focus discussion revealed some important points:

- The first main theme from the three groups of discussion is the method of education. More that 90% of participants believe that memorizing is the only method of the Christian education process in the PC in Egypt. For them only focusing on this method is a natural fruit of the public education system, which mainly depends on this method. A student in each grade until the high school level is required to memorize on heart huge amount of knowledge in each subject every week. Most of this knowledge are not, and cannot be used in the Egyptian context. No wonder, then, that written exams at the end of the year, often at the end of semester, is the only way of student assessment. Here is the image that I always have with many of my schoolmates along years of our educational journey: teachers just give us a number of to keep for certain time to return it back to them at the end of this time. The more a student is able to return of the knowledge s/he had earlier from the teacher the more smartness s/he. As the Christian educators are not professional, pedagogy of the public education system without or with little changes became the pedagogy of Christian education in all Egyptian churches, including the Presbyterian Church. One-directional monologue with imposing some biblical knowledge, as the teacher understands, is the main way in the Christian education process at all ages.

- The second main theme that I concretely conclude from the three group discussions with the Presbyterian pastors and Christian education leaders in Egypt is the teacher-centered paradigm of education. More than 85% of the participant in discussion form pastors and Christian education leaders

Interviews:

The interviews with one theologian and five educators of the Presbyterian Church in Egypt revealed some important themes:

- A consensus has mad by all of the informants that critical thinking parley exists in the education process of the Church in Egypt. While the five educators believe that 20 to 30% is the average of the existence of the critical thinking in the church, theologian Ikram Lamay has a deep conviction that that this percentage never exceeds 10%. Lamay insists that significant lack of using scientific method of thinking in the process of Christian education will never help to create an understanding faith, faith that is able to fulfill the complexity of the contemporary life problems and needs.
- The factors; however, that have made the problem were quite clear for all of the informants, which all reflect the deep influence of the public education system on the Christian education process; lack of democracy, lack of using experience, and lack of creative pedagogy. Indeed, the teacher's image of the Christian education is the same image of the teacher of the public education. Indoctrination, memorization, lack of dialectical, and teacher-centered model of education always leave no space for learner to reflect, analyze, or create, which in turn fail to create critical thinkers.
- Stereotype, says Lamay, is a main reason also of lacking critical thinking. As we stereotype people according their belief, Christian and

Muslim; Orthodox; Pentecost; or according their gender, male and female, in addition to educational and psychological background all together result in lack of critical dialogue.

- Lamay concludes, religious fundamentalism, both Christian and Muslim, illiteracy, and law education all resulted in some taboos, lack of inquiring and understanding. This, in turn, resulted in type of Christians that view the kingdom of God as one rigid form, misunderstanding that Christian faith is so flexible that can take the shape of its contextual culture.

Bibliography

Abdel Fattah, Moataz. "A Failed Attempt to Use Science and Logic." *El Shorouk* weekly newspaper, April 7, 2012. http://www.shorouknews.com/columns/view.aspx?cdate=07042012&id=1df9568b-0799-4380-8715-9541383fdbc5.

Afifi, Sedek. *Moral Education in the Egyptian School*. Cairo: General Egyptian Association of the Book, 2000.

Al Said, Nasr El Din. *Egyptian Affaires: Nation Between the Culture of Homeland and the Culture of Religion*. Cairo: Madboli, 2010.

Aquinas, Thomas. *Summa Theologiae: Latin Text and English Translation, Introductions, Notes, Appendices, and Glossaries*. New York: Blackfriars, 1981.

Aristotle. *Aristotle: On the Heavens*. Translated by William Keith Chambers Guthrie. Cambridge, MA: Harvard University Press, 1939.

———. *Aristotle's Metaphysics: A Revised Text with Introduction and Commentary*. Edited by W. D. Ross. Oxford: Oxford University Press, 1924.

Assad, Maurice. "Christian Education in Egypt: Past, Present, and Future." *Theology Review* 7/1 (1986) 44–61.

Augustine. *The Literal Commentary on Genesis*. Vol. 1. Edited by Johannes Quasten et al. Translated by John Hammond. New York: Paulist, 1982.

Ayers, Robert H. "Language, Logic, and Reason in Calvin's *Institutes*." *Religious Studies* 16/3 (1980) 283–97. http://philpapers.org/rec/AYELLA.

Barth, Karl. *Church Dogmatics*. Vol., 1, Part 2, *The Doctrine of the Word of God*. Edinburgh: T. & T. Clark, 1988.

Berkson, Isaac Baer. *The Ideal and the Community: A Philosophy of Education*. Westport, CT: Praeger, 1970.

Bevan, Edwyn Robert. *Stoics and Skeptics*. Chicago: Ares, 1980.

Bevans, Stephen B. *Models of Contextual Theology*. Maryknoll, NY: Orbis, 2002.

Boisset, Jean. *Sagesse et Saintese dans la Pensee de Jean Calvin*. Paris: Universite de France, 1959.

Boisvert, Raymond. *Dewey's Metaphysics*. New York: Fordham University Press, 1988.

Breen, Quirinus, and John T. McNeill. *John Calvin: A Study in French Humanism*. 2nd ed. Hamden, CT: Archon, 1968.

Brosio, Richard A. *The Relationship of Dewey's Pedagogy to His Concept of Community*. Ann Arbor: University of Michigan School of Education, 1972.

Browning, Don. *Fundamental Practical Theology*. Minneapolis: Fortress, 1995.

Burke, Tom. *Dewey's New Logic: A Reply to Russell*. Chicago: University Of Chicago Press, 1998.

Cahalan, Kathleen A., and Gordon S. Mikoski, eds. *Opening the Field of Practical Theology: An Introduction*. Lanham, MD: Rowman & Littlefield, 2014.
Calvin, John. *Calvin: Institutes of the Christian Religion*. Edited by John T. McNeill. Translated by Ford Lewis Battles. 1559 translation ed. Louisville: Westminster John Knox, 1960.
———. *Calvin's Complete Bible Commentaries*. Edited and translated by Joseph Haroutunian. Grand Rapids: Christian Classics Ethereal Library, 1958. http://www.ccel.org/ccel/calvin/calcom.html.
———. *Commentary on Deuteronomy*. Edited and translated by Joseph Haroutunian. Grand Rapids: Christian Classics Ethereal Library, 1958.
———. *Commentary on Ephesians*. Edited and translated by Joseph Haroutunian. Grand Rapids: Christian Classics Ethereal Library, 1958.
———. *Commentary on Matthew, Mark, Luke*. Vol. 1. Enhanced version, 1.1 edition. Grand Rapids: Christian Classics Ethereal Library, 2009.
———. *Commentary on Philippians, Colossians, and Thessalonians*. Enhanced version, 1.1 edition. Grand Rapids: Christian Classics Ethereal Library, 2009.
———. *Commentary on Psalms*. Edited and translated by Joseph Haroutunian. Grand Rapids: Christian Classics Ethereal Library, 1958.
———. *Commentary on Romans*. Enhanced version, 1.1 edition. Grand Rapids: Christian Classics Ethereal Library, 2009.
———. *Commentaries on the Epistle of Paul the Apostle to The Romans, 4:16*. Edited and translated by Joseph Haroutunian. Grand Rapids: Christian Classics Ethereal Library, 1958. 1990.
———. *Commentary on the Epistles of Paul the Apostle to the Corinthians*. Edited and translated by Joseph Haroutunian. Grand Rapids: Christian Classics Ethereal Library, 1958.
———. *Commentary Upon the Acts of the Apostles*. Vols. 1–3. Edinburgh: T. & T. Clark, 1859.
———. *Institutes of the Christian Religion*. Rev. ed. Peabody, MA: Hendrickson, 2007.
———. *Institutes of The Christian Religion*. Vol. 2. Translated by Henry Beveridge. Whitefish, MT: Kessinger, 2010.
———. *Institutes of the Christian Religion, 1536 Edition*. Grand Rapids: Eerdmans, 1995.
———. *John Calvin: Commentary on Psalms, Volume 4*. Edited and translated by Joseph Haroutunian. Grand Rapids: Christian Classics Ethereal Library, 1958.
———. *The John Calvin Collection: Twelve Classic Works*. Kindle ed. N.p.: Waxkeep, 2012.
Calvin, John, and J. I. Packer. *John*. Wheaton, IL: Crossway, 1994.
Coleman, Monica A., Nancy R. Howell, and Helene Tallon Russell. *Creating Women's Theology: A Movement Engaging Process Thought*. Eugene, OR: Wipf & Stock, 2011.
Csikszentmihalyi, Mihaly. *Creativity: The Psychology of Discovery and Invention*. New York: HarperCollins, 2013.
De Gruchy, John W. *Christianity and Democracy: A Theology for a Just World Order*. Cambridge: Cambridge University Press, 1995.
Dewey, John. *The Child and the Curriculum*. Chicago: University of Chicago Press, 2011.
———. "Christianity and Democracy." A Sunday Morning Service's Talk. Michigan: March 27, 1892.

———. *A Common Faith*. New Haven: Yale University Press, 1991.
———. "The Crucial Role of Intelligence." *Teachers College Record* 1/1 (1935) 9–10. Carbondale: Southern Illinois University, 1987.
———. *Democracy and Education*. New York: Simon & Brown, 2012.
———. *Democracy and Education: An Introduction to the Philosophy of Education*. New York: The Free Press, 1966.
———. "Democracy and Education in the World of Today." *Schools: Studies in Education* 9/1 (Spring 2012) 96–100.
———. "Democracy and Educational Administration." In *Problems of Men*. New York: Philosophical Library, 1946.
———. "The Democratic Faith and Education." In *Problems of Men*, 251–60. New York: Columbia University Press, 1944.
———. *Experience and Education*. New York: Free Press, 1997.
———. "From Absolutism to Experimentalism." In *Contemporary American Philosophy*, edited by G. P. Adams and W. P. Montague, 2:12–27. New York: Macmillan, 1930.
———. *How We Think*. Berkeley: University of California Libraries, 1910.
———. *How We Think: A Restatement of the Relation of Reflective Thinking to the Educative Process*. Washington DC: Heath, 1933.
———. *Human Nature and Conduct: An Introduction to Social Psychology*. CreateSpace Independent Publishing Platform, 2012.
———. *Intelligence In The Modern World: John Dewey's Philosophy*. Edited by Joseph Ratner. New York: Modern Library, 1939.
———. *The Later Works of John Dewey, 1925–1953*. 17 vols. Edited by Jo Ann Boydston. Carbondale: Southern Illinois University Press, 2008.
———. *Logic—The Theory of Inquiry*. New York: Searching, 2007.
———. *The Middle Works of John Dewey*. 15 vols. Edited by Jo Ann Boydston. Carbondale: Southern Illinois University Press, 2008.
———. "The New Psychology." *The Andover Review* 2 (September 1884) 278–89.
———. *My Pedagogic Creed*. Chicago: University of Chicago Press, 1897.
———. "My Pedagogic Creed." *The School Journal* 54/3 (January 16, 1897) 77–80.
———. *Reconstruction in Philosophy*. Mineola, NY: Dover, 2004.
———. *The School and Society*. New York: Cosimo Classics, 2008.
Dewey, John, and Arthur Bentley. *Knowing and the Known*. Boston: Beacon, 1960.
Dowey, Edward A., Jr. *Knowledge of God in Calvin's Theology*. Grand Rapids: Eerdmans, 1994.
Dutton, Wendy, Thomas Hart, and Rebecca Patten. "Critical Thinking and the Christian Perspective." September 29, 2005. http://www.studymode.com/essays/Critical-Thinking-And-The-Christian-Perspective-65802.html.
El Fayomi, Mohamed. *Egyptian Man and the Challenges of the Coming Century*. Edited by Nabil Salama. Cairo: Culture House, 1997.
El-Gabalaway, Saad. "The Allegorical Significance of Naguib Mahfouz's *Children of Our Alley*." *The International Fiction Review* 16/2 (1989) 91–97.
El Kholy, Ayman. *Principles of Education: Future Visions for Developing Education in the Twenty-first Century in Egypt*. Beirut: The House of the University Degrees, 2001.
Ennis, Robert H., and Stephen P. Norris. *Evaluating Critical Thinking*. Pacific Grove, CA: Midwest, 1989.
Ess, Charles, ed. *Critical Thinking and the Bible in the Age of New Media*. Dallas: University Press of America, 2004.

Faour, Muhammad. "Religious Education and Pluralism in Egypt and Tunisia." Washington DC: Middle East Center of Carnegie Endowment for International Peace Publications Department, 2012.

Fares, Fayez. *Christian Ethics*. Vol. 1. Cairo: Cultural House, 1982.

———. *The Crisis of Religion and Ethics in the Contemporary Society*. Cairo: Cultural House, 2002.

———. *Self-Awaking in Experiencing God: Enlightening Messages*. Cairo: Cultural House, 2008.

———. "A Study of Theological Education in the United Presbyterian Church of Egypt." MA thesis, Princeton Theological Seminary, 1952.

———. *With Christ*. Cairo: Cultural House, 1990.

Ferrett, Sharon K. *Peak Performance: Success in College and Beyond*. Chicago: Irwin Mirror, 1997.

Field, Richard. "John Dewey (1859-1952)." Internet Encyclopedia of Philosophy. April 2001. http://www.iep.utm.edu/dewey/.

Fisher, Alec. *Critical Thinking: An Introduction*. Cambridge: Cambridge University Press, 2011.

Foda, Farag. *A Discourse about Secularism*. Cairo: Future, 2005.

Fowler, James W. *Stages of Faith: The Psychology of Human Development and the Quest for Meaning*. San Francisco: HarperOne, 1995.

Frankfurt, Harry G. "Peirce's Account of Inquiry." *The Journal of Philosophy* 55/14 (July 3, 1958) 588–92. http://www.jstor.org/stable/2021965.

Freire, Paulo, and Donaldo Macedo. *Pedagogy of the Oppressed*. Translated by Myra Bergman Ramos. New York: Bloomsbury Academic, 2000.

Gardner, Howard E. *Frames of Mind: The Theory of Multiple Intelligences*. New York: Basic, 2011.

———. *Multiple Intelligences: New Horizons in Theory and Practice*. New York: Basic, 2006.

Gee, Wilson, ed. *Research in the Social Sciences: Its Fundamental Methods and Objectives*. New Delhi: Cosmo, 2006.

Gerkin, Charles, V. *Living Human Document: Re-Visioning Pastoral Counseling in a Hermeneutical Mode*. Nashville: Abingdon, 1984.

Geuss, Raymond. *The Idea of a Critical Theory: Habermas and the Frankfurt School*. Cambridge: Cambridge University Press, 1981.

Ginsburg, Mark. "Active-Learning Pedagogies as a Reform Initiative: Synthesis of Case Studies." American Institutes for Research under the EQUIP1 LWA. August 2009. http://citeseerx.ist.psu.edu/viewdoc/download?doi=10.1.1.608.2996&rep=rep1&type=pdf.

Ginsburg, Mark, and Nagwa Megahed. "Global Discourses and Educational Reform in Egypt: The Case of Active-Learning Pedagogies." *Mediterranean Journal of Educational Studies* 13 (2008) 91–115.

Glaeser, Edward. *Triumph of the City: How Our Greatest Invention Makes Us Richer, Smarter, Greener, Healthier, and Happier*. New York: Penguin, 2012.

Graham, Elaine L. *Transforming Practice: Pastoral Theology in an Age of Uncertainty*. Eugene, OR: Wipf & Stock, 2002.

Groome, Thomas H. *Sharing Faith: A Comprehensive Approach to Religious Education and Pastoral Ministry: The Way of Shared Praxis*. San Francisco: Harper San Francisco, 1991.

Habib, Samuel. *The Art of Dialogue*. Cairo: Cultural House, 1994.
———. *Christ Revolted*. Cairo: Culture House, 1995.
———. *Christianity and Human Being, Selected Papers*. Cairo: Culture House, 1998.
———. *Church and State*. Cairo: Culture House, 1990.
———. *The Gospel and Culture*. Cairo: Culture House, 1997.
———. *Liberation Theology*. Cairo: Culture House, 1991.
Halpern, Diane F. *Thought and Knowledge: An Introduction to Critical Thinking*. New York: Psychology, 2013.
Hemdan, Gamal. *The Character of Egypt: Studies of the Arab World, and The Contemporary Islamic World Geography, 4 parts*. Cairo: Dare Al Helal, 1984.
Hickman, Larry A., Stefan Neubert, and Kersten Reich, eds. *John Dewey Between Pragmatism and Constructivism*. New York: Fordham University Press, 2009.
Hildebrand, David L. *Beyond Realism and Antirealism: John Dewey and the Neopragmatists*. Nashville: Vanderbilt University Press, 2003.
Johnson, William Stacy. *John Calvin, Reformer for the 21st Century*. Louisville: Westminster John Knox Press, 2009.
Kant, Immanuel. *Critique of Pure Reason*. Edited by Marcus Weigelt. Translated by Max Muller. Rev. ed. New York: Penguin, 2008.
Kegan, Robert. *The Evolving Self: Problem and Process in Human Development*. Cambridge, MA: Harvard University Press, 1983.
Kendall, R. T. *Calvin and English Calvinism to 1649*. Eugene, OR: Wipf & Stock, 2011.
———. *Lectures on Calvinism*. Lafayette, IN: Sovereign Grace, 2001.
Kremer, Alexander. "Dewey and Rorty on Truth." *E-Journal of American Studies in Hungary* 3/2 (Fall 2007) 162.
Kroner, Richard. *Speculation in Pre-Christian Philosophy*. Philadelphia: Westminster, 1956.
Kuyper, Abraham. *Lectures on Calvinism*. Grand Rapids: Eerdmans, 1943.
Lamay, Ikram. *Church and Vision*. Cairo: Culture House, 1989.
———. "Church Between Alienation and Participation." In *Religious Thoughts and Participation*, edited by Nabil Naguib Salama, 72–73. Cairo: Cultural House, 1995.
———. *Divine Inspiration and Man's Imagination*. Cairo: Culture House, 2000.
———. *Divorce in Christianity*. Cairo: Arabic Cultural Center, 2006.
———. *How We Think Objectively*. Cairo: Culture House, 1990.
———. *The Other Face of Christ Teaching*. Cairo: Culture House, 1991.
Le Coq, John P. "Was Calvin a Philosopher?" *The Personalist* 29 (1948) 29.
Lee, HeeKap. *Faith-Based Education That Constructs: A Creative Dialogue between Constructivism and Faith-Based Education*. Eugene, OR: Wipf & Stock, 2010.
Leith, John H. "Calvin's Theological Method and the Ambiguity of His Theology." In *Reformation Studies Essays in Honor of R. H. Bainton*, edited by F. Littell, 104–14. Richmond, VA: John Knox, 1962.
Lipman, Matthew. *Philosophy Goes To School*. Philadelphia: Temple University Press, 1988.
Mahfouz, Naguib. *Children of the Alley*. Cairo: Dar El Shrook, 2006.
Mahmud, Zaki Naguib. *Renewal of the Arabic Thinking*. Cairo: El Shrok House, 2004.
Mansur, Anis. *Securities Sadat*. Cairo: Dar Al Maarf, 1979.
Marsoobian, Armen T., and John Ryder, eds. *The Blackwell Guide to American Philosophy*. 1st ed. Malden, MA: Wiley-Blackwell, 2004.

Mathewes, Charles T. *Evil and the Augustinian Tradition*. Cambridge: Cambridge University Press, 2007.
McDonnell, Kilian. *John Calvin, the Church and the Eucharist*. Princeton: Princeton University Press, 1967.
Miettinen, Reijo. "The Concept of Experiential Learning and John Dewey's Theory of Reflective Thought and Action." *International Journal of Lifelong Education* 19/1 (January–February 2000) 54–72.
Miller, Henry. "A Scholarly Critique of Dewey and Experimentalism in Education." *Journal of Educational Sociology* 32/3 (November 1958) 133-40. http://www.jstor.org/stable/2264713.
Muller, Richard A. *The Unaccommodated Calvin: Studies in the Foundation of a Theological Tradition*. New York: Oxford University Press, 2001.
Myers, David G. *Psychology*. 9th ed. New York: Worth, 2009.
Naguib, Makram. *Charismatic Movement*. Cairo: House of Culture, 1982.
———. *Conservative or Liberal*. Cairo: Cultural House, 2008.
———. *Religious Thoughts and Responsibility of Progress*. Cairo: Cultural House, 2008.
Nainggolan, Lisa. "Magdi Yacoub: The Man Behind the Mask." *Medscape*, March 27, 2003. https://www.medscape.com/viewarticle/782920.
Nicola, Vines. *Church and Value System: Theology, Enlightenment, and Social Movement*. Cairo: Seven, 2008.
Niebuhr, Reinhold. *Nature and Destiny of Man*. Vol. 1. New York: Prentice Hall, 1940.
Niebuhr, Reinhold, and Edmund N. Santurri. *An Interpretation of Christian Ethics*. Louisville: Westminster John Knox, 2013.
Niebuhr, Reinhold, and Cornel West. *Moral Man and Immoral Society: A Study in Ethics and Politics*. 2nd ed. Louisville: Westminster John Knox, 2013.
Nixon, Leroy. *John Calvin's Teachings on Human Reason*. New York: Exposition, 1963.
Norris, Stephen P., and Robert H. Ennis. *Evaluating Critical Thinking*. Pacific Grove, CA: Midwest, 1989.
Nuovo, Victor. *Calvin's Theology: A Study of Its Sources in Classical Antiquity*. New York: Columbia University Press, 1964.
Ofek, Hillel. "Why the Arabic World Turned Away from Science." *The New Atlantis* 30 (Winter 2011) 3-23. http://www.thenewatlantis.com/publications/why-the-arabic-world-turned-away-from-science.
Osmer, Richard R. "Practical Theology: A Current International Perspective." Annual conference for the Society for Practical Theology in South Africa, January 2009.
———. *Practical Theology: An Introduction*. Grand Rapids: Eerdmans, 2008.
———. "Practical Theology and Contemporary Christian Education: An Historical and Constructive Analysis." Phd diss., Emory University, 1985.
———. *A Teachable Spirit: Recovering the Teaching Office in the Church*. Louisville: Westminster John Knox, 1990.
———. "Teaching as Practical Theology." In *Theological Approaches to Christian Education*, edited by Jack L. Seymour and Donald E. Miller, 216–38. Nashville: Abingdon, 1990.
———. *The Teaching Ministry of Congregations*. Louisville: Westminster John Knox, 2005.
Osmer, Richard R., and Friedrich Schweitzer. *Religious Education between Modernization and Globalization: New Perspectives on the United States and Germany*. Grand Rapids: Eerdmans, 2003.

Palmer, Parker J. *The Courage to Teach: Exploring the Inner Landscape of a Teacher's Life*. San Francisco: Jossey-Bass, 2007.
Parshall, Phil. *The Cross and the Crescent: Understanding the Muslim Heart and Mind*. Downer's Grove, IL: InterVarsity, 2012.
Partee, Charles. *Calvin and Classical Philosophy*. Louisville: Westminster John Knox, 2005.
———. *The Theology of John Calvin*. Louisville: Westminster John Knox, 2008.
Paul, Richard. *Critical Thinking: What Every Person Needs to Survive in a Rapidly Changing World*. 3rd ed. Santa Rosa, CA: Foundation for Critical Thinking, 1993.
Paul, Richard, and Linda Elder. *Miniature Guide to Critical Thinking Concepts and Tools*. Dillon Beach, CA: Foundation for Critical Thinking, 2014.
Paul, Richard, Linda Elder, and Ted Bartell. "California Teacher Preparation for Instruction in Critical Thinking: Research Findings and Policy Recommendations." Foundation for Critical Thinking, 1997.
Peirce, Charles S. *Charles S. Peirce: Selected Writings*. Edited by Philip P. Wiener. Mineola, NY: Dover, 1966.
———. *Writings of Charles S. Peirce: A Chronological Edition*. 8 vols. Bloomington: Indiana University Press, 1982–2009.
Plato. *The Republic Of Plato*. Translated by Allan Bloom. New York: Basic Books, 1991.
Randall, John. "The Religion of Shared Experience." In *The Philosopher of the Common Man*, edited by Sydney Ratner, 106–45. New York: Putnam's, 1940.
Ratner, Joseph. "Introduction to John Dewey's Philosophy." In *The Later Works of John Dewey*, 2:341–44. Carbondale: Southern Illinois University, 1987.
Razik, Taher, and Diaa El-Din A. Zaher. "Egypt." In *Issues and Problems in Teacher Education: An International Handbook*, edited by Howard B Leavitt, 12–15. Westport, CT: Greenwood, 1992.
Rhee, Jung S. "John Calvin's Understanding of Human Reason in His *Institutes*."
Rice, Daniel F. *Reinhold Niebuhr and His Circle of Influence*. Cambridge: Cambridge University Press, 2012.
———. *Reinhold Niebuhr and John Dewey: An American Odyssey*. Albany: State University of New York Press, 1993.
Robertson, William H. "The Greatest Constructivist Educator Ever: The Pedagogy of Jesus Christ in the Gospel of Matthew in the Context of the 5Es." *Christian Perspectives in Education* 1/2. http://digitalcommons.liberty.edu/cpe/vol1/iss2/5.
Rockler, Michael J. "Russell vs. Dewey on Education." http://docs.lib.purdue.edu/cgi/viewcontent.cgi?article=1393&context=eandc.
Rodgers, Carol. "Defining Reflection: Another Look at John Dewey and Reflective Thinking." *Teachers College Record* 104/4 (June 2002) 842–66.
Rousseau, Jean-Jacques. *Emile: Or On Education*. Translated by Allan Bloom. New York: Basic Books, 1979.
Russell, Bertrand. *Education and the Social Order*. New York: Routledge, 2009.
Saiving, Valerie. "The Human Situation: A Feminine View." *The Journal of Religion* 40/2 (April 1960) 100–112. http://www.jstor.org/stable/1200194.
Schweitzer, Friedrich, and Richard Osmer, eds. *Developing a Public Faith: New Directions in Practical Theology*. St. Louis: Chalice, 2003.
Scott, Gordon. "John Dewey and American Social Science." http://www2.hawaii.edu/~manicas/pdf_files/pub/DeweyAndSocialScience.pdf.

Seymour, Jack L. *Theological Approaches to Christian Education*. Nashville: Abingdon, 1990.

Seymour, Jack L., and Donald E. Miller. *Contemporary Approaches to Christian Education*. Nashville: Abingdon, 1982.

Shaw, Perry. "A Christian Educator Looks at Muslim Education." *Christian Education Journal* 5NS (Fall 2001) 91–109.

Shook, John R., and James A. Good. *John Dewey's Philosophy of Spirit, with the 1897 Lecture on Hegel*. New York: Fordham University Press, 2010.

Smith, Adam. *The Wealth of Nations*. New York: Bantam, 2003.

Smith, Kevin G. Review of *Practical Theology: An Introduction* by Richard Osmer. *Conspectus (South Africa Theological Seminary)* 10 (2010) 99.

Solmsen, Friedrich. *Plato's Theology*. Edited by Harry Caplan et al. Cornell Studies in Classical Philosophy 27. Ithaca: Cornell University Press, 1942.

Stratton, John. *Critical Thinking for College Students*. Lanham, MD: Rowman & Littlefield, 1999.

Sumner, William Graham. *Folkways: A Study of the Sociological Importance of Usages, Manners, Customs, Mores, and Morals*. Boston: Forgotten, 2012.

Talisse, Robert B. "Two Concepts of Inquiry." *Philosophical Writings* 20 (2002) 69–81. https://o5c6ca7b-a-62cb3a1a-s-sites.googlegroups.com/site/rtalisse/2concepts_inquiry.pdf.

Tanner, Daniel. "Some Thoughts on John Dewey." *Education and Culture* 22/1 (2006) 76–78.

Van der Walt, B. J. "Philosophical and Theological Influences in John Calvin's Thought: Reviewing Some Research Results." *In Die Skriflig* 44 (2010) 105–27.

Wahba, Mourad. *Fundamentalism and Secularism*. Cairo: House of Culture, 1995.

———. *Owners of Absolute Truth*. Cairo: Family Library, 1999.

Warfield, Benjamin, et al, eds. "Hisotrical Theology." *Presbyterian and Reformed Review* 12 (1901) 466.

Wasfy, Awsam. *The Focus: Is to Be with and Like Him*. Cairo: Sparkle, 2015.

Westbrook, Robert B. "John Dewey (1859–1952)." *Prospects: The Quarterly Review of Comparative Education* 23/1–2 (1993) 277–91.

Witte, John. "Calvin the Lawyer." In *Tributes to John Calvin on His 500th Birthday*, edited by David Hall and Martin Padgett, 1–23. Emory Legal Studies Research Paper, 2010. https://papers.ssrn.com/sol3/papers.cfm?abstract_id=1863624.

Zaki, Andrea. *Jesus and Historical Criticism: The Story of the Conflict Between Salvation and Social Change*. Cairo: Cultural House, 1996.

———, ed. *Towards a Contemporary Arabic Theology*. Cairo: Cultural House, 2007.

Zewail, Ahmed. "Reflections on Arab Renaissance: A Call For Education Reform." *Cairo Review of Global Affairs* (Spring 2011) 36–47.